Evaluating High-Speed Rail

High-speed rail (HSR) is a technological transportation advance that has raised the interest of policy makers and researchers worldwide. The study of HSR is a recent phenomenon but has received increasing attention due to the extension of this mode of transportation around the globe.

Evaluating High-Speed Rail contains some of the most recent and cutting-edge studies on HSR from different disciplines. The book is organized around a variety of key topics related to the evaluation of HSR projects and experiences. These topics include: the economic appraisal and evaluation of HSR projects; the evaluation of indirect and direct effects of HSR; its territorial, redistributive and environmental impacts; its contribution to or limitations with regard to urban growth; and the management of challenges created by the arrival of HSR lines in core cities. It also covers the contribution of HSR to tourism and its impact on intermodal competition, with especial consideration given to air transportation. Chapters analyse the expected effects of introducing on-track competition and designing public–private contracts to develop new lines.

This cutting-edge volume offers rigorous analysis from top researchers in the field with a clear intention to deliver policy implications and provide the latest analysis on the impact of HSR. This book is suitable for students and academics interested in transportation infrastructure, economic impacts of public investments, mobility, planning and urban affairs, as well as researchers and policy makers in the transportation and infrastructure sector.

Daniel Albalate is an Associate Professor at the University of Barcelona, Spain.

Germà Bel is a Full Professor at the University of Barcelona, Spain.

Routledge Studies in Transport Analysis

1 **Maritime Logistics Value in Knowledge Management**
Eon-Seong Lee and Dong-Wook Song

2 **The Management of Maritime Regulations**
Hristos Karahalios

3 **Public Private Partnerships in Transport**
Trends and theory
Edited by Athena Roumboutsos

4 **Climate Change and Adaptation Planning for Ports**
Edited by Adolf K.Y. Ng, Austin Becker, Stephen Cahoon, Shu-ling Chen, Paul Earl and Zaili Yang

5 **Maritime Networks**
Spatial structures and time dynamics
Edited by César Ducruet

6 **Inland Waterway Transport**
Challenges and prospects
Bart Wiegmans and Rob Konings

7 **Evaluating High-Speed Rail**
Interdisciplinary perspectives
Edited by Daniel Albalate and Germà Bel

Evaluating High-Speed Rail

Interdisciplinary perspectives

**Edited by Daniel Albalate and
Germà Bel**

Routledge
Taylor & Francis Group

LONDON AND NEW YORK

First published 2017
by Routledge

2 Park Square, Milton Park, Abingdon, Oxfordshire OX14 4RN
52 Vanderbilt Avenue, New York, NY 10017

Routledge is an imprint of the Taylor & Francis Group, an informa business

First issued in paperback 2019

British Library Cataloguing in Publication Data
A catalogue record for this book is available from the British Library

Library of Congress Cataloging in Publication Data
Names: Albalate, Daniel, 1980- editor. | Bel i Queralt, Germa, editor.
Title: Evaluating high-speed rail : interdisciplinary perspectives / edited by
    Daniel Albalate and Germáa Bel.
Description: Abingdon, Oxon ; New York, NY : Routledge, 2017. | Includes
    bibliographical references.
Identifiers: LCCN 2016012577| ISBN 9781138123595 (hardback) |
    ISBN 9781315648767 (ebook)
Subjects: LCSH: High speed trains. | Transportation—Planning.
Classification: LCC TF1450 .E89 2017 | DDC 385/.22—dc23
LC record available at https://lccn.loc.gov/2016012577

ISBN: 978-1-138-12359-5 (hbk)
ISBN: 978-0-367-87621-0 (pbk)

Typeset in Times New Roman
by Swales & Willis Ltd, Exeter, Devon, UK

Contents

List of figures   vii
List of tables   ix
Notes on contributors   xi

1 An evidence-based review of key issues in high-speed rail   1
   DANIEL ALBALATE AND GERMÀ BEL

2 The economic evaluation of major infrastructure projects:
   Notes on HSR projects   7
   GINÉS DE RUS

3 Financial and social profitability of HSR in Spain   23
   OFELIA BETANCOR AND GERARD LLOBET

4 Direct and indirect effects of high-speed rail   46
   JOHN PRESTON

5 High-speed rail services and tourism expansion: The need for
   cooperation   69
   MARIE DELAPLACE AND SYLVIE BAZIN-BENOIT

6 HSR and the city: Accessibility to stations and intermodality   82
   JORDI MARTÍ-HENNEBERG AND EDUARD J. ALVAREZ-PALAU

7 Environmental performance and implications of high-speed rail   100
   TORBEN HOLVAD, AMANDINE CRAPS AND JAVIER CAMPOS

8 Environmental assessment of high-speed rail   119
   DAVID HOYOS, GORKA BUENO AND IÑIGO CAPELLÁN-PÉREZ

9 Reality and opportunities for on-track competition in HSR   140
PAOLO BERIA AND RAFFAELE GRIMALDI

10 Assessing the competition between high-speed rail and airlines:
A critical perspective   159
FRÉDÉRIC DOBRUSZKES, MOSHE GIVONI, AND CATHERINE DEHON

11 High-speed rail and PPPs: Between optimization and
opportunism   175
YVES CROZET

Index   187

Figures

3.1 HSR network as of December 2013   26
3.2 Probability distribution of the financial NPV in the
Madrid–Barcelona corridor   32
3.3 Probability distribution of the social NPV in the Madrid–Barcelona
corridor   33
3.4 Probability distribution of the financial NPV in the
Madrid–Andalusia corridor   35
3.5 Probability distribution of the social NPV in the Madrid–Andalusia
corridor   36
3.6 Probability distribution of the financial NPV in the Madrid–East
Coast corridor   38
3.7 Probability distribution of the social NPV in the Madrid–East
Coast corridor   39
3.8 Probability distribution of the financial NPV in the Madrid–North
corridor   41
3.9 Probability distribution of the social NPV in the Madrid–North
corridor   42
4.1 The four broad types of HSR   47
4.2 Iso–welfare curves for HSR investments   55
4.3 Wider economic benefits from reductions in imperfect competition   56
4.4 Agglomeration benefits and tax wedge   56
4.5 Employment effects of transport interventions   58
4.6 Investment curve for HS2   60
4.7 Probabilistic analysis of HS2 costs and benefits   63
6.1 HSR network and connection to agglomerations in Europe   83
6.2 Potential user demand for HSR between stations   86
6.3 Average accumulated potential user demand at connected stations   88
6.4 Classification of HSR stations in relation to their cities, by location   89
6.5 Box charts showing the average distance between HSR stations
and their city halls, by location   90
6.6 Travel time between HSR stations and their city halls, on foot
(above) and by public transport (below), by country   92

6.7   Classification of intermodal relationships between HSR stations
      and airports. Global pie chart on the left and pie charts for
      individual countries (DE, ES, FR and IT) on the right   96
7.1   EU-28 final energy consumption share by mode in 2013 (%) –
      Total = 348.5 Mtoe   103
7.2   EU-28 greenhouse gas emissions share by mode in 2012 (%) –
      Total = 1173.2 MteCO$_2$ 104
7.3   The contributors of the transport sector to total emissions of the
      main air pollutants in 2010 (EEA-32)   106
7.4   Exposure to transport noise in Europe based upon the common
      indicators for Lden and Lnight   107
7.5   Share of the country's surface area used by roads and rail,
      EU-15, 1998   108
8.1   Graphic representation of transport in MODE1, MODE2 and
      HSR in two alternative transport systems, one without HSR (above),
      and another one in which an HSR line is put in service (below)   125
8.2   GHG emissions linked to vehicle movement for a Madrid–Barcelona
      journey in five different transport modes (528 km by aeroplane,
      708 km by conventional train, 621 km by car, 632 km by bus and
      627 km by HSR). Low occupancy is 20 per cent in all modes,
      maximum is 100 per cent, and average occupancy is 75 per cent
      in aeroplane, 30 per cent in car, 64 per cent in conventional train,
      61 per cent in bus and 70 per cent in HSR   130
8.3   Environmental balance of Basque Y CO$_2$ emissions and energy
      consumption (central dynamic and static scenarios)   133
9.1   Map of open-access long-distance services in Europe operated
      by newcomers (incumbents' international services excluded)   141
9.2   The network of Italian fast trains operated by Trenitalia on the
      left (Frecciarossa, Frecciargento and Frecciabianca) and NTV on
      the right (Italo). High-speed infrastructure is represented in
      dark grey (our elaboration)   146
9.3   Best available fare (left) and best first-class fare (right), weekly
      average, one day before departure, for different types of train –
      trains from Milan to Ancona   149
9.4   Forms of on-track competition models   154
9.5   Competitive strategies adopted by open-access newcomers in
      Europe (our elaboration)   155
10.1 Trends in the provision of air services on selected routes   165
10.2 Rail vs air passenger-km (EU-28)   166
10.3 The provision of scheduled worldwide air services against distance   167
10.4 The impact of urban systems on a HSR network required to
      connect main cities to each other   168

Tables

3.1	Structure of RENFE and ADIF financial accounts	27
3.2	Scheme of the social accounts	30
3.3	Financial account for the Madrid–Barcelona corridor (expected discounted values)	31
3.4	Social account for the Madrid–Barcelona corridor (expected discounted values)	33
3.5	Financial account for the Madrid–Andalusia corridor (expected discounted values)	34
3.6	Social account for the Madrid–Andalusia corridor (expected discounted values)	36
3.7	Financial account for the Madrid–East Coast corridor (expected discounted values)	37
3.8	Social account for the Madrid–East Coast corridor (expected discounted values)	39
3.9	Financial account for the Madrid–North corridor (expected discounted values)	40
3.10	Social account for the Madrid–North corridor (expected discounted values)	42
3.11	Financial and social IRR	43
4.1	The global extent of HSR in 2014 (route kms)	48
4.2	Objectives of HSR	49
4.3	Impact matrix for a typical HSR scheme	50
4.4	Abstraction and generation factors	53
4.5	Estimates of rail wider economic benefits	59
4.6	Costs and benefits of HS2, phase one – London to Birmingham (£ million, present value)	59
4.7	Costs and benefits of HS2 (PV 2011 prices)	61
4.8	Benefits of HS2 (PV 2011 prices)	62
6.1	Potential user demand for the main stations in each state	87
6.2	Average access distance between HSR stations and their city halls, by station location and country (in km)	91
6.3	Percentage of intermodal transport services available in relation to the location of HSR stations	94

7.1   Average CO_2 emissions per pkm for different modes   105

7.2   Marginal costs from climate change, air pollution and up/
      downstream processes for passenger transport (€/1,000 pkm)   105

7.3   EU-28 gross electricity generation by fuel in 2013 (total
      electricity generation: 3261.5 TWh)   109

7.4   Estimated total cost from climate change, air pollution, up/
      downstream processes and noise for HSR passenger transport
      (million €)   112

8.1   Transport hierarchy approach   123

8.2   GHG emissions linked to construction and maintenance of
      some lines – emissions expressed in terms per pkm assuming a
      lifetime of 60 years   127

8.3   Annual carbon footprint of elements and components linked to
      the construction and maintenance of the Basque Y   131

9.1   List of open-access long-distance services in Europe operated
      by newcomers in 2016   142

9.2   Characteristics of HSR models   143

9.3   Strategies for competitive advantage in the rail market   152

10.1 Comparing trends according to market shares and to absolute
      figures (millions of passengers)   163

10.2 Fuel burnt against distance flown and aircraft size (kg)   166

11.1 Main causes of PPP failures   180

11.2 Main features and financing structure of the four projects   182

Contributors

Daniel Albalate, Barcelona, 1980. Holds an MSc in Economics (University College London, 2007) and a PhD in Economics (Universitat de Barcelona, 2008). He is currently an Associate Professor in the Department of Applied Economics at the University of Barcelona where he coordinates the Pasqual Maragall Chair of Economy and Territory. His research interests focus on the analysis and evaluation of public policies, particularly in the field of transportation.

Eduard J. Alvarez-Palau, Barcelona, 1984. Holds a PhD in Engineering and Transportation Infrastructures (UPC, 2015), an MBA (UOC, 2016) and an MEng in Civil Engineering (UPC, 2008). He has been a research associate with the Campop Group at the University of Cambridge since 2015. He has also been an instructor on the MSc in City Management and Urbanism at the Universitat Oberta de Catalunya since 2009. He is interested in transportations, urbanism and regional planning, and in both historical and current approaches.

Sylvie Bazin-Benoit, Malo-les-Bains, 1968. Holds a PhD in Economics (University of Lille, 1996), on the subject of local policies aiming to attract firms. She is currently a lecturer in the Department of Management, Logistics and Transport at the University of Reims, the department being part of the Institute of Technology. Here, she is in charge of a professional bachelor's degree in logistics management that she has developed. Her research interests focus on the wider effects of high-speed rail in terms of local economic development.

Germà Bel, Les Cases d'Alcanar, 1963. Holds an MA in Economics (University of Chicago, 1988) and a PhD in Economics (University of Barcelona, 1993). He is currently a Full Professor in the Department of Applied Economics at the University of Barcelona where he is the director of the Pasqual Maragall Chair of Economy and Territory. His main areas of research are public sector reforms, local government, privatization, regulation and transportation.

Paolo Beria, Milan, 1978. Holds an MSc in Civil Engineering and a PhD in Urban Projects and Policies (Politecnico di Milano, 2003, 2008). He is an Associate Professor of Transport Economics and director of the TRASPOL Research

Centre on Transport Policy in the Department of Architecture and Urban Studies at the Politecnico di Milano. He is a member of the management board of the Special Interest Group on Transport Economics and Regulation (SIG-E3) of the World Conference on Transport Research. His fields of research are transport planning and geography, assessment of transport projects and policies, and regulation.

Ofelia Betancor, Las Palmas de Gran Canaria, 1967. Holds an MSc in Economics (Queen Mary and Westfield College, University of London, 1993), and two doctorate degrees in Economics (ITS, University of Leeds, 2011 and University of Las Palmas, 1998). She is an Associate Professor of Economics at the University of Las Palmas and is currently the head of the Department of Applied Economic Analysis.

Gorka Bueno, Bilbao, 1970. Holds an MSc and a PhD in Telecommunications Engineering (University of the Basque Country, 1994, 2001). He is currently an Associate Professor in the Department of Electronics Engineering at the University of the Basque Country and is a member of EKOPOL, the Research Group on Ecological Economics and Political Ecology. After undertaking research for 13 years in the field of photovoltaics, at the moment his research interests lie in the area of energy sustainability.

Javier Campos, Las Palmas, 1968. Holds an MSc in Economics (London School of Economics, 1992) and a PhD in Economics (University of Las Palmas, 1996). He works as an Associate Professor of Industrial Organization in the Department of Applied Economics at the University of Las Palmas. His current research areas include empirical and theoretical analysis of competition and regulation in infrastructure sectors. He has also worked as a consultant for the World Bank and the Inter-American Development Bank, where he has gained field experience on infrastructure reform in Latin America.

Iñigo Capellán-Pérez, Valladolid, 1986. Holds an MSc in Electrical Energy and Sustainable Development (Arts et Métiers Paris Tech, Lille, 2008). He is an industrial engineer from the University of Valladolid and Arts et Métiers Paris Tech. He is a member of GEEDS (Research Group on Energy, Economy and System Dynamics at the University of Valladolid). His research interests focus on the analysis and modelling of the energy–economy–environment systems and the transition to renewable energies in the context of the depletion of fossil fuels and climate mitigation.

Amandine Craps, Charleroi, 1989. Holds a BA in Sociology, an MSc in Environmental Studies and an Advanced Master's degree in Transportation Studies (Free University of Brussels (ULB), 2011, 2013, 2014). During 2015 she was a trainee at the European Railway Agency in Valenciennes where she worked particularly on environmental externalities from different transport modes. She is currently pursuing a PhD focusing on mobility matters at ULB and is an educational coordinator at the Interuniversity Centre for Mobility Studies (CIEM) in Brussels.

Yves Crozet is an emeritus professor at Sciences Po Lyon and the University of Lyon II. He was director of the Transport Economics Laboratory (LET) as well as director of the Réseau Ferré de France (RFF). His research specialization is public economics, with a special interest in transport economics.

Ginés De Rus, Linares, 1953. Holds an MSc in Transport Economics and a PhD in Economics (University of Leeds, 1985, 1989). He is Professor of Applied Economics at the University of Las Palmas de Gran Canaria (Spain) and Cost-Benefit Analysis at the University Carlos III de Madrid. He coordinates the research area on transport and infrastructure at FEDEA. His main fields of interest are transport economics, regulation and cost-benefit analysis. He has worked for the European Commission, the European Investment Bank and the World Bank, among others.

Catherine Dehon holds a PhD from the Université Libre de Bruxelles (2001). She is an Associate Professor at the European Centre for Advanced Research in Economics and Statistics (ECARES) at the Solvay Brussels School of Economics and Management, which is part of the Université Libre de Bruxelles.

Marie Delaplace, Saint-Dizier, 1961. Holds a PhD in Economics on the innovations and places (University of Reims, 1994). She is currently Professor in Spatial and Urban Planning at Lab'Urba (Parisian School of Urban Planning) at the University of Paris-Est-Marne-La-Vallée where she coordinates the research group on City, Transport, Tourism and Territory from the LabEX "Urban Futures" initiative. She is a member of the scientific council of the Observatory of the French High-speed Line Bretagne–Pays-de-la-Loire and from 2011 to 2014 she was the facilitator of the French University of Tourism (AsTRES). She has been working on local economic development, and particularly on the wider effects of high-speed rail, for the past 12 years. She is the author of 30 papers in academic journals and books and 50 communications in international conferences on this issue.

Frédéric Dobruszkes holds an MA in Geography, an MA in Transports and a PhD in Geography (Free University of Brussels (ULB), 1995, 1996, 2007). He is currently an FNRS research associate and a lecturer at the same institution. He is also the head of the Brussels-based Interuniversity Centre for Mobility Studies (CIEM) and the vice-president of the Brussels Regional Mobility Commission. His main research interests relate to transport geography and policy. His current focus is mainly on the dynamics of European air transport and on airline/high-speed rail competition.

Moshe Givoni holds a PhD (University College London, 2005), a BA in Economics and Geography and an MBA (Tel Aviv University, 1996, 1999). He is head of the newly established (2014) Transport Research Unit (TRU) and a senior lecturer, both in the Department of Geography and Human Environment at Tel Aviv University. He is also a visiting research associate in the Transport Studies Unit (TSU) at the University of Oxford where he was a senior researcher before joining Tel-Aviv University. He previously held two Marie

Curie Fellowships, including a post-doctoral fellowship in the Department of Spatial Economics at Vrije Universiteit in Amsterdam (2005–2007). His research interests all fall under the subject umbrella of "Moving towards low carbon mobility".

Raffaele Grimaldi, Como, 1983. Holds an MSc in Civil Engineering (Politecnico di Milano, 2007) and will defend his PhD in Transport and Infrastructure (Sapienza Università di Roma, expected spring 2016). He is currently a research fellow at the TRASPOL Research Centre on Transport Policy in the Department of Architecture and Urban Studies at the Politecnico di Milano. His research interests focus on transport planning and evaluation of projects and policies.

Torben Holvad, Aarhus, 1964. Holds an MSc in Economics (Copenhagen University, 1990), an MA and a PhD (European University Institute, Florence, 1991, 1994). He is an economic adviser at the European Railway Agency (France), a senior research associate in the Transport Studies Unit (TSU) at the University of Oxford and an external Associate Professor in the Department of Transport at the Technical University of Denmark (DTU). He has significant expertise in applied economic analysis with particular emphasis on regulation of the transport sector, policy appraisal and evaluation with respect to promotion of sustainability and regional economic development.

David Hoyos, Bilbao, 1974. Holds an MSc in Development Economics (University of Manchester, 1998) and a PhD in Economics (University of the Basque Country, 2009). He is currently an Associate Professor in the Department of Applied Economics III (Econometrics and Statistics) at the University of the Basque Country where he coordinates EKOPOL, a research group on Ecological Economics and Political Ecology. His main area of research concerns the economic valuation of environmental and natural resources. He is also an associate researcher at BC3 (Basque Centre for Climate Change) and HEGOA (Institute of Development and International Cooperation Studies). More information can be found at: www.ehu.eus/david.hoyos.

Gerard Llobet, Barcelona, 1972. Holds a PhD in Economics (University of Rochester, 2000). He is currently an Associate Professor at the Centro de Estudios Monetarios y Financieros (CEMFI). His research covers topics mainly concerned with industrial organization and the economics of innovation. His papers have been published in the *Journal of Political Economy*, the *Review of Financial Economics*, *Management Science*, the *Journal of Marketing Research* and the *Journal of Economics and Management Strategy*, among others. He is also an editor of the economics blog Nada Es Gratis.

Jordi Martí-Henneberg, Reus, 1959. Holds a degree in History and Geography and a PhD (University of Barcelona). He has been invited to the University of Cambridge as a visiting scholar three times, in 2006, 2011 and 2016. He is currently Professor of Human Geography at the University of

Lleida, where he teaches Geography of Europe from 1990. He leads high-profile research projects, mostly funded by the European Union. He is an ICREA Academia researcher for the period 2013–2018.

John Preston, Leeds, 1960. Holds a BA in Geography (University of Nottingham, 1981) and a PhD in Economics (University of Leeds, 1987). He is currently Professor of Rail Transport and head of the Transportation Research Group (TRG) at the University of Southampton. His research on railways has covered demand and cost modelling, operations and capacity management, and economic appraisal and evaluation. He has undertaken studies of high-speed rail for a variety of bodies, including the International Transport Forum.

1 An evidence-based review of key issues in high-speed rail

Daniel Albalate and Germà Bel

High-speed rail (HSR) is a sound, modern innovation in surface transportation. It has become not only a new transportation mode, but a symbol of modernity, efficiency and technological achievement. For this reason, HSR has been expanding rapidly all over the world in order to improve rail services, promote customer satisfaction and compete with other supposedly more polluting alternatives. Nonetheless, debates about its convenience are too often founded on the grounds of intangible and immeasurable outcomes. In the last few years, literature has emerged which sheds some light on the realities and evidences regarding the contributions of this mode of transportation. There is no doubt that HSR often requires a great deal of input to produce positive net welfare impacts. It requires huge investments because it is usually the most expensive infrastructure project in the history of any country. It also requires high-demand from passengers and its general cost in relation to other modes of transportation is far greater.

This book offers a complete review of the recent analyses and cutting-edge research performed in the field of HSR literature. It covers some of the most challenging topics that today deserve the attention of top researchers in the fields of economics, geography, engineering, the environment and planning. In addition, the issues examined in the next ten chapters are of considerable interest to policy makers worldwide and to anybody interested in having a better understanding of what HSR can offer to their community. This better and evidence-based knowledge contributes to a more deliberative and informed democracy and allows better social choices to be made, especially if we take into account how resource consuming HSR might be.

To satisfy this objective, the book is structured into three blocks or research areas. The first block of chapters discusses the economic assessment of HSR projects from both financial and socioeconomic perspectives. This aspect is critical in HSR infrastructure projects given the huge expenditure associated with them. Only a rigorous assessment and evaluation of these investments, usually borne by taxpayers given the traditional means of finance of the public sector, may avoid large welfare losses and financial burdens for both the current and future generations.

Although it is obvious that transportation infrastructure does not need to be financially profitable, its positive externalities and other welfare-enhancing indirect effects should offset the enormous economic cost of building and maintaining the infrastructure.

This block starts with a general methodological discussion presented by Ginés de Rus in Chapter 2, who offers interesting recommendations with regard to rigorously assessing the economic evaluation of large infrastructure projects. Among such, HSR has become a major infrastructure project requiring specific economic evaluation strategies.

Once the methodological framework has been presented, the block moves to an empirical orientation by presenting the economic evaluation of HSR investments in Spain. In Chapter 3, Ofelia Betancor and Gerard Llobet evaluate the Spanish HSR network from both a financial and a socioeconomic perspective. This empirical chapter serves to confirm how demanding this infrastructure is in terms of investment for it to guarantee a positive welfare contribution. In the specific case of Spain, the country with the longest HSR network in Europe, we can confirm after reading the chapter that this mode of transportation was a tremendous mistake with huge financial and economic losses that will have financial consequences over time, and which has also produced negative social returns.

To end this first block, John Preston covers the indirect and wider economic impacts of HSR in Chapter 4. There is an intense scholar and practitioner debate about why and how indirect and wider effects should be included in large infrastructure economic evaluations. The chapter by John Preston offers his view on this controversial and open debate and provides some figures supported by recent evidence and research on the strength of these effects, with particular interest in HSR1 and HSR2 in the UK. These two cases are good examples of extensive research and evaluation being carried out before large infrastructure projects are undertaken and they help to provide early evidence with regard to some of the wider economic effects that are difficult to introduce in cost-benefit models given their complexity.

The second block of chapters opens a discussion on the economic and land use effects of HSR. These chapters offer some specific views on the impact of HSR on affected industries, such as the tourist industry (Chapter 5), on the land used to build the lines (taking into account its accessibility) (Chapter 6) and on the environment (Chapters 7 and 8).

Marie Delaplace and Sylvie Bazin-Benoit analyze one of the more commonly attributed impacts of HSR – on tourism – which is obviously linked to transportation infrastructure supply. The tourist industry is usually lobbying for new and more efficient transportation modes and in this regard, HSR is seen as a potential channel through which more people may arrive at tourist hotspots. There is no doubt that transportation and tourism are closely related economic activities. However, recent research has shown some mixed or even disappointing results. Bazin-Benoit and Delaplace confirm that in areas served by HSR, the actors expect a dynamic economy, in general, and of tourism in particular. Nevertheless, the disappointing *ex post* analyses make it necessary to study what factors are relevant for transforming the arrival of HSR into a development tool. Among them, Bazin-Benoit and Delaplace elaborate on new forms of cooperation between local stakeholders to take advantage of the tourist potential created by HSR. Indeed, tourism is an activity that generally needs cooperation policies between various public and private stakeholders, and this is particularly important during the planning for HSR. By focusing on different French cities, their chapter analyzes the different kinds of cooperation used in the tourism field with regard to HSR.

Constructing railway infrastructure on land near cities has never been easy. It has been a source of social, economic and environmental tension and has required careful handling. For this reason, Jordi Martí-Henneberg and Eduard J. Alvarez-Palau present a critical debate on how good initial planning, appropriate design and carefully selected methods of construction are required to ensure that cities and their railway stations are able to get the most from the arrival of new HSR services. These authors study the impact of HSR stations on the geography of Europe in order to analyze, measure and make an international comparison of their accessibility. On the one hand, demand potential and its expected growth seems to be called into question as the standard criterion for assigning investments in HSR. On other hand, different approaches regarding the type of networks designed have inevitably produced consequences for the location of HSR stations, their accessibility and, therefore, their contribution. The chapter shows how transport policies have allowed different cities to integrate their HSR stations into their daily dynamics in different fashions. Indeed, new transport services have been studied taking into consideration the different modes of transport already available in order to allow acceptable levels of accessibility to HSR stations, whether linked to public or private transport. Unfortunately, the authors show their disappointment at the lack of connectivity between HSR stations and airports in some countries, especially because this limits their intermodal potential for journeys over medium and long distances. The major contribution of HSR appears to be in medium distances, where it can be more efficient than road and air transportation. For this reason, designing a multimodal network appears to be essential to offer the best accessibility and service for the whole set of origin–destination distances.

The environmental contribution of HSR in that it has advantages over air transportation in this respect has been one of the most frequently cited advantages by unconditional supporters of HSR. No doubt in standard situations HSR does appear to be more environmentally efficient in operation than air transportation, but this so-called advantage is far from being that clear when we consider other aspects of the life cycle of this infrastructure and its capabilities for attracting users from the more polluting modes of transportation. In Chapter 7, Torben Holvad, Amandine Craps and Javier Campos contribute to this book elaborating on the environmental performance of HSR and its implications. Overall, during the past couple of decades rail has been promoted in European transport policy in order that a move towards a more sustainable transport system can be effected. This draws notably on the environmental performance of rail compared to other modes of transport. The chapter provides an up-to-date and comprehensive assessment of the environmental performance of HSR.

The environmental implications of HSR are also considered in comparison to other modes of transportation, including conventional rail. The life cycle perspective is of special interest, a consideration going beyond an extensive literature that neglects the different phases of the project. This part of the analysis provides indications of the micro-based environmental implications of HSR. Subsequent analyses look at an aggregated perspective on HSR environmental implications both in isolation and as part of the overall transport system. The authors also provide a challenging discussion on a future perspective of HSR which involves consideration of expected transport scenarios covering both network development and HSR usage in order to determine the likely environmental impacts of HSR over the time period 2030–2050.

David Hoyos, Gorka Bueno and Iñigo Capellán-Pérez also devote Chapter 8 to assessing the environmental contribution of HSR. They focus on the greenhouse gas (GHG) emission and energy consumption balance and, ultimately, they evaluate the conditions under which HSR investments can be considered the right move for sustainable mobility. For this purpose, these authors apply the transport hierarchy approach as a general framework for the assessment of HSR from a sustainable perspective. This framework establishes a priority order for the design and management of transport systems, differentiating between four levels of priority: (1) demand minimization; (2) modal shift and intermodality; (3) efficiency optimization; and (4) capacity increase. New HSR projects, therefore, fall directly into the last option. Taking into account the magnitude of the environmental problem as well as the commitments already signed by the EU, the most important contribution of HSR to sustainable mobility lies in its potential for environmental impact reductions, especially with regard to GHG emission and energy consumption. In an illustrative example, the project Basque Y in Spain, it is shown that net GHG emission and energy consumption reductions are likely to be virtually nil during the useful lifetime of the infrastructure. This example demonstrates the need to assess the environmental performance of HSR on a case-by-case basis.

The third block of chapters relates to the role of institutions, particularly with regard to regulation, competition and the introduction of private participation. On the one hand, we have two chapters exploring the potential and realities of competition. Chapter 9 examines on-track competition, while Chapter 10 considers and contributes to the extensive emerging literature on intermodal competition. Paolo Beria and Raffaele Grimaldi examine the very first case, unique in the world so far, of HSR on-track competition in Chapter 9.[1] On-track competition is slowly coming to the fore in the battlefield of the rail market, and is trying to open niche long-distance markets behind the front line of regional franchises. Their chapter aims at revising – under different perspectives (normative, analysis of current and potential markets, competitors' behaviour) – the current and expected cases of on-track competition, with particular focus on the only one actually belonging to the high-speed segment – that in Italy. While detailed traffic figures are not available, the effects of competition can be analyzed empirically looking at supply and at fare strategies. The text concludes by generalizing the results, in order to shed light on the conditions for the development of the high-speed open access market in Europe.

Intermodal competition is also of essential interest if we take into account the fact that part of the environmental effects and a large share of social benefits depend on the operational attractiveness of HSR with respect to other modes of transportation. Chapter 10 is devoted to intermodal competition. This chapter, offered by Frédéric Dobruszkes, Moshe Givoni and Catherine Dehon, examines competition between HSR and airlines as being a fundamental issue to consider with regard to taking advantage of the supposed environmental efficiency gains of this mode of rail transportation in comparison to air travel. These authors suggest that the supposed environmental benefit is now inevitably at the core of any new HSR project or of many plans that aim to reduce the environmental footprint of medium-distance mobility, and especially as far as air travel is concerned. This critical aspect of HSR is evaluated in the chapter by moving from HSR project rhetoric to the evidence-based outcomes in terms of intermodal impacts of HSR services. The authors highlight some of the most common methodological misunderstandings in this debate and discuss the limitations affecting the power of HSR to reduce air travel.

On the other hand, the last chapter of this book, contributed by Yves Crozet, considers the limited role of privatization in the development of this mode of transportation by drawing on the French experience with public–private-partnerships (PPPs). During the last 20 years, PPPs have been applied in the rail sector, especially for HSR. A review of these PPPs shows that some of them have partly or totally failed. Beyond the evidence that PPP is a good option to optimize the risks in that these are shared between public and private partners, the fact that some unexpected risks do arise has to be emphasized. These can occur especially because of opportunistic behaviours from both sides of the contract. After a description of the attractiveness of PPPs, the chapter proposes a brief inventory of difficulties encountered by HSR PPPs. The main learning outcome from this review is that some huge risks remain for the public authorities. The state is very often the lender of last resort and sometimes the operator of last resort because it is usually highly unacceptable to simply close the service down. Such a result can be explained by the fact that public decision makers behave like "risk lovers".

To conclude this introductory chapter, all the chapters in the book offer a particular contribution and present different viewpoints with regard to the new, modern and controversial mode of rail transportation – HSR. The book reviews the current state of knowledge in relation to some specific issues that we consider the main topics and challenges underlining a consideration of HSR. This, therefore, implies that, inherently, the book will also help to identify new lines of research, the results of which will ultimately offer more certainty of what HSR has to offer, taking into account the impacts that it will have. The book will also help to identify further challenges regarding the introduction of HSR which will need to be addressed if this impressive project is going to reach its full potential in any country.

Note

1 Spain prepares for the liberalization of part of its network by introducing on-track competition for the Madrid–Valencia link. This liberalization has not been implemented yet at the time of writing this chapter.

2 The economic evaluation of major infrastructure projects

Notes on HSR projects[1]

Ginés de Rus

1. Introduction

In the 1970s and first half of the 1980s, the net stock of public capital in the US grew at 1.6 per cent, approximately three times lower than the annual growth rate during the previous 20 years. Aschauer (1989) linked this reduction in infrastructure investment to the productivity slowdown in that period, particularly during the first half of the 1980s. Following this main contribution, many other studies have found similar causal relations between infrastructure and economic growth (Munnel, 1990; Deno, 1991; Deno and Eberts, 1991; Eisner, 1991; García-Mila and McGuire, 1992).

In a second wave of econometric research, the estimations were much less optimistic (Evans and Karras, 1994; Holtz-Eakin, 1994; Holtz-Eakin and Schwartz, 1995; Holtz-Eakin and Lovely, 1996). Beyond the discussion on the value of the elasticities, the research on the economic impact of public infrastructure investment has shown that the estimated elasticities of productivity with respect to the stock of public capital are very sensitive to the present level of this stock. Aschauer's high elasticities correspond to a period of low growth in the net stock of public capital. For example, in the case of Spain, de la Fuente and Vives (1995), Goerlich and Mas (2001) and Mas et al. (1996), among others, obtained higher elasticities in the 1970s than in the 1990s when the core infrastructure network was already built (from 0.14 to 0.02).

Moreover, the aggregate approach, followed in the econometric estimations, can only provide an average approximation of what happened in the past. Therefore, their estimates are not going to help much with the key question of where and in which type of infrastructure the marginal investment should be assigned (Gramlich, 1994). This problem is crucial in the allocation of resources and it is mainly addressed within the realm of the public sector. This is the main concern of this chapter: how the economic evaluation of transport projects can be improved by detecting some of the weaknesses of their actual application.

The somewhat naive and common belief in the economic benefits of transport infrastructure investment, disregarding the opportunity cost of the resources employed in specific projects, rests on some type of "availability cascade" (Kuran and Sunstein, 1999) consisting of a self-reinforcing process through which a collective belief develops without critical thinking or any empirical justification. People usually believe that infrastructure investment is good (and the bigger, faster or taller the better) because other people have adopted this belief. The political discourse reinforces this idea, emphasizing the benefits, overlooking the costs and presenting some irrelevant short-term demand effects as benefits of the specific project (Crompton, 2006). The mantra is: investment in public infrastructure is good for the country. It creates jobs and increases productivity.

This cognitive bias found some academic support in the economic literature of the 1980s and its overoptimistic elasticities of productivity with respect to the stock of public capital. The overflow of papers based on the aggregate approach contrasts with the lack of any practical interest in its results for the key questions regarding infrastructure investment decisions in the real world (Gramlich, 1994).

Infrastructure investment consists of giving up present consumption for future consumption. Reliable transport in the future requires deviating resources in the present to build basic infrastructure to keep up with demand growth and technological change for future needs. It is an intertemporal trade-off. This is the key point when speaking on investment, and the choice of an appropriate social discount rate is the conventional approach to make the flow of sacrifices and the benefits homogenous over time to determine whether the sacrifice is worthy. Unfortunately, this trade-off is not the only one that practitioners must face in the decision-making process.

The economic evaluation of infrastructure investment requires consideration of some additional trade-offs. Going back to first economic principles, we start with the basic question: is the society better off with the project? To answer this question we need to address which model we previously had in mind and the scope and validity of cost-benefit analysis. In section 2, the basic framework for the evaluation of projects and the issue of the social planner model versus the interest group competition model are discussed along with the role of cost-benefit analysis in these alternative worlds.

Pricing and investment is the content of section 3. Both subjects are interconnected and cannot be treated independently. Investment in capacity requires forecasting demand, which is sensitive to the level and the structure of charges. Furthermore, once the infrastructure is built, pricing decisions are highly conditioned by sunk costs given the degree of specificity of the assets already built.

Moreover, the substitutability and complementarity of some infrastructures are additional reasons for addressing the price–investment decision jointly, which also has significant long-term consequences beyond allocative efficiency in the short term. This is the content of section 4, which includes a discussion of the short- versus long-term consequences of major infrastructure investment projects. This discussion includes the optimal timing of investment but fundamentally concerns the issue of long-term equilibria when mutually exclusive systems or networks compete to solve a common problem. Section 5 deals with incentives in the application of cost-benefit analysis and section 6 concludes.

2. A model for the economic evaluation of projects

The economic evaluation of infrastructure projects through cost-benefit analysis requires a clear understanding of the difference between what economists would like to measure and what they *can* measure. We are interested in welfare changes, but we have to address the monetary measures of utility changes. Although cost-benefit analysis is trying to measure changes in social surplus brought about by a project, the analysis is carried out with money as an alternative to estimating the actual changes in individuals' utility, and finally in social welfare through some type of conversion of individual utility into social wellbeing.

Therefore, although money is only an instrument in the economic appraisal of transport infrastructure investment, it is the common unit in which economists express changes in utility and welfare. This has a price in terms of some well-known ambiguities when comparing or aggregating monetary changes of individuals who differ in their level of income, among other personal characteristics.

When the objective is the maximization of social welfare and public funds are limited, the maximum net present value must be calculated for the set of projects, given their interrelation and the existence of a budget constraint. In practice, many projects are subject to individual evaluation without considering the consequences of their implementation with respect to other projects linked with the former through relationships of complementarity or substitutability and the long-term implications of some decisions. Even so, the common assumption is that the government tries to maximize welfare and conduct cost-benefit analysis to guide its decisions.

An alternative view (Becker, 1983) explains a government's action by the political power of different interest groups. A new infrastructure investment decision could be the consequence of lobbying by contractors and/or the economic agents of the region receiving direct benefit, instead of the outcome of the maximization of a social welfare function. In this case, the consequences of investing in a particular project with far-reaching consequences are much more serious and deserve a detailed treatment (see sections 4 and 5).

There is a well-documented body of evidence showing that the *ex ante* benefits and costs in many projects are usually overestimated and underestimated, respectively (Flyvbjerg et al., 2002; 2005). The tendency of people to base their forecasts on the "inside view" in which planned actions and intention dominate the "outside view" based on the statistical evidence from the *ex post* outcomes of similar projects (Kahneman and Tversky, 1979; Kahneman, 1994), leads to the so-called "planning fallacy", which explains the poor results of many infrastructure projects with apparently positive *ex ante* evaluation.

It is crucial to look at the cause of the difference between forecasted and actual outcomes in the planning fallacy. In many cases it is not a problem of individuals' tendencies to disregard relevant statistical information and base the predicted results on planned actions and intentions (cognitive bias), but of strategic misrepresentation. In this latter case, inaccuracy is deliberate (Flyvbjerg, 2013); hence, we have to look to the institutional design in which the planning and economic evaluation of infrastructure projects takes place.

Though many of the projects approved by the government do not support the view of a social planner pursuing the maximization of social welfare, the analyst can go ahead with the economic evaluation of a project as if the government were pursuing the general interest of society.

The existence of a benevolent government is not required to conduct a cost-benefit analysis. A more prosaic view is compatible with its defense in public policy. We can assume the existence of a government pursuing the maximization of the probability of its re-election, for example, and at the same time estimating the welfare effects of projects. Cost-benefit analysis can help provide relevant information to the economic agents about the associated costs and benefits of government interventions as it is an investment in public infrastructure (Becker, 2001).

It is quite risky to quantify impacts without a clear analytical framework. To derive rules for the practitioner of cost-benefit analysis we need a model. A rigorous approach is needed to derive practical rules to avoid double counting and other errors in the valuation of transport benefits and costs. We assume the existence of a rational individual (or household) who maximizes utility subject to the usual constraints. We overlook here problems derived from distorted preferences (see Adler and Posner, 2001; Brennan, 2014).

The utility of this representative household is affected by the project, so it can be a winner, a loser or be indifferent to the implementation of the project. As utility cannot be measured, economists estimate the monetary valuation of utility changes, typically the compensating variation or the maximum amount of money that given to or taken from the individual leaves him indifferent to the project compared with the situation without the project (the counterfactual).[2]

There are well-known problems when converting this monetary compensation into welfare changes as individuals differ in income and personal characteristics. The so-called social marginal utility of income is expected to be different among individuals even assuming a utilitarian social welfare function where the social marginal utility is identical for all individuals. Moreover, changes in utility happen in different periods of time, and another weighting is required to calculate the net present value of the projects given the preferences of individuals between present and future consumption. This is the issue of discounting (see Burgess, 2011; Moore et al., 2013a, 2013b).

In practice, the Kaldor–Hicks compensation criterion is explicitly or implicitly followed. The conventional calculus of the net present value implies a social marginal utility of income equal for all the individuals in society. This presumes an optimal distribution of income or, perhaps, the possibility/desirability of dealing with equity separately (for distributional issues see Layard and Walters, 1978).

Although we do not cover the mechanics of cost-benefit analysis (see other chapters in this book), it is important to stress that the household's monetary valuation is based on the impact of a project on prices, income (both external and coming from labor or profits) and taxes, plus the impact on attributes such as air quality, noise, safety or comfort. Hence, when an infrastructure project changes the level of pollution and the generalized price of transport, for example, it is essential to have the model in mind to ask the right questions and avoid double counting.

Johansson (1993) posits general equilibrium cost-benefit rules for marginal and large projects that affect the environment. The core approach is general and can be applied to any other government intervention, such as the provision of transport infrastructure. The key idea is that the economy is composed of households and firms, ultimately owned by the former. The indirect utility function of a representative consumer is a function of prices, wages, exogenous income, firms' profits, taxes and public goods. Under the assumption of well-behaved functions and prices adjusting to equate supply and demand, the monetary valuation of the utility change produced by a large project can be approximated through the conventional rules of adding consumer, producer and taxpayer surpluses, as long as the consumer's willingness to pay does not include any change in exogenous income, profits or taxes.

Cost-benefit analysis can be contemplated as a set of shortcuts to circumvent the impossible task of measuring the total effects of an infrastructure project in the economy. This involves the effects on many households and markets during the lifespan of the project. The good news is that under some conditions, particularly in a state of continuous adjustment of prices to equate supply and demand, it is possible to approximate the net present value concentrating the effort in the primary market. The bad news is that the conventional approach loses validity when the project produces significant price changes.

We now move to a more formal discussion of the cost-benefit analysis framework with the aim of making explicit the assumptions behind the practical rules followed to try to answer the demanding question of whether society should put public money into particular infrastructure projects. The general equilibrium cost-benefit rules (Johansson, 1993) will be our basic framework.

Let us assume the existence of an economy with identical households, where firms are ultimately owned by households. The representative household consumes private goods and a public good, interpreted here as the *level* of public infrastructure, and supplies a vector of different type of labor. The indirect utility function of the economy's representative household is written as:

$$V = V\big[p, w, Y + \Pi(p, w, z) - \tau, z\big]$$
$$= \max_{x^d, L^s} \big\{ U(x^d, L^s, z) \;\; s.t. \;\; Y + \Pi + wL^s - \tau - CV - px^d = 0 \big\} \tag{1}$$

p: price vector
w: factor prices vector
Y: exogenous income
Π: profit income
τ: lump sum tax collected by the government
x^d: private goods vector
L^s: labor vector
z: public good
CV: compensating variation

Firms, owned by households, maximize profits (Π):

$$\Pi = pF(L, z, K) - wL - 1.K, \tag{2}$$

where the price of capital is equal to 1.

The government controls the variable z. The upgrading of a road changes the magnitude of z, but the increase in z requires the use of real resources as production factors and other produced goods.

Totally differentiating the indirect utility function (1) and the profit function (2), the cost-benefit rule (3) is obtained. The reduction in total travel time and accidents following the upgrading of the road can be interpreted as a small change in z and evaluated according to (3).

$$dV / V_y = (x^s - x^d)dp + (L^s - L^d)dw +$$
$$\left[(V_z / V_y)dz + pF_z dz - dC - dCV \right] = 0 \tag{3}$$

Even if the change in the level of infrastructure affects other markets, if prices adjust to reach a new equilibrium, the first two terms in (3) net out and so we can concentrate the effort in the primary market. With a project cost, calculated at initial prices, equal to dC, the term dCV measures the representative household's willingness to pay (net of project costs). Applying the Kaldor–Hicks potential compensation criteria, a dCV equal to zero corresponds to a net present value (*NPV*) equal to zero.

We can then calculate the *NPV* of a small infrastructure project from the terms within brackets in (3): the households' direct willingness to pay plus the direct impact on profits minus the project costs. Changes in profits or costs due to changes in prices are not accounted for in the evaluation if demand equals supply in the new equilibrium.

The first three terms in brackets in (3) account for the change in resources and willingness to pay due to the infrastructure investment. In (3) the access to the infrastructure is free. In the next section we discuss the effect of charging for the use of the infrastructure. In the case of large projects, the general equilibrium rule is a generalization of (3) as long as the project does not lead to significant price changes.

3. Pricing and investment

The social appraisal of infrastructure projects requires addressing pricing explicitly. Investment and pricing cannot be separated out in cost-benefit analysis. Dupuit's rule of charging zero for the use of an uncongested bridge is an *ex post* rule. In the *ex ante* evaluation, when the bridge is still a project, the total willingness to pay for capacity (assuming free access) has to be at least as high as construction costs (otherwise, the bridge should not be built) but to tell whether this is the case, we need to know the price. Price determines demand and, therefore, total willingness to pay for capacity. The price to be charged has to be known in advance to carry out the economic evaluation of the investment.

Moreover, when Dupuit's bridge is congested a positive price is optimal to internalize the cost imposed on other users (Hotelling, 1938). In this case, the total willingness to pay for capacity could be lower than construction costs compared with the previous case given free access in both cases. The same happens when a budget constraint is binding or there is intermodal competition. The point is that pricing determines the volume of demand, which affects optimal capacity, costs and social surpluses.

This can be observed in expression (3) where the household's gross willingness to pay is composed of a direct effect on utility $(Vz/Vy)dz$, and the direct effect on profits $pF(z)dz$. When a price is introduced for the use of the infrastructure, the values of both terms usually change. Although a proportion of the price effect is a transfer that nets out in the first term of (3), unless demand is perfectly inelastic, there are changes in quantities as well as in social surplus (negative if price is above the marginal cost as is the case when all costs are fixed). Therefore, if demand elasticity is positive, in absolute terms, dCV cannot be estimated without previous knowledge of the price to be charged.

The optimal first-best pricing rule is to charge the social marginal cost: zero in the uncongested Dupuit's bridge and positive in other circumstances when costs vary with use, externalities or significant relationships exist with other markets. In the presence of budget constraints, following the optimal pricing rule also solves the problem when there are no indivisibilities in capacity provision and there is perfect information on demand, as short- and long-term marginal costs coincide.

This set of assumptions does not represent the real world. The common context of infrastructure investment is a second-best world with indivisibilities, imperfect information on costs and particularly on demand, relevant connections with other markets (e.g. intermodal competition) and the pervasive existence of budget constraints.

The first problem once we abandon the first-best world is that short- and long-term marginal costs are different and given the high proportion of fixed costs in the short term the economic consequences of applying short- or long-term marginal costs pricing are significant.

Infrastructure pricing and investment in a first-best world consist of maximizing total willingness to pay net of costs, including producer and user costs (mainly time in the case of transport infrastructure). Under the assumptions of absence of indivisibilities and separability of operating and capacity costs, the first-best rules for pricing and investment are straightforward. Let us consider the case of investing in road or airport capacity. In both areas the user cost is mainly time, and congestion is the immediate consequence of insufficient capacity.

The regulator charges an access price that includes the unit producer cost and the time costs imposed on others (delays as a consequence of congestion) due to the increase in the number of users (the user cost is already paid by the passenger and any environmental externalities are assumed to be internalized).

The investment rule is: increase capacity until the reduction in delay costs equals the additional producer cost of expanding capacity. The interrelation between pricing and investment is now evident. Pricing according to marginal social costs and expanding capacity according to the reduction of congestion costs allow the internalization of capacity costs and, under some quite demanding conditions, cost recovery (Mohring, 1976). The optimal price changes the values of $(Vz/Vy)dz$ and $pF(z)dz$ but the final value of dCV is the highest possible given the application of first-best marginal cost pricing.

The real world of infrastructure investment is characterized by indivisibilities and demand uncertainty. Moreover, the private sector is involved in the construction and operation of public infrastructure. The departure from short-term marginal cost pricing is, therefore, unavoidable. It could be possible to introduce second-best pricing that minimizes efficiency losses. The idea is to deviate from marginal cost fulfilling the budget constraint at a firm level (see Johansson and Kriström, 2012) or at an aggregate level (Nash and Samson, 2001). The practical difficulties of this proposal seem obvious when infrastructure such as airports, roads, ports and railways not only competes within a nation but also in a supranational dimension.

Charging short-term marginal costs when total willingness to pay is lower than capacity costs also has long-term consequences, as demand will grow given the misleading price signal in terms of the incremental costs of capacity expansion. This is particularly worrying in the case of alternative technologies to solve the same common problem.

The issue of intermodal competition is also crucial for pricing and investment decisions. Marginal social cost pricing in the primary market is suboptimal in the presence of distortions in secondary markets and when there are significant links with the primary market, but particularly when there are intermodal consequences as is the case, for example, of investment in HSR infrastructure that disregards the effects on air transport.

Public investments in dedicated HSR infrastructure that compete directly with air transport serve as an excellent case for the analysis of access pricing, investment and intermodal competition (de Rus and Socorro, 2014). Currently, some countries with a well-developed airport network are investing, or considering the possibility of investing in HSR infrastructure for distances (500–600 km) in which both modes of transport compete and where the total volume of demand in the corridor seems insufficient to justify expensive additional infrastructure with comparative advantages in the case of massive demand but extremely inefficient with low traffic.

The generalized cost of transport includes the monetary price, time and service quality. When the government invests in HSR infrastructure, the former equilibrium usually changes with a significant variation in the modal split and the allocation of resources. When the determinant of the change in modal split is the price charged by the government for the HSR infrastructure, it is crucial to know the content of these charges. If the government is applying short-term marginal cost pricing it is fundamental to evaluate beforehand the options for medium-distance intercity passengers before construction costs are sunk.

De Rus and Socorro (2014) show that with airlines in competition and the government charging access prices for airports and rail infrastructure, a positive net present value is not a sufficient condition to invest in HSR. The necessary and sufficient condition implies a positive difference in social welfare for the cases in which the new infrastructure is and is not constructed and optimal pricing is applied. This is not a result derived from the presence of uncertainty and the irreversibility of the investment, but from the interaction of pricing and investment decisions and the need to consider alternative policies based on pricing and regulation.

The consequences of recognizing these interdependences for public investment are paramount. The institutional design of the ministry of transport and public works in many countries where the division of management units is usually based on technological characteristics (road, air or rail) may result in the overall picture being lost and an investment being made in costly infrastructure with an evident reduction in social welfare.

4. The economic effects of large projects

Once we abandon the assumption of perfect divisibility, we see projects as incremental changes. Then, a narrower range of sizes may be available and capacity design has to be explicitly considered. There are also different technologies available to solve a common transport problem. The evaluation of large projects is difficult when significant price changes are expected and the economic consequences of a particular project may seriously affect the allocation of resources in the long term.

In the case of a large project, we can still follow the insight of expression (3) as long as the first two terms in parenthesis vanish once the project is implemented. In expression (3) the evaluation is conducted following the changes in willingness to pay and changes in resources. An alternative and equivalent approach is to add surpluses as changes in prices which do not add value (transfers) net out in the process of aggregation.

Following Johansson (1993), the social willingness to pay can be expressed as the consumer surplus (through a compensated demand), and the change in profits and taxes:

$$V(p^1, w^1, Y^1 + \Pi^1 - \tau^1 - CV, z^1) = V(p^1, w^1, Y^0 + \Pi^0 - \tau^0 - CV^p, z^1) = V^0 \quad (4)$$

Where V^0 refers to the level of utility attained without the project and CV^p denotes the partial willingness to pay for the project as a user of the infrastructure, excluding any effects on lump sum income, profits and taxes. Superscripts 1 and 0 denote with and without the project. The difference between CV and CV^p is the following:

$$CV = CV^p + \Delta Y + \Delta \Pi - \Delta \tau \quad (5)$$

where ΔY, $\Delta \Pi$ and $\Delta \tau$ are the change in exogenous income, profits and taxes, with and without the project.

This is the standard approach of defining the effect of the project as the sum of the consumer compensating variation, producer surplus and taxpayer surplus. The problem with large projects with significant impacts on prices in secondary markets is the near impossibility for the individuals to give a sound answer to the questions involved in expression (5). This shows a serious weakness of cost-benefit analysis when there are significant price effects on the rest of the economy and the assumption of supply equaling demand through the adjustment of prices becomes untenable.

Even assuming either more or less invariance of prices in the rest of the economy or the possibility of measuring the effects of price changes through other methods, there is a quite disturbing problem associated with large projects, which in principle seems to be manageable through planning and evaluation. This is the existence of multiple equilibria in the long term and the possibility of ending up with a bad equilibrium when the evaluation concentrates on individual projects and loses the larger picture of the long-term intermodal effects. This is again a reminder of the inadequacy of dealing with a project in isolation, disregarding relevant interactions with other markets and the dynamic process during the lifespan of the project.

If the reader looks at the keyboard of the topmost row of letters of his/her computer, it is highly probable that the first six letters spell out QWERTY. This is far from offering an explanation as to the efficiency of this arrangement of letters as opposed to an alternative layout. David (1985) shows that other arrangements, such as the DSK (the Dvorak Simplified Keyboard), were clearly superior and allowed faster typing. Nevertheless, the initial design, invented to address the problem of the typewriter keys clashing and jamming if struck in rapid succession, still remains as the standard for computers long after the old typewriter and the tendency to jam have disappeared.

The reasons why QWERTY became the dominant keyboard arrangement are: technical interrelatedness, economies of scale and quasi-irreversibility of investment (David, 1985). The lessons to be drawn from the sequence of facts and changes and influences explaining the inefficient standard arrangement of the keyboard currently provide some hints for the explanation of what is going on at present with mutually exclusive infrastructure investment, which shows the three features already mentioned above and the possibility of ending up with a practically irreversible and suboptimal system in the long term.

The economic planning of infrastructure and the evaluation of particular projects need to look to these insights. Some major transport infrastructure projects present these characteristics, and the decision concerning a particular project influences the future with a type of dynamic process in which initial investment favors the lock-in of, perhaps, a less efficient technology than the next best alternative. This is the case of addressing medium-distance intercity mobility in low-density countries with a choice of regional air transport or an HSR network (de Rus, 2011; 2012).

The long-term effects on the allocation of resources can be dramatic. The case of HSR versus air transport is illustrative in countries where both systems can be considered mutually exclusive. In countries with low population density, the usual base case is a network of airports with enough capacity to provide infrastructure for point-to-point medium-distance trips. HSR infrastructure is a technology for high-volume corridors; it is expensive and a high proportion of its costs is sunk. The irreversibility of investment is one of its main characteristics. Hence, unless it is carefully evaluated, looking at the alternatives and the long-term consequences of the investment, it may well be that the initial decision to introduce HSR ends up with an undesirable equilibrium in which the wrong technology displaces a cheaper, more efficient, financially sustainable and reversible alternative.

5. Incentives and institutional design

One crucial and mostly neglected issue in cost-benefit analysis is the explicit consideration of institutional design. The benevolent planner assumption is harmless when deriving the general equilibrium rules for the economic evaluation of projects but it turns out to be inadequate when we move from theory to the practical application of these rules.

When we apply a model to the real world,

> it is reasonable to ask whether it is based on assumptions that are generally in accord with what we know about the world and are capturing factors that are of first-order importance. In other words, we use the background knowledge that we have about the world we live in (knowledge that is based ultimately on empirical evidence) to filter out models that are not useful for understanding what happens in the economy or for making policy decisions.
>
> (Pfleiderer, 2014)

Cost-benefit analysis is carried out by public agencies within a specific governance structure, which inevitably affects the incentives required to deliver a sound assessment of projects. The construction of white elephants almost everywhere and the extension and frequency of contract renegotiation of the concessions for the construction and operation of transport infrastructure, worldwide, show that something must be wrong with the institutional design where public agencies plan and evaluate infrastructure projects (Flyvbjerg et al., 2003; Guasch and Straub, 2006).

The investment in infrastructure with private participation requires several stages from the initial planning process to the end of the concession. These phases, including the economic evaluation, are usually implemented within the same public authority without any clear separation of the different tasks involved. This favors the construction of white elephants, given the particular objectives of politicians (e.g. to be re-elected) and the role of investing in infrastructure projects to reach these objectives. The common governance structure reduces the incentive to conduct a rigorous cost-benefit analysis and reduces the incentives to minimize costs in the construction and operation along the lifespan of projects.

Engel, Fisher and Galetovic (2014) provide a proposal to change the institutional design in which the provision of infrastructure with public–private partnerships takes place. This proposal separates the project planning, design and delivery from the economic evaluation of projects and forms them into independent units. It also separates the unit awarding the contracts for the construction and operation of the project and the unit supervising the compliance with these contracts. Another unit addresses renegotiation and conflict resolution.

The creation of an independent agency conducting cost-benefit analysis sheltered from political interference could be an important step in the search for the best projects for society and would reduce the risk of costly inefficiencies associated with the present governance structure. The Public Investment System (SNI) in Chile is an interesting experience illustrating the application of some of these principles. It is probably the most consolidated investment appraisal system in Latin America. The SNI covers different infrastructure areas and it separates the agency promoting projects from the agency evaluating them (Gómez-Lobo, 2012).

Another remarkable initiative is the Major Projects Authority (MPA) in the UK. Launched in 2011, "It is a collaboration between the Cabinet Office, HM Treasury and departments and has the fundamental aim of significantly improving the delivery success rate of major projects across central government."[3]

A related issue concerning institutional design is the presence of various levels of government. Projects are evaluated in a context in which different levels of government are implied and where the objectives of the agents involved are not usually aligned. This is probably one of the main issues concerning the practical application of cost-benefit analysis at present. If the incentive of agent A is to get his project approved and financed by agent B, and a positive net present value is a requirement to get the project through, the incentives to overestimate benefits and underestimate costs are evident, as is the loss of incentive to reduce costs and charge users to raise revenues. This separation between who promotes and who pays also affects the decisions on infrastructure capacity and technology.

There are several reasons explaining why some supranational organizations finance infrastructure projects or why national governments finance regional projects. Some of the alleged ones are: to enable countries and regions to converge; to improve regional competitiveness and create jobs; and to promote international territorial cooperation. De Rus and Socorro (2010) have analyzed the consequences of the existence of two different levels of government regarding national infrastructure investment when a national project is financed by a supranational organization in a context of asymmetric information. This analysis is equally valid for a national government financing infrastructure projects in its regions.

The practical implications of this analysis are significant as they apply to the institutional design in the European Union where the European Commission co-finances national and cross-frontier infrastructure projects of its member countries. It is also relevant for the common case of a national government financing regional projects in many countries with a structure of regional governments. The basic scheme has two stages. In the first, a supranational (national) planner selects and finances projects presented by a national (regional) government. In the second stage, the national (regional) government selects a type of contract for the construction, maintenance and operation of the infrastructure projects. The role of cost-benefit analysis in this framework changes substantially from a method that selects projects with the objective of maximizing welfare to an obstacle that has to be overcome to get access to public funds.

6. Conclusions

Cost-benefit analysis is largely the quantification in monetary terms of the incremental changes in welfare, as derived from the implementation of a transport project, with respect to a counterfactual. If the incentives are adequate, the evaluation is carried out with the aim of examining whether society is expected to be better off with the project. There are several reasons why this may not be the case in the real world and unless the governance structure changes, we have enough evidence to suspect that the economic evaluation will not serve the public interest, playing the role of another administrative procedure to be overcome for the interest groups to obtain access to public funds. This is basically the case with the supranational co-financing of transport infrastructure projects like HSR and with the financing of regional projects from the budget of the central government.

We believe that the institutional design is so important for the social significance of the economic evaluation of infrastructure projects that unless the promoters of projects are interested in a sound evaluation, cost-benefit analysis will play a minor role in the decision of what new infrastructure projects to construct and when and where to construct them.

Once this problem is solved the practitioner has to deal explicitly with the issue of pricing. The relation between pricing and investment is paramount and nothing relevant can be obtained without the consideration of the relationship between pricing, demand and capacity, particularly when significant relationships exist between different transport infrastructures, such as HSR and airports. The main conclusion in this area is the inadequacy of conducting cost-benefit analysis without an explicit consideration of pricing and its effects on social surplus, particularly when infrastructures are characterized by intermodal competition.

Finally, the long-term effects of projects should be considered in the planning and evaluation procedures. Some major infrastructure projects, particularly the development of HSR, show technical interrelatedness, economies of scale and quasi-irreversibility of investment. These features can lead to locking into a less efficient technology than the next best alternative, unless the evaluation of the initial investment explicitly takes into consideration the dynamic process associated with this initial investment and its probable consequences in the long term. This is not an easy task, but a short-term evaluation disregarding the long-term effects can lead to profound consequences in the allocation of resources.

Notes

1 This chapter is an abridged version of FEDEA Working Paper 2014–16. The author is indebted to Per-Olov Johannson for his comments and suggestions. The responsibility for opinions expressed and for any remaining errors are solely those of the author.
2 This adds another difficulty for the practitioner as the counterfactual is dynamic. The world changes with and without the project and the prediction has to cover the lifespan of the project, which is quite long in the case of transport infrastructure.
3 https://www.gov.uk/government/groups/major-projects-authority

References

Adler, M.D. and E.A. Posner (2001). *"Implementing cost-benefit analysis when preferences are distorted"*, in M.D. Adler and E.A. Posner (eds), *Cost-benefit analysis: Legal, economic and philosophical perspectives*, Chicago and London: The University of Chicago Press, pp. 269–312.

Aschauer, D.A. (1989). *"Is public expenditure productive?"*, Journal of Monetary Economics, 23, pp. 177–200.

Becker, G.S. (1983). *"A theory of competition among pressure groups for political influence"*, The Quarterly Journal of Economics, 98(3), pp. 371–400.

Becker, G.S. (2001). *"A comment on the conference on cost-benefit analysis"*, in M.D. Adler and E.A. Posner (eds), *Cost-benefit analysis: Legal, economic and philosophical perspectives*, Chicago and London: The University of Chicago Press, pp. 313–316.

Brennan, T.J. (2014). *"Behavioral economics and policy evaluation"*, Journal of Benefit-Cost Analysis, 5(1), pp. 89–109.

Burgess, D.F. and R.O. Zerbe (2011). *"The most appropriate discount rate"*, Journal of Benefit-Cost Analysis, 4(3), pp. 391–400.

Crompton, J.L. (2006). *"Economic impact studies: Instruments for political shenanigans?"*, Journal of Travel Research, 45, p. 67.

David, P.A. (1985). *"Clio and the economics of QWERTY"*, The American Economic Review, 75(2), pp. 332–337.

de la Fuente, A. and X. Vives (1995). *"Infrastructure and education as instruments of regional policy: Evidence from Spain"*, Economic Policy, 20, pp. 11–54.

de Rus, G. (2011). *"The BCA of HSR: Should the government invest in high speed rail infrastructure?"*, Journal of Benefit-Cost Analysis, 2(1), pp. 1–28.

de Rus, G. (2012). *"Economic evaluation of the high speed rail"*, Stockholm: Ministry of Finance, Expert Group on Environmental Studies.

de Rus, G. and P. Socorro (2010). *"Infrastructure investment and incentives with supranational funding"*, Transition Studies Review, 17(3), pp. 551–567.

de Rus, G. and P. Socorro (2014). *"Access pricing, infrastructure investment and intermodal competition"*, Transportation Research Part E, 70, pp. 374–387.

Deno, K.T. (1991). *"Public capital and the factor intensity of the manufacturing sector"*, Urban Studies, 28(1), pp. 3–14.

Deno, K.T. and R. Eberts (1991). *"Public infrastructure and regional economic development: A simultaneous equation approach"*, Journal of Urban Economics, 30, pp. 329–343.

Eisner, R. (1991). *"Infrastructure and regional economic performance: comment"*, New England Economics Review, (Sept/Oct), pp. 47–58.

Engel, E., R.D. Fisher and A. Galetovic (2014). *"The economics of public–private partnerships"*, New York: Cambridge University Press.

Evans, P. and G. Karras (1994). *"Is government capital productive? Evidence from a panel of seven countries"*, Journal of Macroeconomics, 16(2), pp. 271–279.

Flyvbjerg, B. (2013). *"Quality control and due diligence in project management: Getting decisions right by taking the outside view"*, International Journal of Project Management, 31, pp. 760–774.

Flyvbjerg, B., M.K.S. Holm and L.B. Buhl (2002). *"Underestimating costs in public works projects: Error or lie?"*, Journal of the American Planning Association, 68(3), pp. 279–295.

Flyvbjerg, B., N. Bruzelius and W. Rothengatter (2003). *"Megaprojects and risk: An anatomy of ambition"*, Cambridge, UK: Cambridge University Press.

Flyvbjerg, B., M.K.S. Holm and L.B. Buhl (2005). *"How (in)accurate are demand forecasts in public works projects? The case of transportation"*, Journal of the American Planning Association, 71(2), pp. 131–146.

García-Mila, T. and M.T. McGuire (1992). *"The contribution of publicly provided inputs to state economics"*, Regional Science and Urban Economics, 22, pp. 229–241.

Goerlich, F. and M. Mas (2001). *"Capitalización y crecimiento"*, vol. I, in *La evolución económica de las provincias Españolas (1955–1998)*, Bilbao: Fundación BBVA.

Gómez-Lobo, A. (2012). *"Institutional safeguards for cost benefit analysis: Lessons from the Chilean National Investment System"*, Journal of Benefit-Cost Analysis, 3(1), pp. 1–28.

Gramlich, E.M. (1994). *"Infrastructure investment: A review essay"*, Journal of Economic Literature, 32(3), pp. 1176–1196.

Guasch, J.L. and S. Straub (2006). *"Renegotiation of infrastructure concessions: An overview"*, Annals of Public and Cooperative Economics, 77(4), pp. 479–493.

Holtz-Eakin, D. (1994). *"Public-sector capital and the productivity puzzle"*, The Review of Economics and Statistics, 76(1), pp. 12–21.

Holtz-Eakin, D. and A.E. Schwartz (1995). *"Spatial productivity spillovers from public infrastructures: evidence from state highways"*, Working Paper No. 5004, Washington, DC: National Bureau of Economic Research.

Holtz-Eakin, D. and M.E. Lovely (1996). *"Scale economies, returns to variety and the productivity of public infrastructure"*, Regional Science and Urban Economics, 26(2), pp. 105–123.

Hotelling, H. (1938). *"The general welfare in relation to problems of taxation and of railway and utility rates"*, Econometrica, 6(3), pp. 242–269.

Johansson, P-O. (1993). *"Cost-benefit analysis of environmental change"*, Cambridge, UK: Cambridge University Press.

Johansson, P-O. and B. Kriström (2012). *"The economics of evaluating water projects. Hydroelectricity versus other uses"*, Heidelberg: Springer Verlag.

Kahneman, D. (1994). *"New challenges to the rationality assumption"*, Journal of Institutional and Theoretical Economics, 150, pp. 18–36.

Kahneman, D. and A. Tversky (1979). *"Prospect theory: An analysis of decisions under risk"*, Econometrica, 47, pp. 313–327.

Kuran, T. and C.R. Sunstein (1999). *"Availability cascades and risk regulation"*, Stanford Law Review, 51(4), pp. 683–768.

Layard, R. and A. Walters (1978). *"Income distribution"*, in R. Layard and S. Glaister (eds), *Cost-benefit analysis*, 2nd edn, Cambridge, UK: Cambridge University Press, pp. 179–198.

Mas, M., J. Maudos, F. Pérez and E. Uriel (1996). *"Infrastructures and productivity in the Spanish regions"*, Regional Studies, 307, pp. 641–649.

Mohring, H. (1976). *"Transportation economics"*, Cambridge, MA: Ballinger.

Moore, M.A., A.E. Boardman and A.R. Vining (2013a). *"More appropriate discounting: The rate of social time preference and the value of the social discount rate"*, Journal of Benefit-Cost Analysis, 4(1), pp. 1–16.

Moore, M.A., A.E. Boardman and A.R. Vining (2013b). *"The choice of the social discount rate and the opportunity cost of public funds"*, Journal of Benefit-Cost Analysis, 4(3), pp. 401–409.

Munnel, A.H. (1990). *"How does public infrastructure affect regional economic performance"*, New England Economic Review, (Sept/Oct), pp. 11–32, Boston, MA: Federal Reserve Bank of Boston.

Nash, C. and T. Samson (2001). *"Pricing European transport systems. Recent developments and evidence from case studies"*, Journal of Transport Economics and Policy, 35(3), pp. 363–380.

Pfleiderer, P. (2014). *"Chameleons: The misuse of theoretical models in finance and economics"*, Working Paper No. 3020, Palo Alto, CA: Stanford University.

3 Financial and social profitability of HSR in Spain

Ofelia Betancor and Gerard Llobet

1. Introduction

The high-speed railway (HSR) has become the priority of the infrastructure policy in Spain. More than 3,100 kilometres of HSR were in operation in September 2015. This network makes Spain the country with the second largest network in the world, way behind China (16,000 kilometres) but ahead of other supporters of HSR like Japan (2,664 kilometres), France (2,036 kilometres), or Germany (1,334 kilometres).[1] The lines under construction will extend the network in the coming years to beyond 4,000 kilometres.

The total cost of the network already in operation is likely to exceed €50,000 million expressed in monetary units of 2015. This investment effort, mostly carried out in the last 15 years, has been undertaken in parallel with an ambitious airport capacity expansion and a large highway construction plan. Surprisingly, until 2015 no analysis commissioned by the Spanish government to measure the social returns of these new infrastructures, if such a one exists, has been made public.

Many experts have been concerned about the potential lack of social profitability of this investment. Authors such as de Rus and Inglada (1997) and de Rus (2011; 2012), among others, studied the first two lines, Madrid–Seville and Madrid–Barcelona and showed that, under reasonable assumptions, society will not recover the infrastructure construction costs. More recently, Betancor and Llobet (2015) conducted, at the request of FEDEA (Fundación de Estudios de Economía Aplicada), the first systematic analysis of all the lines in operation in Spain, including a social profitability analysis as well as a financial profitability one. In this chapter we summarize the main findings of this study.[2]

Our analysis is carried out over the network in operation in December 2013. This network included four main corridors that we denote as: Madrid–Andalusia, Madrid–Barcelona, Madrid–East Coast and Madrid–North. The construction of this network has been carried out by a state-owned company, ADIF (Administrador de Infrastructuras Ferroviarias). Another state-owned company, RENFE Operadora (referred to in the rest of this chapter simply as RENFE), has been in charge of providing train services.[3]

Our financial profitability results suggest that, although in general the revenues cover the costs of operation, it is very unlikely that they will eventually cover a significant proportion of construction costs during a reasonable time span. Regarding the social profitability analysis, the results point in a similar direction. Social benefits might compensate for a larger proportion of the construction costs but not so much as to make the investment socially profitable. The only exception is the Madrid–Barcelona corridor, for which society could, in the most optimistic scenario, just barely recover the whole cost of the investment.

It is important to point out that one of the main challenges in this work was information collection. Although we requested data from both companies, ADIF and RENFE, we received no response. For this reason, our analysis has been conducted using the scant public information available and secondary sources. Most data has come from the annual report of the Observatorio del Ferrocarril, an institution funded by ADIF and RENFE that provides somewhat disaggregate information on traffic. We complemented this source with data available in *Ferropedia*, a wiki about the Spanish railway system set up and maintained over the years by train enthusiasts aiming to put together the information that filtered through from public reports, budget estimates, etc.[4] Computation of the financial and social analysis also required some assumptions that are in great part inspired by de Rus (2012). As a verification of our approach we cross-checked our estimates with the data released in February 2014 by the Spanish government at the request of the parliament and published in the *Boletín Oficial de las Cortes Generales* (BOCG). This data included total costs, revenues and profits disaggregated at the origin–destination level for 2012, making the comparison with our work easier.

In this chapter we start by describing, in section 2, the Spanish approach to HSR. In section 3 we describe the methodology and the data we use in our analysis, and our main assumptions. Section 4 summarizes the results for all the lines in operation by the end of 2013 and section 5 discusses how robust our results are in relation to our main assumptions. Section 6 concludes.

2. The Spanish HSR

The deployment of HSR in Spain, commonly referred to as AVE (Alta Velocidad Española), can be described as the result of two construction phases. The first phase corresponds to the construction of the line from Madrid to Seville that took place between 1988 and 1992. No further investment took place until 1998 when the government presented a plan to extend the HSR network to the rest of the country. This second phase started with the works for the Madrid–Barcelona line (finished in 2008) and was followed by the works for the Madrid–Valladolid (2008), Madrid–Málaga (2008), Madrid–Valencia (2010) and Madrid–Alicante (2013) lines. These construction works extended the network to 2,515 kilometres by the end of 2013, the date at which our analysis is conducted.[5] This HSR network stands in contrast to the existing conventional network of 11,663 kilometres as reported in Observatorio del Ferrocarril en España (2014).

All HSR lines were constructed using the *international track gauge* of 1,435 mm. This made the lines incompatible with the existing network constructed mainly with the *Iberian gauge* of 1,668 mm and also some 1,250 kilometres of *meter gauge* tracks in the north. To allow trains to connect cities that were served with a combination of international and Iberian gauge tracks, gauge-changing technologies and facilities were developed. As a result, the new network allows high-speed trains to make use of the new infrastructure while others equipped with gauge-changing technology might serve locations for which the HSR only covers some segments, albeit at lower speeds even in the high-speed part of the route. Thus, the benefits of HSR in Spain stem both from the high-speed services (AVE) but also from the improved conventional train services that make use of the mixed technology. RENFE gave these the commercial name of Alvia.[6] Due to the fact that Alvia trains do not reach speeds above 250 kph they are not considered HSR.

Figure 3.1 shows the existing lines at the end of 2013. These lines can be classified in four different corridors, which will be the unit of our analysis and which we describe next.

1   The **Madrid–Barcelona corridor** includes HSR services between these two cities and intermediate stops together with a connection to Huesca. RENFE also provides AVE services from Barcelona to Seville and Málaga bypassing Madrid, and Alvia services from Madrid and Barcelona to cities like Pamplona and Bilbao.

2   The **Madrid–Andalusia corridor** includes the services Madrid–Seville and Madrid–Málaga. It also includes the aforementioned services connecting with Barcelona and, among others, Alvia services to Huelva and Cadiz.

3   The **Madrid–East Coast corridor** connects Madrid with Valencia and Alicante, but also with Alvia services to other cities like Castellón.

4   The **Madrid–North corridor** connects Madrid with Valladolid over about 200 kilometres, and it is used to feed traffic to the whole of the north of Spain using Alvia trains, from Galicia in the north-west to the Basque Country in the north. It is also the area where most of the future expansion of the network will occur.[7]

3. Methodology and data

For each of the corridors we conduct a financial and social profitability analysis using the methodology that we discuss next. These analyses are based on several common assumptions. The most important of them is that we evaluate the corridors as if there were no additional investment for completing them. This assumption is appropriate for several reasons. First, it does not force us to make assumptions on the construction and operating costs and revenues of lines that do not exist yet. Second, it is a useful benchmark in the evaluation of future expansions of the network since our work could be used, in turn, as the proper counterfactual for that analysis. Finally, to the extent that the profitability of a line is increasing due to the size of the cities served and, with the exception of Bilbao, all big cities are connected through HSR, our analysis constitutes a likely upper bound on the eventual profitability of the services.

Figure 3.1 HSR network as of December 2013.

Another important assumption refers to the counterfactual scenario utilized. To that aim, we assume that without HSR the conventional line would be in service for the whole of the duration of the project. Again, our analysis constitutes an upper bound on the profitability of the HSR infrastructure, as there could be better alternatives, such as waiting to build the HSR or adopting a new technology that may come about in the future.

3.1. Financial profitability

This analysis aims to study the profitability for the public purse of the investment in HSR. In order to do this we take into account the vertical separation between construction and management of the infrastructure, carried out by ADIF, and the operation of trains, conducted by RENFE. We adopt a 50-year time span starting at the beginning of infrastructure construction. This span is larger than the 30-year one recommended by the European Commission in order to accommodate Spanish specificities, such as the two phases in the construction of the infrastructure.[8] We are also discounting revenue and cost flows at a 5 per cent real rate, as recommended by European Commission (2008) guidelines.

In our analysis all the results are reported as the difference between the net present value (NPV) obtained when the infrastructure is in place and the corresponding counterfactual. We conduct our analysis in two steps. First, we analyze the present value of the net revenues of ADIF and RENFE, ignoring the cost of the infrastructure. We then compare how much of the cost of construction could be covered with these revenues. Unless stated otherwise, all figures are reported in euros (2013 value).

The structure of ADIF and RENFE's accounts is summarized in Table 3.1. ADIF's costs include the maintenance and operation of tracks, stations, etc. The main source of revenue is access charges. RENFE's costs obviously include access charges but also the cost of buying/leasing trains and operating them. Revenues arise from the sale of tickets mainly to passengers of HSR services. As we will see, except in the Madrid–North corridor, Alvia trains constitute a residual part of RENFE revenues.

Passenger data are obtained from Observatorio del Ferrocarril en España (2014) that provides historical data for most lines. We complemented this source when necessary with data from *Ferropedia*. Traffic is assumed to grow at a rate that mimics the long-term growth rate of the Spanish GDP. Following de Rus (2012) we have fixed this rate at an annual 2 per cent. Notice that this rate is likely to underestimate the growth rate in the first years after inauguration, when the HSR typically takes a large market share from the plane. However, this process was essentially completed at the point of assessment of those HSR lines for which the plane was a relevant competitor, the Madrid–Seville and Madrid–Valencia lines, for example, where in 2013 the plane constituted less than 10 per cent of the total traffic. Interestingly, this has not been the case for the Madrid–Barcelona line where, five years after the opening of the line, the plane still commanded a stable market share of about 50 per cent. Furthermore, a long-term annual increase in traffic similar to GDP seems to be consistent with the limited evidence for Spain. For the Madrid–Seville line, the growth rate of traffic between 1995 and 2013 has been roughly the same as the one of the Spanish GDP during that time although the number of passengers has fluctuated substantially more.[9]

The number of passengers is also used to compute the average price of tickets using the revenue data published by the Spanish government in February 2014 in the BOCG. The price is kept constant in real terms during the entire span of investment. This assumption is consistent with the prices observed for most lines

Table 3.1 Structure of RENFE and ADIF financial accounts.

RENFE		ADIF	
Revenues		**Revenues**	
	Passengers		Access charges
Costs		**Costs**	
	Access charges		Infrastructure maintenance
	Maintenance and operation		
	Trains acquisition		

and it reflects the competition that the train faces mainly from the plane, for which fare reductions have been common in recent decades.[10]

We assume that the number of trains RENFE operates increases as the number of passengers rises to keep a constant load factor of 70 per cent.[11] The cost of these trains is imputed using the historical value of the trains already operating on the line and assuming them to last for 30 years. The acquisition cost of trains is amortized over their lifetime. The annual cost of maintenance and operation, which includes items such as wages and energy costs, is estimated to be €9 million per train, following de Rus (2012).

The third item in RENFE's costs is the payment of access charges. According to the report by ADIF in 2014,[12] the access charges were composed of five main concepts: an access fee based on the line and total traffic, a capacity fee, a circulation fee, a traffic fee and a railway station fee. Alvia trains are also subject to a gauge change usage fee. Using the formulae provided by ADIF, we obtained the fees paid by RENFE for each line. For the purposes of computing the usage fees it is assumed that 40 per cent of the trains circulate during peak hours, 40 per cent during shoulder hours and 20 per cent during off-peak hours.

Regarding ADIF, maintenance costs are assumed to be 109,000 euros per kilometre of track. As Albalate and Bel (2010) report, the Minister of Public Works stated in 2008 that this cost reached 100,000 euros per kilometre and 200,000 per kilometre of tunnel. Our cost corresponds to the inflation-adjusted lower bound. This cost is kept constant over the time span of the project, assuming that, although over time there will be cost improvements, they will be compensated for by the additional costs associated with increases in traffic.

The information on construction costs is typically obtained from the public budgets that specify expenditures for each line. In a few cases, such as for the Madrid–Barcelona corridor, we have used the audited costs figure which indicates an overrun of about 45 per cent over the budgeted costs. Thus, the costs we attribute to each corridor are likely to be a lower bound. Furthermore, we exclude from our analysis the construction costs (and revenues) of the stations and other infrastructures, which often cannot be uniquely attributed to a specific corridor.

As discussed before, the values obtained are compared with a counterfactual scenario computed in the following way: we keep constant the number of passengers before the HSR started to operate and we impute the cost of acquisition and maintenance of similar lines; the price is set to half the price of the HSR ticket; and, furthermore, we assume that the HSR allows a reduction in the cost of maintenance of the legacy network of about 25 per cent, since most traffic is diverted to the new infrastructure with commuter and freight trains becoming the main users of the old infrastructure.

Finally, the model incorporates risk factors that provide a distribution of the net value of the project. We report the average of these present values. In particular, we simulate our model including random realizations of the growth rate of traffic (1.5–2.5 per cent) and the occupation load factor of each train (65–70 per cent).

3.2. Social profitability

Social profitability is also estimated for the four corridors as mentioned above. These accounts balance social costs and benefits of a project, this is, opportunity costs of the new railway infrastructure and services against social benefits. In turn, social benefits are passengers' travel time savings, new users' willingness to pay and avoided costs. Time savings accrue when passengers change their mode of transport to HSR from planes, conventional trains, buses and private cars. There are also benefits from generated demand as demonstrated by changes in willingness to pay, net of resources. Finally, avoided costs are also a source of benefits as other transport activities are reduced when demand deviates to HSR, for example, there are fewer road transport accidents and there is a reduction in congestion.[13]

The social analysis, as in the case of the financial one, is counterfactual. It is the result of a comparison of social welfare in the situations with and without the project. Changes in welfare are estimated based on changes in willingness to pay and resources, as applied also in de Rus (2012).

The welfare approach of the social HSR accounts is in contrast to the financial one that concentrates on firms' (ADIF and RENFE) profitability. Hence, although the basic variables used in the assessments are the same (traffic levels, investment and maintenance costs, etc.), there are important differences that arise from the elements that comprise the welfare measure as compared with those that comprise firms' profits. Another important difference is shown by the need to correct by shadow prices in order to incorporate the opportunity costs of resources committed to the project or the need to use the appropriate social discounting rate. We use a 3.5 per cent financial discount rate, as recommended in European Commission (2008) guidelines. The project life is 50 years as well, with treatment of uncertainty based on a risk analysis that results in a statistical distribution of the social NPV of projects. As in the case of the financial profitability assessment, statistical distributions are assumed for the rate of traffic growth over time (uniform distribution between 1.5–2.5 per cent), train load factors (uniform distribution between 65–75 per cent) and in-vehicle values of time (normal distributions).

It is also important to bear in mind that social and financial analyses are not independent. Obviously, only those projects with a positive social profitability are feasible candidates. However, under public budget restrictions it may also happen that even the best investment projects will not be carried out. Therefore, our work provides two complementary views of the same problem.

Table 3.2 shows the basic structure of the social account. As already mentioned, social costs are derived from the infrastructure and operation of rail services and are corrected by shadow prices. Travel time savings are obtained assuming that a given proportion of traffic deviates from other modes available in the same corridor.[14] In general, the largest deviations come from planes and conventional trains. Besides, these savings distinguish between access/egress, waiting and in-vehicle times. Values of time applied are those suggested for Spain in HEATCO

(2006). As indicated in the same source, these values change over time according to changes in national income, with a 0.7 degree of elasticity. We also assume that 60 per cent of traffic arises for business purposes and 40 per cent for leisure reasons.

Finally, our estimates do not include environmental impacts. According to the new evidence available, the possible social benefits that may arise are not large when all impacts are considered and the whole project life taken into consideration, which includes the construction phase. This issue is discussed at length in de Rus (2011) and de Rus (2012).

4. Results

We now briefly summarize the results of our analysis for the four corridors. A more detailed discussion with a list of all the parameters is available in Betancor and Llobet (2015).

4.1. Madrid–Barcelona

The cost of the Madrid–Barcelona corridor reached, according to the Spanish Tribunal de Cuentas,[15] €8,967 million. Most of the 8 million passengers in 2013 travelled from or to these two cities and, to a minor extent, the intermediate city of Zaragoza. Passengers from Barcelona to Seville and Málaga constituted the second largest source of traffic, followed by Alvia services. According to

Table 3.2 Scheme of the social accounts.

Social costs
Infrastructure investment
Infrastructure maintenance
Investment in trains
Maintenance and operation of trains
Social benefits
Time savings
- Conventional train
- Car
- Bus
- Plane
Willingness to pay (WTP) of generated demand
Avoided costs
- Conventional train
- Car
- Bus
- Plane
Reduction in accidents
Reduction in congestion

the official data as of 2012, these corridors generated revenue for RENFE of about €425 million, from which €407 million came from AVE services. Once we attribute half of the revenue from Barcelona to Seville and Málaga to this corridor (and the other half to the Madrid–Andalusia corridor) the total revenue becomes €376 million. The methodology discussed in the previous section delivers cost estimates in 2013 that are very close to those reported in the BOCG for all the lines.

Table 3.3 presents the results of our financial profitability analysis. If we ignore the investment cost, we observe that over the lifetime of the infrastructure RENFE and ADIF would obtain a present value of profits close to €3.5 billion at the time of the building of the infrastructure, which started in 1998. About €2 billion of these profits is allocated to ADIF and €1.5 billion to RENFE. In particular, passenger revenues imply over €5 billion for RENFE, while total costs of €3.6 billion correspond mostly to access charges of €2.7 billion. Maintenance and train acquisition costs are less than €900 billion. ADIF faces total maintenance costs of €755 million.

Table 3.3 Financial account for the Madrid–Barcelona corridor (expected discounted values).

RENFE				
Revenues		**5,094,943,522 €**	Discounting year	1998
	Passengers	5,094,943,522 €	Investment span	50 years
			Monetary units	2013
Costs		**3,627,396,813 €**	Real financial discount rate	5.00%
	Access charges	2,752,009,705 €		
	Maintenance and operation	659,229,493 €		
	Trains acquisition	216,157,614 €		
Balance		**1,467,546,709 €**		

ADIF				
Revenues		**2,752,009,705 €**		
	Access charges	2,752,009,705 €	Operating profits RENFE+ADIF	3,464,420,874 €
Costs		**755,135,540 €**	Investment cost	7,541,229,929 €
	Maintenance and operation	755,135,540 €		
			Total balance Madrid–Barcelona	−4,076,809,055 €
Balance		**1,996,874,165 €**	Ratio: Operating profits/ Investment cost	**45.94 %**

Hence, while running the HSR service is quite a profitable business it is not enough to cover the construction costs. As the table indicates, the present value of the cost of the infrastructure in 1998 is over €7.5 billion. Overall, operation profits would be enough to cover about 46 per cent of the cost of the infrastructure.

Figure 3.2 simulates the model for different values of the load factor and growth rate of the demand. The results do not change substantially, but show that in the best scenario the profits from the service are likely to leave about €3.7 billion uncovered.

The social account for this corridor is shown in Table 3.4. Social profitability is negative too, and slightly larger than €1.6 billion.[16] The largest social benefits come from travel time savings when passengers shift from other modes of transport (49 per cent), and mainly when they change from conventional trains to AVE. These are followed by avoided costs (35 per cent), most importantly for not operating air transport. Necessarily, the largest cost component is infrastructure, followed by maintenance and operation of trains.

Figure 3.3 shows the probability distribution of the social NPV after application of risk analysis. It can be seen that the probability concentrates on negative values. Although some positive or close to zero NPVs may be obtained, their probability is very low. Remember that getting a NPV equal to zero means that the society is in the same situation as it would be without the project.

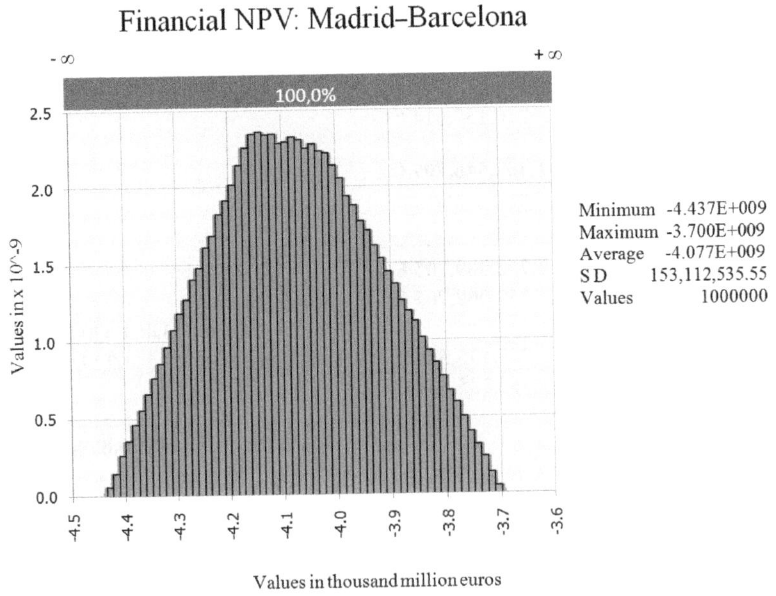

Figure 3.2 Probability distribution of the financial NPV in the Madrid–Barcelona corridor.

Table 3.4 Social account for the Madrid–Barcelona corridor (expected discounted values).

Social costs	−13,676,539,106 €
Infrastructure investment	**−7,999,813,335 €**
Infrastructure maintenance	**−1,084,033,720 €**
Investment in trains	**−1,016,841,490 €**
Maintenance and operation of trains	**−3,575,850,561 €**
Social benefits	*12,045,053,435 €*
Time savings	**5,916,199,443 €**
- Conventional train	3,689,384,198 €
- Car	1,085,807,530 €
- Bus	322,560,500 €
- Plane	105,590,048 €
- Savings Alvia	712,857,167 €
WTP of generated demand	**1,397,586,318 €**
Avoided costs	**4,167,088,570 €**
- Conventional train	1,164,870,186 €
- Car	1,047,002,056 €
- Bus	115,735,854 €
- Plane	1,839,480,475 €
Reduction in accidents	**537,313,433 €**
Reduction in congestion	**26,865,672 €**
NPV	**−1,631,485,672 €**

Discounting year 1998
Monetary units 2013
Real social discounting rate 3.5%

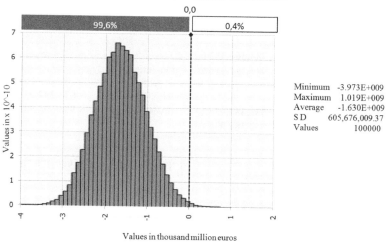

Social NPV: Madrid–Barcelona

Minimum   -3.973E+009
Maximum   1.019E+009
Average   -1.630E+009
S D   605,676,009.37
Values   100000

Values in thousand million euros

Figure 3.3 Probability distribution of the social NPV in the Madrid–Barcelona corridor.

4.2. Madrid–Andalusia

The Madrid–Andalusia corridor turns out to be less profitable. The reason is the much lower number of passengers that use the train in that corridor. In 2013 about 5.5 million passengers used AVE and Alvia services. The HSR had already diverted almost all traffic from the plane. The train had, in relation to the plane, a market share of 90 per cent and 80 per cent for the lines Madrid–Seville and Madrid–Málaga, respectively.

Total revenues in 2012 for this corridor amounted to €335 million, once we imputed 50 per cent of the revenues from the Barcelona–Seville and Barcelona–Málaga lines. Our cost estimates for each line are consistent with the data published in the BOCG.

Table 3.5 shows that the NPV of profits of ADIF and RENFE in 1987 is estimated to be around €635 million. RENFE's profits are slightly over €200 million.

Table 3.5 Financial account for the Madrid–Andalusia corridor (expected discounted values).

RENFE				
Revenues		2,526,003,990 €	Discounting year	1987
	Passengers	2,526,003,990 €	Investment span	50 years
			Monetary units	2013
Costs		2,322,745,557 €	Real financial discount rate	5.00%
	Access charges	1,107,423,086 €		
	Maintenance and operation	1,091,067,582 €		
	Trains acquisitions	124,254,889 €		
Balance		203,258,433 €		
ADIF				
Revenues		784,364,382 €		
	Access charges	784,364,382 €	Operating profits	
			RENFE+ADIF	635,237,880 €
Costs		352,384,934 €	Investment cost	5,584,608,585 €
	Maintenance and operation	352,384,934 €		
			Total balance Madrid–Andalusia	−4,949,370,705 €
Balance		431,979,447 €	Ratio: Operating profits/ Investment cost	11.37 %

In particular, RENFE obtains revenues in excess of €2.5 billion and faces costs of over €2.3 billion. Half of these costs correspond to access charges, whereas the maintenance and operation of trains constitutes a similar amount. ADIF incurs a total maintenance cost of about €352 million.

The profits of €635 million would only cover about 11 per cent of the €5.5 billion of infrastructure costs. The rest of the infrastructure costs would eventually be assumed by the public purse. Introducing different values of the load factor and the demand rate of growth does not change the results substantially, as shown in Figure 3.4. An important caveat of the analysis of this corridor is that, as already discussed, almost 20 years have passed between the inauguration of the Madrid–Seville line and the opening of the Madrid–Málaga line, which means that the 50-year time span of the latter line is substantially shorter than in the other cases. As we show in the next section, however, the results do not change much if we extend the time span to 100 or 150 years.

The results of the social account (see Table 3.6) also show a negative profitability of slightly over €3.3 billion. Main social benefits come from travel time savings (42 per cent), followed by avoided costs (40 per cent). Again, the main components are time savings for traffic deviated from conventional trains and air transport avoided costs. Figure 3.5 shows a probability distribution of the NPV that is always negative.

4.3. Madrid–East Coast

The Madrid–East Coast corridor delivers results very similar to the ones obtained for the previous corridor. The two main lines that constitute this corridor,

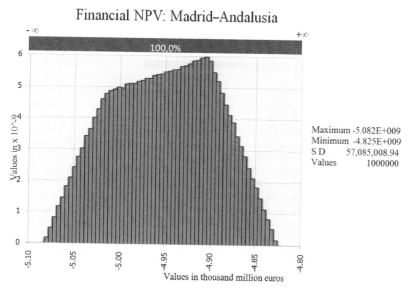

Figure 3.4 Probability distribution of the financial NPV in the Madrid–Andalusia corridor.

Table 3.6 Social account for the Madrid–Andalusia corridor (expected discounted values).

Social costs	*–9,873,614,686 €*
Infrastructure investment	**–6,125,533,626 €**
Infrastructure maintenance	**–966,651,671 €**
Investment in trains	**–558,028,630 €**
Maintenance and operation of trains	**–2,223,400,760 €**
Social benefits	*6,510,141,425 €*
Time savings	**2,714,982,748 €**
- Conventional train	1,903,120,376 €
- Car	430,005,363 €
- Bus	117,396,056 €
- Plane	0 €
- Savings Alvia	264,460,953 €
WTP of generated demand	**910,331,669 €**
Avoided costs	**2,580,879,640 €**
- Conventional train	718,438,032 €
- Car	502,254,166 €
- Bus	30,307,146 €
- Plane	1,329,880,295 €
Reduction in accidents	**289,473,684 €**
Reduction in congestion	**14,473,684 €**
NPV	**–3,363,473,261 €**

Discounting year 1987
Monetary units 2013
Real social discounting rate 3.5%

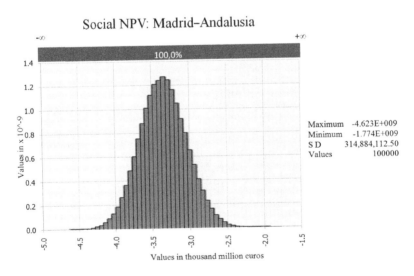

Figure 3.5 Probability distribution of the social NPV in the Madrid–Andalusia corridor.

Madrid–Valencia and Madrid–Alicante, were inaugurated in 2010 and 2013, respectively. This corridor generated revenues that exceeded €145 million in 2012, two-thirds of which were attributable to the Madrid–Valencia line. As in the case of the Madrid–Andalusia line, the market share of the plane became irrelevant after the arrival of the HSR. It is also important to point out that in the following years revenues will have increased substantially since the HSR line between Madrid and Alicante only started to operate in mid 2013, replacing the Alvia trains used for that route. Our analysis incorporates an estimate of this increase in traffic.

Table 3.7 shows that RENFE and ADIF would obtain operating profits of about €564 million during the duration of the project. RENFE would obtain profits of €258 million and ADIF of about €306 million. Passengers would contribute

Table 3.7 Financial account for the Madrid–East Coast corridor (expected discounted values).

RENFE				
Revenues		**2,104,656,171 €**	Discounting year	2003
	Passengers	2,104,656,171 €	Investment span	50 years
			Monetary units	2013
Costs		**1,846,139,335 €**	Real financial discount rate	5.00%
	Access charges	872,472,626 €		
	Maintenance and operation	880,226,619 €		
	Trains acquisitions	93,440,091 €		
Balance		**285,516,835 €**		

ADIF				
Revenues		**872,472,676 €**		
	Access charges	872,472,626 €	Operating profits	
			RENFE+ADIF	564,717,357 €
Costs		**566,272,104 €**	Investment cost	5,882,108,651 €
	Maintenance and operation	566,272,104 €		
			Total balance Madrid–East Coast	−5,317,391,294 €
Balance		**306,200,522 €**	Ratio: Operating profit/ Investment cost	**9.60 %**

to a present value of revenues for RENFE of €2.1 billion. RENFE's cost would be around €1.8 billion, almost half of which would correspond to access charges of €872 million, with a similar figure for maintenance and operation costs. ADIF's cost would amount to €566 million.

As in the previous cases, although operating profits are positive, these would only cover about 9.6 per cent of the cost of construction. Figure 3.6 shows that this result is unlikely to be affected much if we introduce uncertainty about our parameters.

Again, the social results (see Table 3.8) are negative and close to €3.7 million. The main benefits arise from time savings (48 per cent) and avoided costs (41 per cent). Figure 3.7 presents the probability distribution of the social NPV, with negative values that in the best case scenario reach €2.5 billion.

4.4. Madrid–North

The last corridor we discuss is Madrid–North. This corridor is special in that only 200 kilometres were in operation in 2013. As a result, very few of the trains using the corridor make use of the high-speed features. Instead, most are Alvia trains that make use of the infrastructure from Madrid to Valladolid, where they switch to the conventional network. The available information indicates that total revenue of this corridor was around €65 million in 2012 and we can approximate the number of passengers to be around 2 million in 2013. Operational costs of these lines are more difficult to approximate as most previous studies have focused on HSR and not on these mixed trains. Once we compared our results with those provided in the BOCG it turned out that we had underestimated the costs with regard

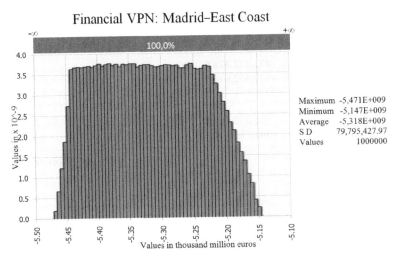

Figure 3.6 Probability distribution of the financial NPV in the Madrid–East Coast corridor.

Table 3.8 Social account for the Madrid–East Coast corridor (expected discounted values).

Social costs	−9,549,466,680 €
Infrastructure investment	**−6,368,163,311 €**
Infrastructure maintenance	**−959,048,399 €**
Investment in trains	**−366,714,922 €**
Maintenance and operation of trains	**−1,855,540,049 €**
Social benefits	*5,890,370,090 €*
Time savings	**2,817,516,537 €**
- Conventional train	1,309,575,953 €
- Car	475,806,933 €
- Bus	120,830,319 €
- Plane	811,384,356 €
- Savings Alvia	99,918,977 €
WTP of generated demand	**378,753,854 €**
Avoided costs	**2,421,022,775 €**
- Conventional train	698,465,048 €
- Car	359,946,622 €
- Bus	48,827,698 €
- Plane	1,313,783,407 €
Reduction in accidents	**260,256,410 €**
Reduction in congestion	**12,820,513 €**
NPV	**−3,659,096,590 €**

Discounting year 2003
Monetary units 2013
Real social discounting rate 3.5%

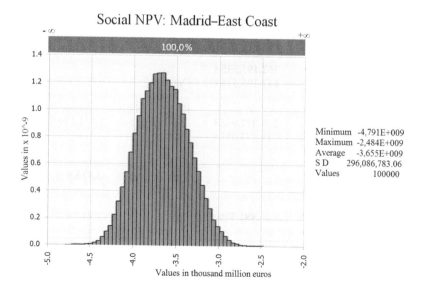

Social NPV: Madrid–East Coast

Minimum -4,791E+009
Maximum -2,484E+009
Average   -3,655E+009
S D   296,086,783.06
Values   100000

Values in thousand million euros

Figure 3.7 Probability distribution of the social NPV in the Madrid–East Coast corridor.

to some lines by up to 10 per cent, indicating that our analysis provides an upper bound on the profitability of the corridor.

Surprisingly, the present value of profits is estimated to be negative, although losses are small. As Table 3.9 shows, ADIF and RENFE would incur, in total, losses of about €54 million. These losses would be allocated to ADIF, whereas RENFE would make a profit of €12 million. Interestingly, compared to other cases, access charges are small in relation to the cost of maintenance and operation of the trains. These results suggest that ADIF subsidized these services much more than in the other corridors.

These negative operational profits, of course, would imply that the cost of infrastructure of €3.8 billion would not be covered by passenger revenues. These

Table 3.9 Financial account for the Madrid–North corridor (expected discounted values).

RENFE				
Revenues		**923,662,070 €**	Discounting year	2002
	Passengers	923,662,070 €	Investment span	50 years
			Monetary units	2013
Costs		**911,547,548 €**	Real financial discount rate	5.00%
	Access charges	152,195,535 €		
	Maintenance and operation	693,209,902 €		
	Trains acquisitions	66,142,110 €		
Balance		**12,114,523 €**		
ADIF				
Revenues		**152,195,535 €**		
	Access charges	152,195,535 €	Operating profits RENFE+ADIF	–54,766,997 €
Costs		**219,077,055 €**	Investment cost	3,871,149,596 €
	Maintenance and operation	219,077,055 €		
			Total balance Madrid–North	**–3,925,916,593 €**
Balance		**–66,881,520 €**	Ratio: Operating profits/ Investment cost	**–1.41 %**

results would not change in any meaningful way when we introduce uncertainty about the parameters of the model (see Figure 3.8).

The social account (see Table 3.10) again shows a negative profitability slightly above €3 billion. In this case, the main benefits accrue from avoided costs (43 per cent), time savings (30 per cent) and willingness to pay from generated traffic (22 per cent). Interestingly, our estimates indicate that the shift in traffic from private cars and the plane is detrimental to society when all the components of time are considered. This is mainly due to the fact that only a small section of the corridor can be operated at high speed at the time of analysis. To avoid further damaging the project we assume these components to be equal to zero. Figure 3.9 shows the probability distribution of the social NPV in this case.

5. Robustness analysis

Our analysis showed that the results would not change much if the growth rate of the demand and the load factor change within a reasonable range. For the social analysis, values of time have also been considered as statistical variables. Two other parameters of the model are important for our conclusions: the project time span and the discount rates. In this section we study how sensitive the results are when these two parameters change. In order to do so, we extend the horizon from 50 to 100 and 150 years. We also compute the internal rate of return (IRR) of the project, which allows us to see at what discount rates the corridors become financially and socially profitable.

Table 3.11 summarizes how the results change when the horizon is extended. We have left out the Madrid–North corridor since, as we have seen, even financial

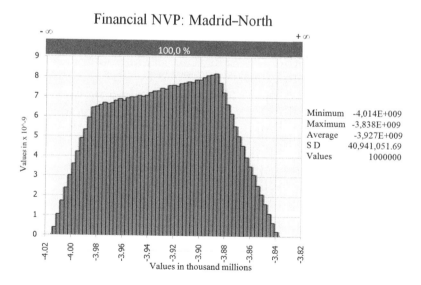

Figure 3.8 Probability distribution of the financial NPV in the Madrid–North corridor.

Table 3.10 Social account for the Madrid–North corridor (expected discounted values).

Social costs	*−5,122,644,289 €*
Infrastructure investment	**−4,058,706,870 €**
Infrastructure maintenance	**−304,517,219 €**
Investment in trains	**−222,909,933 €**
Maintenance and operation of trains	**−536,510,267 €**
Social benefits	*1,836,431,772 €*
Time savings	**560,979,572 €**
- Conventional train	516,915,675 €
- Car	0 €
- Bus	44,063,896 €
- Plane	0 €
WTP of generated demand	**403,832,985 €**
Avoided costs	**782,803,426 €**
- Conventional train	236,012,215 €
- Car	250,866,598 €
- Bus	69,401,149 €
- Plane	226,523,463 €
Reduction in accidents	**85,526,316 €**
Reduction in congestion	**3,289,474 €**
NPV	**−3,286,212,517 €**

Discounting year 2002
Monetary units 2013
Real social discounting rate 3.5%

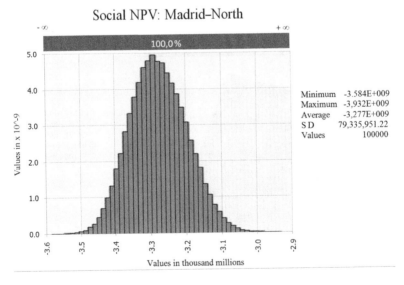

Minimum -3.584E+009
Maximum -3,932E+009
Average -3,277E+009
SD 79,335,951.22
Values 100000

Figure 3.9 Probability distribution of the social NPV in the Madrid–North corridor.

Table 3.11 Financial and social IRR.

Evaluation time span	Financial IRR	Social IRR
Madrid–Barcelona		
50 years	1.73%	2.55%
100 years	3.68%	4.95%
150 years	4.00%	5.44%
Madrid–Andalusia		
50 years	<0	0.15%
100 years	1.40%	3.69%
150 years	2.24%	4.38%
Madrid–East Coast		
50 years	<0	0.31%
100 years	1.52%	3.55%
150 years	2.33%	4.27%

variable costs are not covered, making an IRR calculation meaningless. Instead, we focus on the other three corridors. In all of them, as expected, the IRR rises as the time span increases, both for the financial and social analysis. In all three corridors, time spans of 100 years lead to a social IRR of above 3.5 per cent, which would make these investments socially profitable. From a financial point of view, however, only the Madrid–Barcelona corridor would deliver an IRR of above 3 per cent in the 100-year time span. The other two corridors would lead to an IRR of around 1.5 per cent and 2.3 per cent in the 100- and 150-year time spans, respectively.

It is important to emphasize that, although useful for illustration purposes, these time spans are quite implausible. It is reasonable to think that the tracks will be in place in 100 years' time, but it is also reasonable to expect that the technology will have become obsolete by then and have been superseded by new and faster alternatives. In other words, a time span of 100 years constitutes an unrealistic commitment of not adopting a better technology, incompatible with this infrastructure, during that period of time.

6. Conclusions

The results described in this chapter point out that the investment in HSR is unlikely to lead to benefits for the Spanish society. Even in the most favourable case, the Madrid–Barcelona corridor, the benefits are unlikely to outweigh the cost of infrastructure construction. This is true both if we focus on the revenue that the government is likely to obtain from passenger tickets and if we also account for the social effects that this infrastructure might have.

As we have discussed during the previous sections, we have tried to make assumptions in our work that err on the side of caution. Beyond the natural uncertainty in this kind of project, the lack of public information has forced us to take a conservative stand on many relevant variables of the analysis. We have also settled for a counterfactual that is quite extreme, as it implies that no alternatives to the HSR, such as upgrading part of the existing infrastructure, were available.

Our results are in line with other studies which have found that most HSR projects lead to a negative social value. Albalate and Bel (2015) summarize many of these studies and show that only the Tokyo–Osaka line in Japan, the Paris–Lyon line in France, and the Jian–Qhindao line in China are found to be socially profitable.

However, the case of Spain is special in many respects. The different governments that have been in power in Spain during the last 25 years have had confidence in the HSR as a solution to a railway infrastructure that was in need of a radical overhaul. These same governments have also fostered the creation and expansion of airports and highways aimed at improving the mobility of the Spanish population. The resulting situation of overcapacity makes it unlikely that Spanish society will ever recover the cost of all the infrastructures.

Part of the problem arises, most likely, from the lack of an *ex ante* cost-benefit analysis of these infrastructures. It is only now, with the results of studies like ours, that the public in Spain is becoming aware of the social cost of these infrastructures.

Acknowledgments

We are grateful to Ginés de Rus and Angel de la Fuente for helpful comments and suggestions. Ginés de Rus also gave us access to the computer code used in previous assessments. Possible errors are our sole responsibility.

Notes

1 This information is based on data from the International Union of Railways and has been updated with more recent data.
2 This study is available at: http://documentos.fedea.net/pubs/eee/eee2015-08.pdf.
3 Until 2005, railway operations and infrastructure construction were both carried out by RENFE (Red Nacional de los Ferrocarriles Españoles). Following a European Directive, the Spanish government vertically separated this company, creating ADIF, which took charge of construction and administration of the infrastructure, and RENFE Operadora, which took charge of train operations.
4 See www.ferropedia.es.
5 These lines were complemented with connections to nearby cities such as Huesca, Toledo and Girona.
6 In some cases the lines are also used for regional services that are subject to Universal Service Obligations and they are operated by a different unit of RENFE.
7 As can be seen in Figure 3.1, the HSR network also includes a small portion from A Coruña and Ourense which we have ignored in our analysis because it is not connected to the rest of the HSR infrastructure.
8 We should not interpret this assumption as saying that after 50 years the infrastructure becomes useless. On the contrary, it means, for example, that after 50 years the technology would be superseded by a better technology that would make the current investments obsolete. It is important to point out that the first HSR was inaugurated in Japan in 1964 and, thus, the HSR is a mature technology that could be disrupted in the near future.

9 Changes in population are unlikely to have a positive impact on the number of passengers. According to the Spanish Statistical Office (INE) the population in Spain is expected to fall from 46.5 million in 2014 to 44.1 million in 2044 (see www.ine.es/prensa/np870.pdf).

10 As an anecdote, it is worth mentioning that the price of the air shuttle between Madrid and Barcelona, which is the busiest route in Spain, is the same in real terms as when it was inaugurated in 1974.

11 Our occupation factor measures the number of passengers-km per seat-km available even for those trains that are under maintenance. RENFE typically reports a ratio of number of passengers over available seats. This measure leads to higher occupation rates. Suppose, for example, that a passenger gets off at an intermediate station and another one gets on the train at the same station. Our measure would be identical to the case in which the same passenger stayed for the duration of the trip. According to the alternative measure, however, the number of passengers per available seat would increase to two. The Observatorio del Ferrocarril en España (2014) reports an average occupation in 2013 of 61.3 per cent for our measure and 74.3 per cent for the alternative one.

12 See www.adif.es/ca_ES/conoceradif/doc/CA_Dred_Completo.pdf.

13 In order to estimate impacts on road traffic accidents and congestion we apply available evidence as obtained in de Rus (2012). According to this source, the relative weight of these components over total social profits reached 4.6 per cent and 0.2 per cent, respectively.

14 We apply the same percentages as in de Rus (2012) for Madrid–Barcelona and Madrid–Andalusia. For the other corridors we adopt similar figures.

15 Spanish Court of Auditors.

16 Remember that monetary units are expressed as discounted values in euros (2013 value).

References

Albalate, D. and G. Bel (2010). "*Cuando la economía no importa: Auge y esplendor de la alta velocidad en España*", Revista de Economía Aplicada, 19(55), pp. 171–190.

Albalate, D. and G. Bel, (2015). "*La experiencia internacional en alta velocidad ferroviaria*", Estudios sobre la Economía Española, 2015/02, Madrid: FEDEA.

Betancor, O. and G. Llobet (2015). "*Contabilidad financiera y social de la alta velocidad en España*", Estudios sobre la Economía Española, 2015/08, Madrid: FEDEA.

de Rus, G. (2011). "*The BCA of HSR: Should the government invest in high speed rail infrastructure?*", Journal of Benefit-Cost Analysis, 2(1), pp. 35–79.

de Rus, G. (2012). "*Economic evaluation of the high speed rail*", Stockholm: Ministry of Finance, Expert Group on Environmental Studies.

de Rus, G. and V. Inglada, (1997). "*Cost-benefit analysis of the high-speed train in Spain*", The Annals of Regional Science, 31, pp. 175–188.

European Commission (2008). "*Guide to cost-benefit analysis of investment projects: Structural funds, Cohesion Fund and Instrument for Pre-accession*", Brussels: European Commission, Directorate General Regional Policy.

HEATCO (2006). "*Deliverable 5: Proposal for harmonised guidelines*", Stuttgart: HEATCO.

Observatorio del Ferrocarril en España (2014). "*Informe 2013*", Madrid: Observatorio del Ferrocarril en España.

4   Direct and indirect effects of high-speed rail

John Preston

1. Background and introduction

This chapter draws on an International Transport Forum Round Table that considered the economics of investment in high-speed rail (HSR). This round table included presentations from China, Chinese Taipei, France, Italy, Korea, India, Japan and the UK, along with a summary and conclusions paper (Preston, 2014)[1]. This work has been updated here with respect to recent developments, particularly in the UK, along with a more detailed consideration of the role of wider economic benefits.

In the rest of this introductory section we will briefly define HSR, posit four key classifications and examine the global extent of HSR. In section 2, we will assess the objectives of HSR schemes and their key costs and benefits. We will make a key distinction between direct and indirect effects. We will define direct effects as the traffic impacts of HSR services. We will define indirect effects as the traffic impacts on non-HSR services (air, car, classic rail, coach) as well as the non-traffic impacts, principally related to economic development, but also considering environmental and social impacts. In section 3, we will outline the key demand and supply (cost) features of HSR. In section 4, we will examine the balance between costs and benefits and the role of wider economic benefits. In section 5 we will review the recent experience of HS2 in the UK, before drawing some conclusions in section 6.

In defining HSR, we use the definitions of EC Directive 96/48, itself derived from the work of the International Union of Railways (UIC) (Council of the European Union, 1996). Thus, HSR services are those operating on dedicated new lines capable of operating speeds of 250 kph or more or on upgraded existing lines capable of speeds of 200 kph or more. However, the work of Campos et al. (2009) indicates that there are four broad types of HSR, as illustrated by Figure 4.1, each of which might be expected to have a different mix of direct and indirect effects.

Model 1 (exclusive exploitation) is where there is separate infrastructure for HSR and classic rail. This is the model used by the initial Shinkansen services in Japan from 1964, but Japan has moved away from this model with the development of the mini-Shinkansens from 1992, with HSR operating on conventional alignments that have been enhanced to standard gauge. We might expect that the direct impacts of

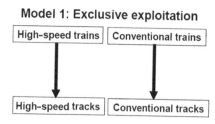

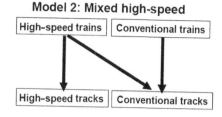

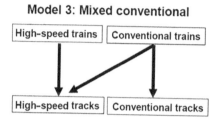

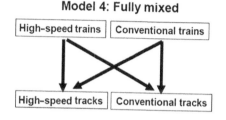

Figure 4.1 The four broad types of HSR.

HSR are maximised under the exclusive exploitation model. Model 2 is referred to as mixed high speed. This is still a predominantly segregated system but with high-speed trains occasionally using conventional tracks, in particular to access central railway stations. This was the basis of the French TGV system developed from 1981 onwards. Model 3 (mixed conventional) permits conventional trains to use high-speed tracks, so that other cities off (or beyond) the HSR route can be served. This was the essence of the Spanish AVE system developed from 1992 onwards, permitting cities such as Malaga to be served off the HSR trunk route between Madrid and Seville. Model 4 (fully mixed) allows complete interchange between high-speed and conventional services, both for passengers and freight. This is the basis for the German ICE network developed from 1988 onwards. It might be expected that the indirect impacts of HSR are maximised under this model.

At least three further nuances to this categorisation might be added. The first relates to the location of termini and intermediate stations. These may be in established central termini (London St Pancras, Paris Gare du Nord and Gare du Lyons), in new locations on the edge of the central area (Shin Osaka, Lyon Part-Dieu, Euralille) or at the edge of the city itself (typical in China and Chinese Taipei and also for some greenfield intermediate stations in France). It may be hypothesised that central locations will maximise the direct benefits of HSR but out-of-town locations may maximise indirect benefits, particularly where there is provision for car-based park and ride or scope for unlocking land for development. The second relates to the extent of grade separation and the preponderance of elevated sections and tunnels. For fully segregated systems, such as in Chinese Taipei, such structures account for the vast majority of the system (and hence lead to higher costs). For mixed systems, the preponderance of such structures is much reduced (as are costs but also benefits). The third relates to the extent to which a network of HSR lines and services exists, with the expectation that direct effects will be greater, the greater the extent of the HSR network. However, so will indirect effects, with the balance between the two effects a matter of empirics.

The extent of HSR systems is shown by Table 4.1 (from UIC as of 1 September 2014). Four nations (China, Japan, Spain and France) dominate the list, accounting for 80 per cent of the HSR system build. The rapid pace of growth can be ascertained due to the fact that by 1 April 2015 UIC was reporting 29,792 km of HSR route in operation (up 30 per cent). Two recent extremes may be noted. The first is the 'build it and see' approach of China and Spain which has led to a very rapid development of national HSR networks. The second is the 'paralysis by analysis' approach of the UK and the US, where there have been a large number of feasibility studies but very little in terms of system build (Perl, 2012; Preston, 2012). In between, there has been the more gradual expansion of the Japanese and French systems, albeit against a background of concern that network economies may have been exhausted (Crozet, 2013) and that further extensions will not be viable.

2. Objectives and impacts

As might be expected from what after all are mega-projects, HSR projects have multiple objectives. Of course, speeding up services (and the improved connection between places this engenders) is always present as an aim, but perhaps not as dominant as might be thought. For both the Tokaido Shinkansen and TGV Sud-Est, enhancing capacity was arguably just as important an objective, and one of the most effective ways to enhance capacity for rail services is to segregate fast and slow services. In both Japan and France, promotion of national champions in the railway supply industry was also an important factor, along with government-led initiatives to modernise the sector. In France, an important prestige factor was associated with the desire to establish leadership of the supply industry at the European level and to develop export markets (e.g. Korea).

Table 4.1 The global extent of HSR in 2014 (route kms).

	Built	*Under construction*
China	11,132	7,571
Japan	2,664	779
Spain	2,515	1,308
France	2,036	757
Rest of world	4,607	2,339
Total	22,954	12,754

Source: International Union of Railways, 2014.

Table 4.2 Objectives of HSR.

	Impact	France	Japan	China	Italy	UK	Chinese Taipei	Spain
Speed	Direct	✓	✓	✓	✓	✓	✓	✓
Capacity	Direct/ Indirect	✓	✓	✓	✓	✓(HS2)	✓	
Reliability	Direct				✓	✓(HS1)		
Economic development	Indirect			✓		✓	✓	
Environment	Indirect					✓(HS2)		
Supply industry	Indirect	✓	✓	✓				✓
Prestige	Indirect	✓		✓	✓			✓
Political integration	Indirect			✓				✓

Source: Preston, 2014.

For Italy and the UK, where there are perceived (and actual) problems with the reliability of conventional services, the reliability of HSR is an attraction.

For both China and Spain, HSR has been seen as an important tool for nation-building and political integration (Albalate and Bel, 2012). In China, Chinese Taipei and the UK, it has been argued that HSR brings wider economic benefits. In the UK, this is often cast in terms of rebalancing regional economies, attracting development to more peripheral regions from the core region of London and the south-east as a result of places being better connected. In China and Chinese Taipei, it is more about developing new areas of urban growth around out-of-town HSR stations – and hence may be more associated with expanding places (Leunig, 2011). The environmental credentials of HSR have also been pushed, most notably at COP15 in Copenhagen in 2009 (Oxera, 2009). In the UK, HS2 was originally promoted as a tool in reducing carbon emissions, although this would depend on reducing the carbon intensity of electricity generation and the embodied carbon in construction, and on maximising abstraction from air and car. What seems clear from the above is that, over time, the indirect effects of HSR have been perceived as becoming relatively more important.

An impact matrix for a typical HSR scheme is given by Table 4.3. To simplify matters, a vertically integrated monopolist is assumed. In reality, infrastructure and operations are likely to be vertically separated and horizontal separation means there could also be competition between HSR operators, as exists at the time of writing in Italy and Sweden. Similarly, we assume only one governmental body – typically of a highly centralised state. In reality, devolution means that regional and local governmental bodies will also be involved – which is particularly a feature of mature systems in France and Japan.

For rail operators, the key costs relate to the construction and operation of HSR and are thus a direct impact. For a horizontally integrated rail operator, operating costs will include adjustments to classic rail services. Horizontal separation adds further complexities and increased scope for competition. A rail operator may

Table 4.3 Impact matrix for a typical HSR scheme.

Incidence group	Costs	Benefits
Rail operator (Direct)	Construction costs Operating costs	Increased operating revenue Increased other revenue (Grants and subsidies)
HSR users (Direct)	Higher (net) fares	Faster services More reliable services More comfortable services (Indirect tax reductions)
Other transport users (Indirect)		Congestion relief on competing rail, road and air services
Other transport operators (Indirect)	Reduced revenue	Reduced operating costs Reduced capital investments
Government (Direct)	(Grants and subsidies) (Indirect tax losses)	
Wider society (Indirect)	Noise and vibration Land take Visual intrusion Social exclusion Shadow price of public funds	CO_2 emissions reductions Accident reductions Additional wider economic benefits

Notes: Fiscal transfers between government and other groups identified in brackets. Revenue will also have a transfer element and this needs to be taken into account.

receive support from the government in terms of capital grants and (less commonly) operating subsidies, although these are pecuniary transfers. In cases of public ownership, the support may take the form of the write-off of historic debts. This may reflect general support for the rail system and, hence, attribution to HSR is difficult and depends on accounting conventions.

For rail operators, the key benefit comes in the form of increased revenue from fares from HSR users, but where the industry is vertically integrated and outputs are diversified (as in Japan) this may also come from commercial developments in and around HSR stations. This is again a direct impact. However, fare revenues need to be treated with caution (Sugden, 1972). Fares are a transfer between rail users and operators, but if we are concerned with the distributional impacts of HSR these transfers should be highlighted. Furthermore, HSR revenue abstracted from other modes is also a transfer and ideally should be highlighted as such, along with the reductions in operating costs and user benefits of these other modes as a result of the competitive response by the operators of these rival modes or services. Typically, rail revenue is expressed as the net increase over the classic rail system, with the operating cost reductions of the classic rail system (and the impact on user benefits) also taken into account. For other modes (air, car, coach) the usual assumption is that these are perfectly competitive markets and that the HSR revenue gains from these modes reflect the reductions in capital and operating costs that take place, with no impact on the benefits to remaining users of the rival modes. A similar assumption with respect to the wider economy applies to generated revenue. An alternative approach is to directly estimate the cost reductions of the other modes or the changes in government support for such modes where they are state controlled (e.g. state-owned airlines).

HSR users may be expected to pay higher fares than for classic rail services, and a substantial proportion may be expected to be abstracted from classic rail. HSR fares may also be expected to be higher than coach fares. HSR fares may be lower than air fares (although this may not be the case where low-cost carriers are present) and lower than out-of-pocket motoring costs where tolled motorways are the norm, but higher where motorways are free at the point of use. Intermodal comparisons may be distorted by indirect taxation. In particular, motoring is usually more highly taxed than rail travel.

HSR users benefit from the increased reliability, speed and comfort of services (including the guarantee of a seat in pre-booking systems) and, despite likely increases in out-of-pocket costs, generalised costs of travel will have reduced, both for abstracted traffic and for generated traffic, with the resultant changes in benefits often estimated by the rule of half, although more precise estimation techniques (such as numerical or direct integration) are preferable (Nellthorp and Hyman, 2001). This is another direct impact.

Overall, it may be expected that there are benefits to other users of the transport system, largely due to congestion relief. These are indirect impacts. On classic rail, where there is latent demand, as is believed to exist in London and south-east England, released capacity may permit enhancements to commuter and regional services, increasing frequencies and reducing overcrowding, which will have reduced also due to transfers to HSR. Some train paths may also be released for rail freight services. However, where large amounts of classic rail demand are abstracted by HSR, there will be reductions in the frequency of classic rail services, possibly initiating a spiral of decline. Intermediate stations that are bypassed by HSR may particularly suffer reductions in service, as initially occurred in the cases of Arras and Dijon in France, although in both cases service levels have subsequently been strengthened. On the road system, there may be reduced congestion due to some modal shift to both HSR and classic rail services, although these benefits may be limited where origins and destinations are dispersed. For air services, there will be reductions in those that directly compete, to the disadvantage of remaining air travellers. However, where hub airports are congested, reduced short- and medium-haul services will release slots for long-haul flights. Where airport slots are not allocated using market mechanisms, this may even lead to commercial (and social) gains. Furthermore, HSR can be a complement to air services where hub airports are connected to the HSR network as in the cases of Amsterdam, Frankfurt and Paris (Charles de Gaulle), and this in turn may reduce landside congestion at these airports. In certain circumstances, avoided expenditure on air and road systems as a result of HSR investments may be considered a benefit.

Governments may be expected to be adversely affected where grants and subsidies are required and where there are reductions in the indirect tax take as a result of the switch of traffic from heavily taxed road to more lightly taxed rail. These may be interpreted as direct impacts.

Costs and benefits to wider society may be classified in three indirect impact categories related to the sustainability concept. First, environmental benefits may relate to reductions in emissions of carbon and other air pollutants but there may be issues along HSR routes with respect to noise and vibration, land take (and the resultant impacts on biodiversity and on water courses), severance and visual intrusion.

Second, the main social impact is likely to be the reduction in accidents as a result of the transfer of traffic to HSR, which has an excellent safety record. Although some of these benefits accrue to transport users, the majority may be seen as accruing to wider society. Pagliara et al. (2016) also highlight the fact that HSR may engender social exclusion and fieldwork suggests that geographical exclusion is an issue in Italy, whereas economic exclusion is a feature in the UK. This, in turn, suggests that the higher fares in the UK are having an exclusionary effect.

Third, there are economic impacts. A key feature of these is that they should be additional. Changes in patterns of economic activity may be redistributive rather than generative, although this redistribution may have benefits when it leads to more regionally balanced patterns of economic development. Changes in land values may similarly be redistributive rather than generative, with increased values close to HSR lines at the expense of locations further away. Moreover, these changes in values may be simply downstream manifestations of the changes in the generalised cost of travel and hence changes in accessibility, so to include them would be double counting unless HSR has reduced imperfections in land markets (Mohring, 1993). Another economic impact is the shadow price of public funds, which largely arises due to the distortion effects on the economy of taxation. In the UK, this deadweight loss might be equivalent to 20 per cent of government support; in France (with a higher tax regime) the figure may be more like 30 per cent. In some countries (e.g. Sweden) this deadweight loss is taken into account explicitly; in others, such as the UK, it is taken into account implicitly by looking for a benefit-cost ratio (BCR) of at least 1.5, although this is also driven by the opportunity cost of alternative investments.

3. Demand and supply

In an appendix, 52 data points on the usage of HSR schemes of varying degrees of maturity are presented. The mean usage is 26 million passengers per annum, but there is considerable variation, as indicated by a standard deviation of 23.4 million. Factors that might explain this demand include: the size of cities served (in terms of population and income), distance, speed, service frequency, fares, station accessibility, competition and time since opening – with long build-ups over time being a feature. Cultural issues may also be a factor, with national boundaries tending to deter traffic as may regional borders (e.g. between Catalonia and Castille in Spain). For example, Shires (1998) estimated that for the European Union, crossing a national boundary reduced passenger traffic by between 30–60 per cent.

For day trips, a travel time (one way) of three hours is recognised as a key threshold. The journey time difference between rail and air will be approximately two hours (although that can be considerably narrowed when check-in and access/egress times are taken into account). Around this level, the mode split between air and rail is around 50:50. Where the time difference is less, rail share increases sharply, *in extremis* eradicating air as a mode (e.g. Paris–Brussels). This pattern may be replicated by an S-shaped logistic curve (see, for example, Esplugas et al., 2005).

Table 4.4 shows that sources of HSR traffic are context specific, varying from scheme to scheme and according to the definition of what constitutes generated travel (e.g. the treatment of re-distributed traffic), but evidence from five existing HSR schemes in Europe suggests around 30 per cent of HSR demand is abstracted from air, 30 per cent from classic rail, 15 per cent from road (predominantly car) and 25 per cent is generated. In developing economies (such as China), where domestic air markets are not yet mature, abstraction from air will be lower and generation will be higher. For road, abstraction from car may be lower in developing economies but abstraction from bus and coach may be higher. Indirect effects might be expected to be greatest where there is substantial abstraction from car, such as for the Thalys services.

Given the amount of grade separation required HSR has substantial capital costs. Campos et al. (2009) estimate a mean construction cost of €22 million per km (2005 prices) and a standard deviation of €10 million. More generally, these costs may vary from below €10 million per route km (in China) to over €100 million per km (in the UK, for the High Speed 1 (HS1) approaches to London). Factors that explain these variations include wage rates, land costs, the extent of planning regulations and of health and safety regulations, the quantity and type of structures (in turn related to topography and geology), track type (slab compared to ballast) and operating speeds. In China, increasing speeds from 250 to 350 kph appeared to lead to a near doubling of capital costs per route km (Wu, 2013).

Table 4.4 Abstraction and generation factors.

Route	Paris–Lyons[1]	Madrid–Seville[2]	Madrid–Barcelona[3]	Thalys[4]	Eurostar[4]
% HST traffic generated from:	1980 to 1985	1991 to 1996 forecast	'Before HSR' to 'After HSR'	Range not given	Range not given
Induced	29	50	20	11	20
Road	11	6	10	34	19
Classic rail	40*	20	10	47	12
Air	20	24	60	8	49

Sources: [1]Bonnafous, 1987; [2]de Rus and Inglada 1997; [3]Segal, 2006; [4]Coto-Millán et al., 2007, all quoted in Preston, 2009. Atkins et al. (2015) have estimated that for domestic HS1 services 77 per cent of demand comes from rail, 11 per cent from car, 2 per cent from coach and 10 per cent generated.

Note: *All Paris–Lyon's 'after' rail travel is presumed to be by HST (i.e. no conventional rail following introduction of HST), since alternative journey time is ~5 hours compared to ~2 hours by HST.

There are also considerable variations in operating costs, which are again substantial, with infrastructure maintenance around €100,000 per track km per annum and train services costs (capital, operating and maintenance) around €0.06 per seat km. Rolling stock acquisition costs may vary between €33,000–65,000 per seat. Overall, HSR has higher energy and maintenance costs than classic rail, but the high speeds lead to high utilisation of rolling stock and accompanying staff, thus offsetting these costs to some extent. To the extent that higher costs reflect higher service quality, they should be associated with greater direct and indirect effects, with the balance again a matter for empirical study.

Track access charges and prices should equilibrate demand and supply but HSR is rarely operating in perfectly competitive markets and government intervention is the norm. This partly explains the large variations in HSR prices, for example €0.20 per passenger km for the Tokaido Shinkansen, €0.12 for TGV Sud-Est and €0.06 in China. There are similar variations in track access charges, typically varying between 25–45% of HSR revenues, depending on the emphasis placed on full cost recovery. In pricing, it is important to distinguish between the revenue yield approaches typified by SNCF (France) and Eurostar and the more traditional mileage charge plus supplement typified by DB (Germany) and JR (Japan). The former might be seen to be an attempt to implement perfect (first order) price discrimination, the latter an attempt to implement multi-part tariffs. As a result of the variations in prices there will also be variations in load factors. Typically, they will be quite high – such as the 70 per cent achieved by the TGV service in France. In Germany, a load factor of 50 per cent is more typical for ICE services, although this is due in part to the shorter distance between city pairs and the greater churn this engenders. Another important factor is the extent of competition. The head-on competition between Trenitalia and NTV in Italy has reduced average fares by 30 per cent (Croccolo and Violi, 2013). Clearly, higher prices and track access charges will reduce the direct and indirect effects of HSR.

4. Cost, benefits and wider economic benefits

One approach to HSR appraisal that has been championed by de Rus, drawing on his extensive experience of undertaking cost-benefit analyses of HSR in Spain (de Rus and Inglada, 1997; de Rus and Nombela, 2007; de Rus and Nash, 2009; de Rus, 2012), is to develop iso-welfare curves for HSR investments. This approach is illustrated by Figure 4.2.

These iso-welfare lines illustrate the value of first year time savings required to cover investment costs, given a fixed level of demand, and assumptions concerning the amount of generated traffic and the annual rate of growth of benefits. For example, suppose we assume mean construction costs of €22 million/km (as above) and a value of time of around €25.5 per hour, based on latest UK values, assuming 50 per cent business/50 per cent leisure (Department for Transport, 2015). If we also assume a mean time saving of 90 minutes for a 500 km journey (and this would be substantially less for traffic abstracted from air – see, for

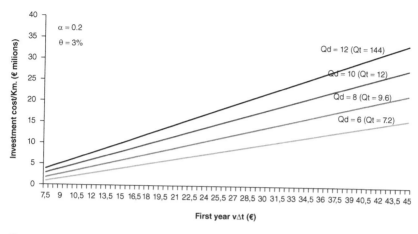

Figure 4.2 Iso-welfare curves for HSR investments.

example, Oxera, 2009) this would give a value of time savings of €38.25. These calculations of time savings are on the generous side but reflect that less than 50 per cent of non-revenue benefits may be attributed to reductions in train journey times (see Table 4.8). Under such a set of assumptions, the breakeven ridership would be in excess of 9 million abstracted trips and almost 11 million trips in total – substantially in excess of the levels achieved in Spain, but not elsewhere in the world.

However, it has long been postulated that HSR may have additional economic benefits that are not captured by a conventional cost-benefit analysis – these are referred to as wider economic benefits. For example, Blum et al. (1997) highlighted the importance of reductions in imperfect completion in transport-using sectors, the promotion of economics of scale and agglomeration benefits and the benefits from regional rebalancing.

As Figure 4.3 indicates, there may be potential gains from trade from connecting places that are not accounted for in a conventional cost-benefit analysis that assumes perfect competition (Dodgson, 1973). Assuming a transport-using sector is monopolised, private benefit will be determined by the marginal revenue curve, and the private benefits of a transport-related cost reduction in a transport-using sector will be denoted by the areas A and B. However, this neglects the social benefits of expanded trade given by the quadrilateral C. These gains may be particularly large where transport promotes competition and/or permits specialisation and hence increased outputs. However, HSR has little impact on freight, which might be expected to be the main driver for changes in competition in primary and secondary economic activities, but HSR can have important impacts on business passenger travel, which will be important for tertiary and quaternary economic activities. In the UK, these benefits are measured by an uplift on business travellers' time savings and account for around 32 per cent of full network wider economic benefits for HS2 (see Table 4.8).

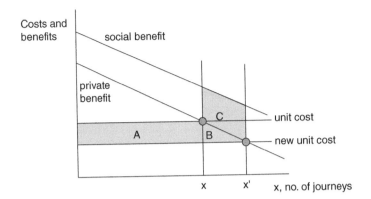

Figure 4.3 Wider economic benefits from reductions in imperfect competition.

There may be additional economic benefits from expanding places e.g. expansion of the City of London into Docklands or by expanding a city's suburbs. In Figure 4.4, it is assumed that there is a post-tax wage gap between the higher wages in an urban area and the surrounding rural areas, but that this diminishes with city size. At prevailing commuter costs, the number of workers in the city is given by X. If commuting costs reduce, this increases to X*. The conventional benefits to existing commuters are given by the area α and those to generated commuters are given by the area β. These benefits are included in a conventional cost-benefit analysis. However, there are additional benefits related to the additional income tax raised (ε) and the increased productivity (δ). As can be seen from Figure 4.4,

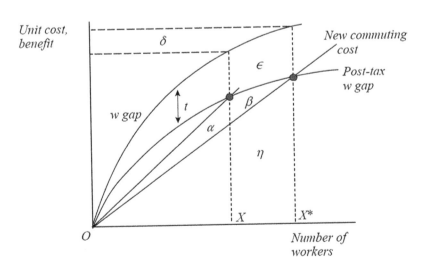

Figure 4.4 Agglomeration benefits and tax wedge.

the benefits could be substantial, but HSR has limited direct impact on commuter markets – although there are exceptions (e.g. Ciudad Real in Spain). For HS2, such benefits are estimated based on a methodology developed by Graham (2007) that determines productivity gains based on an elasticity with respect to a city's effective density (in essence a measure of mass). Agglomeration benefits are found to account for around 63 per cent of full network wider economic benefits for HS2.

However, for a scheme like HS2 these benefits are largely as a result of improvements to the classic rail network and enhancements to commuter services to London and the other major cities. Work by Graham and Melo (2010) shows that although economic theory does not preclude the existence of wider economic benefits across inter-regional distances, the empirical evidence suggests that these may be very small, at least in relative terms. For example, a transport investment that directly affects 25 per cent of long-distance rail trips by increasing speeds by 25 per cent might increase output by only 0.0006 per cent. This is because of the small proportion of long-distance rail trips in the total travel market. It might be argued that there are certain key business markets, focused on major city centres, where rail has a much larger market share. Work undertaken in the UK by KPMG (2013) attempted to examine labour and business connectivity by assessing the relationships between labour productivity, rail connectivity and road connectivity, using a framework that permits land use to change over time. However, these connectivity indicators are correlated with each other (and other indicators such as the quality of labour and land). Furthermore, bi-directional causality needs to be addressed. It is plausible that high-productivity areas attract transport investments as well as being generated by such investments. KPMG inferred a causal relationship between productivity and rail connectivity and estimated that this could lead to benefits of £15 billion per annum by the year 2037 (at 2013 prices), although this would include conventional benefits. This would represent an increase in GDP of 0.8 per cent in 2037 – a figure that is several orders of magnitude different from the theoretical estimations of Graham and Melo. The £15 billion per annum compares to the gross benefits (excluding indirect tax adjustment) of around £74 billion (2011 prices) for the whole HS2 network over a 60-year project life and with an interest rate of 3.5 per cent for the first 30 years and 3 per cent for the next 30. The KPMG methodology thus seems to give much higher estimates of benefits that many may consider implausible. If £15 billion per annum is discounted over 60 years in a similar manner then a present value of benefits of around £398 billion, some 5.4 times the original estimate, is obtained.

Venables et al. (2014) speculate that there may be further socio-economic benefits of increased employment. In Figure 4.5, there are two thresholds for transport costs to permit economic development and hence employment: T* (site 1) and T^ (site 2). At site 1, the social benefits of development are above the private benefits. At site 2, the social benefits of development are below the private benefits. Reducing transport costs to permit development of site 1 will unlock additional social gains: examples might include non-marginal changes in land prices, improved coordination between complementary firms

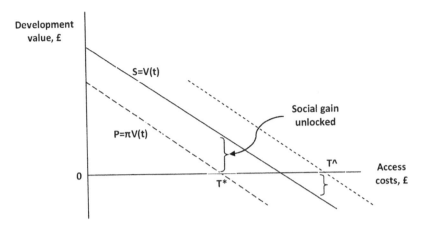

Figure 4.5 Employment effects of transport interventions.

and improved coordination to reduce low-level skills traps and the discouraged worker effect. Reducing transport costs to permit development of site 2 will lead to some additional social losses (and too much development) due to business stealing.

However, HSR may have limited regeneration potential. For example, for HS1 the development of Ashford and Ebbsfleet has been slow and has stalled since the economic downturn of 2008 (Preston and Wall, 2008; Atkins et al., 2015). Development at Stratford has been more substantive but can be related to intra-urban transport investments such the Jubilee Line, the Docklands Light Railway and Crossrail. For HS2, these employment benefits account for 5 per cent of the full network wider economic benefits, although HM Treasury remains sceptical of such benefits given an assumption of full employment. These benefits could be more substantial in economies characterised by widespread underemployment or unemployment. There could also be a danger that the employment created by HS2 is typified more by site 2 than site 1 and these benefits are hence negative.

Table 4.5 brings together some of the evidence on wider economic benefits from a number of rail studies. This gives a range of additional wider economic benefits compared to traditional benefits of between 13–80 per cent. Empirical work for the Eddington Review suggests multipliers on BCR of 1.09 for international gateways and 1.07 for inter-urban corridors, compared to 1.24 for urban networks (Eddington, 2006). This suggests a multiplier for HSR towards the bottom end of the range given in Table 4.5.

5. Case study: HS2

Although the UK is something of a laggard in terms of HSR, it has a long and well-documented history in appraisal and evaluation. The only existing service

Table 4.5 Estimates of rail wider economic benefits.

Study	Multiplier	Context
Oosterhaven & Elhorst (2003)	1.20	Randstad Maglev
	1.80	Randstad–Groningen Maglev
Department for Transport (2005)	1.56	London Crossrail
Atkins (2008)	1.70	UK HSR
Greengauge 21 (2009)	1.13	UK HSR
HS2 (2010)	1.13	London–Birmingham
HS2 (2012)	1.21	London–Birmingham
HS2 (2013)	1.27	Full network
Docherty et al. (2009)	1.26	Glasgow–Edinburgh HSR

is HS1, between the Channel Tunnel and central London, developed as a Public–Private Partnership, with London and Continental Railways (LCR) given the award in 1996. The railway itself opened in two phases: in 2004 (from the Channel Tunnel to mid Kent) and in 2007 (from mid Kent to central London), with domestic HSR commencing in 2009. The out-turn project costs were £6.2 billion for 108 km of new line, 18 per cent over budget and some 11 months late. The National Audit Office estimated an *ex ante* BCR of 1.5 in 2001(1.75 if regeneration is included – implying a multiplier of 1.17) and an *ex post* BCR of 0.8 in 2012. A more recent evaluation by Atkins et al. (2015) estimates a BCR of 0.53 without wider economic benefits and 0.64 with wider economic benefits (implying a multiplier of 1.21), in part due to additional financing costs of £4.8 billion in present value terms and 2010 prices.

Despite the problematic nature of HS1, the UK government has continued to examine the case for HSR linking London to Birmingham and onwards to Leeds and Manchester. Somewhat inevitably, this has become known as HS2 and has

Table 4.6 Costs and benefits of HS2, phase one – London to Birmingham (£ million, present value).

		2010	2012	2013
1	Transport user benefits	28.7	19.0	24.6
2	Other benefits		Less than 0.1	0.4
3	Net benefits (1 + 2)	28.7	19.0	24.8
4	Capital costs	17.8	18.8	21.8
5	Operating costs	7.6	8.6	8.2
6	Total costs (4 + 5)	25.5	27.4	29.9
7	Revenues	15.0	13.9	13.2
8	Indirect taxes	−1.5	n.s.	−1.2
9	Net cost to government (6−7−8)	11.9	13.4	17.9
10	BCR (3/9)	2.4	1.4	1.4

Sources: HS2 Ltd, 2010; 2012; 2013. n.s. = not stated.

Note: Adding other benefits raises the BCR to 2.7 in 2010 and to 1.7 in 2012 and 2013. Prices in 2010 and 2012 refer to 2009, in 2013 they refer to 2011.

been subject to a series of cost-benefit analyses, three of which are presented in Table 4.6.

It can be seen that the initial appraisal for phase one (London to Birmingham) in 2010 resulted in a standard BCR of 2.4, which increased to 2.7 when wider economic benefits were included (implying a multiplier of 1.13). However, subsequent analysis in 2012 indicated that capital costs had been underestimated and benefits overestimated, with the BCR reducing to 1.4 (1.7 if wider economic benefits are included – implying a multiplier of 1.21). The rise in costs was partly associated with environmental mitigation measures. Further estimates in 2013 gave the same BCRs, albeit with higher costs and benefits and with a change in the treatment of indirect taxes, which were now treated as a benefit change and hence appeared on the numerator in the BCR calculation.

Figure 4.6 gives the investment curve for the project. Major construction is scheduled to start in 2017, following completion of Crossrail – continuity of work for the civil engineering industry is a factor here. It can be seen that expenditure for phase one (London to Birmingham) peaks in around 2019, whilst that for phase 2 (Birmingham to Leeds/Manchester) peaks in 2021. Phase one is scheduled to open in 2025, with phase two opening in 2031, although there are plans to bring some sections of phase two (Birmingham to Crewe) forward in time. Benefits in present value terms are forecast to increase up to 2036, but are then capped to be constant in undiscounted terms.

Table 4.7 gives some more details of the breakdown of costs and benefits in 2013. It can be seen that the full network is more beneficial than phase one, indicating some network economies exist, at least initially. In addition, it is noticeable that over two-thirds of transport user benefits accrue to business users.

Table 4.8 indicates that around 70 per cent of the full network transport benefits can be classified as direct, associated with reduced journey times, improved

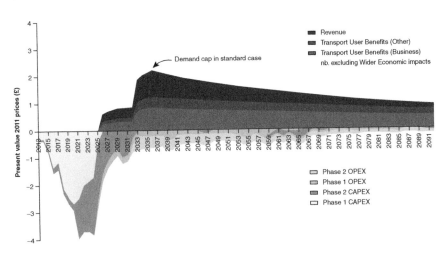

Figure 4.6 Investment curve for HS2.

Table 4.7 Costs and benefits of HS2 (PV 2011 prices).

	BCR components		Phase one (£billion)	Full network (£billion)
1	Transport user benefits	Business	£16.9	£40.5
		Other	£7.7	£19.3
2	Other quantifiable benefits		£0.4	£0.8
3	Loss to government of indirect taxes		−£1.2	−£2.9
4	Net transport benefits = (1) + (2) + (3)		£23.8	£57.7
5	Wider economic impacts (WEIs)		£4.3	£13.3
6	Net benefits including WEIs = (4) + (5)		£28.1	£71.0
7	Capital costs		£21.8	£40.5
8	Operating costs		£8.2	£22.1
9	Total costs = (7) + (8)		£29.9	£62.6
10	Revenues		£13.2	£31.1
11	Net costs to government = (9) − (10)		£16.7	£31.5
12	BCR without WEIs (ratio) = (4)/(11)		1.4	1.8
13	BCR with WEIs (ratio) = (6)/(11)		1.7	2.3

Source: HS2 Ltd, 2013.

reliability and improved access and interchange as a result of a number of new stations, whilst 30 per cent may be classed as indirect, related to impacts on the classic rail network (due to reduced waiting time and overcrowding) and reduced congestion on the roads.

Whilst the initial analysis in 2010 was based on a deterministic point estimate, subsequent analysis has been probabilistic. For example, Figure 4.7 shows that there is a 65 per cent chance that the phase one scheme will exhibit medium value for money (BCR>1.5).

The National Audit Office (2013) has raised concerns about the initial cost-benefit analysis, unclear objectives and project management. There have been particular difficulties in modelling competition (especially within rail) and realistic pricing policies. The primacy of travel time savings has come under particular scrutiny. One line of argument, associated with David Metz (Metz, 2008), is that time savings have little meaning if there is a constant travel time budget, with higher speeds dissipated by longer trips. The counter argument is that the increased travel distances that HSR permits allow a better matching of people with economic activities and, assuming perfectly competitive markets, these benefits will be accurately reflected by time savings. Given the ability to use time productively on trains (Lyons et al., 2007), there are concerns about whether the value of time for business users is too high, particularly for those abstracted from classic rail. Moreover, strong growth in business travel in the recent past may have been due to changes in company car taxation (Le Vine and Jones, 2012) and this may be a one-off increase. There might also be concerns over competition from 'disruptive' technologies, whether they are autonomous road vehicles, video conferencing or car sharing.

Table 4.8 Benefits of HS2 (PV 2011 prices).

Grouped benefit	Disaggregated benefit	Phase one		Full network	
		Benefit value (£m)	Percentage of total	Benefit value (£m)	Percentage of total
Transport user benefits	Improved access	£1,094	4%	£1,115	2%
	Reduction in crowding	£4,068	14%	£7,514	11%
	Improvements in interchange	£810	3%	£4,146	6%
	Reductions in waiting	£3,508	12%	£8,081	11%
	Reductions in walking	£404	1%	£1,330	2%
	Reductions in train journey time	£11,518	41%	£31,007	44%
	Greater reliability on the HS2 network	£2,624	9%	£5,496	8%
	Benefits to road users	£568	2%	£1,162	2%
	Total	**£24,594**	**87%**	**£59,852**	**84%**
Wider economic impacts	Agglomeration (businesses closer together)	£2,413	9%	£8,706	12%
	Imperfect competition (increased output due to reduced costs)	£1,692	6%	£4,053	6%
	Increased labour force participation	£235	1%	£535	1%
	Total	**£4,341**	**15%**	**£13,293**	**19%**
Other impacts	Reduction of car noise	£10	0%	£27	0%
	Carbon	£43	0%	£101	0%
	HS1 link	£287	1%	£458	1%
	Reduction in car accidents	£123	0%	£334	0%
	Noise from HS2 trains	–£55	0%	–£133	0%
	Total	£407	1%	E788	1%
	Loss to government of indirect tax	–£1,208	–4%	–£2,912	–4%
	Total	**£28,134**	**100%**	**£71,020**	**100%**

Source: HS2 Ltd, 2013.

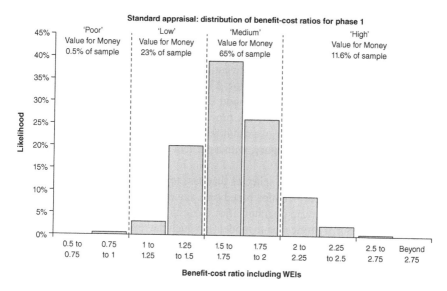

Figure 4.7 Probabilistic analysis of HS2 costs and benefits.

6. Conclusions

Overall, we conclude that there is a reasonable body of evidence on the direct and indirect impacts of HSR, that these costs and benefits are substantive and that the balance between costs and benefits will be context specific. Given this evidence, we suggest a four-stage test for HSR:

1   Does HSR make a commercial return? Based on Crozet (2013), the key patronage threshold seems to be around 20 million passengers per annum. From the appendix, we find that 22 schemes (or combination of schemes) pass this threshold, some 42 per cent of our data set. The majority of schemes in this category are from East Asia, although the TGV Sud-Est is a notable exception.

2   Does HSR make a social return based on impacts to the rail system? Here we suggest the key demand threshold may be around 9 million abstracted passengers per annum. However, this is based on a relatively generous assumption of the proportion of end-to-end users, the magnitude of time saving benefits and the value of travel time. Ignoring the issues surrounding trip generation, we find that 35 of the schemes in the appendix pass this threshold (67 per cent of the data set).

3   Does HSR make a social return when quantitative benefits to the rest of the transport sector and wider economic and environmental factors are taken into account? In such circumstances, we might expect a lower threshold. However, our review of the evidence suggests that this uplift in wider benefits for HSR may only be 25 per cent, reducing the annual demand threshold

to around 7 million. We find 39 of the schemes in the appendix pass this threshold (75 per cent).

4   Does HSR represent a social improvement when other qualitative factors are taken into account? There may be circumstances where demand is so low and/or costs high, that no conventional cost-benefit analysis will show a social return. Examples include the AVE in Spain and the Channel Tunnel. For the former, de Rus (2012) found BCRs of 0.66 and 0.58. For the latter, which is not exclusively an HSR project, Anguera (2006) found a BCR of only 0.38. From the above, we can infer that something like one in four HSR schemes fall into this category, with a particular concentration in Europe.

With respect to delivery, HSR schemes that pass tests one or two may be amenable to Public–Private Partnerships based on a stand-alone model (where revenue risk is borne by the private operator). For those that go ahead based on passing tests three and four, a services-sold model (in which the revenue risk remains with the public sector) is more likely.

Acknowledgement

An earlier version of this paper was presented to the International Workshop on Advances in Research on Surface Transportation held at the University of Barcelona, 24 November 2015.

Note

1 See: www.internationaltransportforum.org/jtrc/DiscussionPapers/jtrcpapers.html.

References

Albalate, D. and Bel, G. (2012). "*The economics and politics of high speed rail: Lessons from experiences abroad*", Lanham, MD: Lexington Books.

Anguera, R. (2006). "*The Channel Tunnel. An ex-post economic evaluation*", Transportation Research Part A: Policy and Practice, 40(4), 291–315.

Atkins Ltd (2008). "*Because transport matters: High speed rail*", London: Atkins Ltd.

Atkins Ltd, AECOM and Frontier Economics (2015). "*First interim evaluation of the impacts of high speed 1. Final report. Volume 1 – main report*", London: Atkins Ltd.

Beria, P. (2015). "*High-speed rail in Italy: Is it a story of success?*", Paper presented at the International Workshop on Advances in Research on Surface Transportation, University of Barcelona, 24 November 2015.

Blum, U., Haynes, K.E. and Karlsson, C. (1997). "*The regional and urban effects of high-speed trains*", The Annals of Regional Science, 31, 1–20.

Bonnafous, A. (1987). "*The regional impact of the TGV*", Transportation, 14, 127–137.

Campos, J., de Rus, G. and Barron, I. (2009). "*A Review of HSR services around the world*", In de Rus, G. (Ed), *Economic analysis of high speed rail in Europe*, Bilbao: Fundación BBVA, pp. 19–32.

Chang, J. (2013). "*High speed rail in Taiwan*", Presentation to ITF Roundtable, New Delhi, India, 19 December 2013.

Coto-Millán, P., Inglada, V. and Rey, B. (2007). *"Effects of network economies in high-speed rail: The Spanish case"*, Annals of Regional Science, 41, 911–925.

Council of the European Union (1996). *"The interoperability of the trans-European high-speed rail system"*, Council Directive 96/48/EC, 23 July 1996, Brussels: CEC, available at http://eur-lex.europa.eu/LexUriServ/LexUriServ.do?uri=CELEX:31996L0048:en:HTML [accessed 23 November 2015].

Croccolo, F. and Violi, A. (2013). *"New entry in the Italian high speed market"*, Discussion Paper 29, Paris: International Transport Forum.

Crozet, Y. (2013). *"High speed rail performance in France: From appraisal methodologies to ex-post Evaluation 2"*, Discussion Paper 26, Paris: International Transport Forum.

Department for Transport (2005). *"Transport, wider economic benefits and impacts on GDP"*, Discussion Paper, London: DfT.

Department for Transport (2015). *"Provision of market research for value of travel time savings and reliability: Non-technical summary report"*, London: DfT, available at www.gov.uk/government/publications/values-of-travel-time-savings-and-reliability-final-reports [accessed 23 November 2015].

de Rus, G. (2012). *"Economic evaluation of the high speed rail"*, Stockholm: Ministry of Finance, Expert Group on Environmental Studies, available at www.ems.expertgrupp.se/Default.aspx?pageID=3 [accessed 23 November 2015].

de Rus, G. and Inglada, V. (1997). *"Cost-benefit analysis of the high-speed train in Spain"*, Annals of Regional Science, 31, 175–188.

de Rus, G. and Nombela, G. (2007). *"Is investment in HSR socially profitable?"*, Journal of Transport Economics and Policy, 41(1), 3–23.

de Rus, G. and Nash, C. (2009). *"In what circumstances is investment in HSR worthwhile?"*, In de Rus, G. (Ed), *Economic analysis of high speed rail in Europe*, Bilbao: Fundación BBVA, pp. 51–70.

Docherty, I., Shaw, J., Preston, J. and Hepworth, M. (2009). *"High speed ground transport: Glasgow–Edinburgh corridor"*, Glasgow: SPT.

Dodgson, J.S. (1973). *"External effects and secondary benefits in road investment appraisal"*, Journal of Transport Economics and Policy, 7(2), 169–185.

Eddington, R. (2006). *"The Eddington transport study"*, London: DfT.

Esplugas, C., Teixeira, P., Lopez-Pita, A. and Saña, A. (2005). *"Threats and opportunities for high speed rail transport in competition with low costs carriers"*, Paper presented at the International Conference on Competition and Ownership in Land Passenger Transport, Lisbon, Portugal, 4–8 September 2005.

Graham, D.J. (2007). *"Agglomeration, productivity and transport investment"*, Journal of Transport Economics and Policy, 41(3), 317–343.

Graham, D.J. and Melo, P. (2010). *"Advice on the assessment of wider economic impacts: A report for HS2"*, London: Imperial College.

Greengauge 21 (2009). *"Fast forward. A high-speed rail strategy for Britain"*, Kingston upon Thames: Greenguage 21.

HS2 Ltd (2010). *"High speed rail. London to the West Midlands and beyond"*, London: DfT.

HS2 Ltd (2012). *"Economic case for HS2: Updated appraisal of transport user benefits and wider economic benefits"*, London: DfT.

HS2 Ltd (2013). *"The economic case for HS2"*, London: DfT.

International Union of Railways (2014). *"High speed lines in the world"*, Paris: UIC, available at http://old.uic.org/IMG/pdf/20140901_high_speed_lines_in_the_world.pdf [accessed 23 November 2015].

Jun, L. (2013). *"Presentation to Round Table New Delhi, India"*, Department of Railway Research, Seoul: Korean Transport Institute.

KPMG (2013). *"High speed rail: Consequences for employment and economic growth. Technical Report"*, London: HS2 Ltd.

Kurosaki, F. (2013). *"Shinkansen investment before and after JNR reform"*, Discussion Paper 27, Paris: International Transport Forum.

Leunig, T. (2011). *"Cart or horse: Transport and economic growth"*, Discussion Paper 04, Paris: International Transport Forum.

Le Vine, S. and Jones, P. (2012). *"On the move. Making sense of car and train travel trends in Britain"*, London: RAC Foundation.

Lyons, G., Jain, J. and Holley, D. (2007). *"The use of travel time by rail passengers in Great Britain"*, Transportation Research Part A: Policy and Practice, 41(1), 107–120.

Metz, D. (2008). *"The myth of travel time savings"*, Transport Reviews, 28(3), 321–336.

Mohring, H. (1993). *"Maximising, measuring, and not double counting transportation improvement benefits: A primer on closed- and open-economy cost-benefit analysis"*, Transportation Research Part B: Methodological, 27(6), 413–424.

Nash, C.A (2013). *"When to invest in high speed rail"*, Discussion Paper 25, Paris: International Transport Forum.

National Audit Office (2012). *"Department for Transport. The completion and sale of high speed 1"*, HC1834, London: TSO.

National Audit Office (2013). *"High speed 2: A review of early programme preparation"*, London: TSO.

Nellthorp, J. and Hyman, S. (2001). *"Alternatives to the rule of half in matrix based appraisal"*, Paper presented at the European Transport Conference, Cambridge, 10–12 September 2001.

Oosterhaven, J. and Elhorst, J.P. (2003). *"Modelling interactions between the economy, the environment and transportation at the local and regional level, with an application to Dutch Maglev projects"*, Paper presented at the TRIP research conference on the Economic and Environmental Consequences of Regulating Traffic, Copenhagen, 2–3 February 2003.

Ortega, A., Guzman, A., Preston, J. and Vassallo, J. (2016). *"The price elasticity of demand of high speed rail lines in Spain. The impact of the new pricing scheme"*, Paper presented at the Transportation Research Board Annual Meeting, Washington, DC, 10–14 January 2016.

Oxera (2009). *"Sustainability performance of the railteam network"*, Brussels: Oxera.

Pagliara, F., de Pompeis, V. and Preston, J. (2016). *"Travel cost: Not always the important element of social exclusion"*, Paper presented at the World Conference on Transport Research, Shanghai, 11–14 July 2016.

Perl, A. (2012). *"Assessing the recent reformulation of United States passenger rail policy"*, Journal of Transport Geography, 22, 271–281.

Preston, J. (2009). *"The case for high speed rail: A review of recent evidence"*, London: RAC Foundation.

Preston, J. (2012). *"High speed rail: About time or a waste of time?"*, Journal of Transport Geography, 22, 308–311.

Preston, J. (2014). *"The economics of investment in high speed rail: Summary and conclusions"*, Discussion Paper 2013-30, Paris: International Transport Forum.

Preston, J. and Wall, G. (2008). *"The ex-ante and ex-post economic and social impacts of the introduction of high speed trains in south-east England"*, Planning Practice and Research, 23(3), 403–422.

Segal, J. (2006). *"High speed rail – the competitive environment"*, Paper presented at the European Transport Conference, Strasbourg, 18–20 September 2006.

Shires, J.D. (1998). *"Barriers, borders and frontiers: The cost of transport"*, Transport Studies Unit Reference 873, Oxford: University of Oxford.

Sugden, R. (1972). *"Cost benefit analysis and the withdrawal of rail services"*, Bulletin of Economic Research, 1(24), 23–32.

Venables, A.J. (2004). *"Evaluating urban transport improvements: Cost-benefit analysis in the presence of agglomeration"*, London: LSE.

Venables, A.J. (2007). *"Evaluating urban transport improvements. Cost-benefit analysis in the presence of agglomeration and income taxation"*, Journal of Transport Economics and Policy, 41(2), 173–188.

Venables, A. and Gasiorek, M. (1999). *"The welfare implications of transport improvements in the presence of market failure: The incidence of imperfect competition in UK sectors and regions"*, London: DETR.

Venables, A.J., Laird, J. and Overman, H. (2014). *"Transport investment and economic performance. Implications for project appraisal"*, London: DfT, available at www.gov.uk/government/uploads/system/uploads/attachment_data/file/386126/TIEP_Report.pdf [accessed 23 November 2015].

Wu, J. (2013). *"The financial and economic assessment of China's high speed rail investments: A preliminary analysis"*, Discussion Paper, Paris: International Transport Forum.

Appendix 1: Database of HSR demand

Source	Line/City pair)	Level of demand (m pa)	Year
Nash, 2013 (Table 3.2)	TGV Sud-Est	19.2	1987*
	TGV Atlantic	29	1995*
	TGV Nord	20	1994
	TGV Connexion	16.6	2000*
	TGV Rhone-Alpes	18.5	1995
	TGV Mediterrane	20.4	2001
	Madrid–Seville	3.6	1998*
	Madrid–Barcelona	5.4	2009
	Tokyo–Osaka	80	1970*
	Seoul–Busan	28	2010*
National Audit Office, 2012 (In Nash, 2013)	HS1 international	9.7	2011
	HS1 domestic	8.4	2011
	Tokaido–Sanyo	128.3 (207.4)	1984 (2011)
	Tohuku	24.1 (76.1)	1984 (2011)
Kurosaki, 2013 (Table 2 and Table 5)	Joetsu	11.3 (34.8)	1984 (2011)
	Hefei–Nanjing	21.3	2012
	Beijing–Tianjin	21.0	2012
Wu, 2013	Qingdao–Jinan	28.0	2012
	Shi–Tai	22.6	2012
	Hefei–Wuhan	11.0	2012
	Coastal HSL	15.1	2012
	Wuhan–Guangzhou	19.7	2012
	Zhenghou–Xian	5.8	2012
	Chengdu–Dujiangyan	4.7	2012
	Shanghai–Nanjing	29.2	2012
	Shanghai–Hangzhou	28.3	2012
	Nanchang–Jiujiang	30.2	2012
	Changchun–Jilin	8.4	2012
	Hainan East Circle	6.4	2012
	Beijing–Shanghai	24.8	2012
	Italy HS network	Over 12.1	2012
	Chinese Taipei HSR	36.6	Average 2007–13.
Croccolo and Violi, 2013.	G-Line (Gyeongbu)	22.2 (39.1)	2004 (2011)
	H-Line (Honam)	4.2 (7.3)	2004 (2011)
Chang, 2013	Madrid–Barcelona	5.2	2011
Jun, 2013	Madrid–Seville	2.8	2011
Ortega et al., 2016	Madrid–Valencia	2.4	2011
	Turin–Milan	1.5 (4)	2011 (2013)
Beria, 2015	Milan–Bologna	6.5 (13)	2011 (2013)
	Bologna–Florence	11 (18)	2011 (2013)
	Florence–Rome	9.5 (17.5)	2011 (2013)
	Rome–Naples	3 (7.5)	2011 (2013)

5 High-speed rail services and tourism expansion

The need for cooperation

Marie Delaplace and Sylvie Bazin-Benoit

1. Introduction

In cities served by high-speed rail (HSR), local actors expect there to be an expansion in the tourism sector. Indeed, HSR can be perceived as an opportunity for renewed attractiveness, particularly in the field of tourism. However, the literature on this subject is highly controversial. A few cities have experienced a growth in visitor numbers; but, a decrease in the average duration of tourist stays sometimes occurs. A number of elements may affect the link between HSR and tourism; this article focuses on the forms of cooperation that exist between actors, which seem to be one of the key elements of this reported dynamism. After all, a tourist destination incorporates numerous products and services realized by various stakeholders in a given place. The production of this destination requires coordination between these stakeholders. The arrival of a HSR service can incite them to work together so as to take full advantage of the best possible accessibility for their area.

Section 2 puts forward the controversial results of the literature concerning the link between HSR and tourism. By analyzing the French case, section 3 highlights the determinants that could explain this heterogeneity and, more particularly, the types of cooperation in question.

2. HSR and tourism: A review

2.1 Types of tourism which could potentially benefit from HSR

Urban tourism and business tourism appear to be the main types of tourism likely to benefit from a HSR service (Mannone, 1995; Amiard, 1997; Kamel and Matthewman, 2008; Masson and Petiot, 2009; Urena et al., 2009; Bazin-Benoit et al., 2010; 2011; Delaplace and Perrin, 2013).

Urban tourism has increased significantly due to the growth in short stays and, in the French case, due to the reduction of working time (in particular, the 35-hour week) up until the 2000s. This is usually short-stay tourism (two or three days, in general)—for instance, during weekends—which mainly concerns individuals or couples from different socio-economic groups. Compared to car journeys, traveling by HSR allows passengers to get to their destination faster while being able to relax and at the same time avoid road congestion and the increasing difficulties associated with accessing the heart of the city, especially if the destination station is located in the city center. Compared to air travel, it also saves the time lost in travel between the airport and the heart of the city. All forms of tourism that take place in the heart of the city in question could therefore benefit from HSR services. This is the case, for example, for event-related tourism, as well as for business tourism, sometimes also referred to as "MICE" (meetings, incentives, conferencing, exhibitions). This type of tourism, undertaken for business purposes, is also a form of short-stay tourism (two or three days), but during the week. It is characterized by both individual and collective travel. The decision to travel depends mainly on companies or administrations, with particular importance accorded to reduced travel time. These journeys are made by socio-professional groups with a high income and a relatively low sensitivity to price, but a high sensibility to the quality and speed of the rail service. Like other types of tourism, this tourism is characterized by a shortening of the average stay. Business tourism establishments are generally located in the downtown areas of cities. Indeed, location, along with accessibility and accommodation capacity, is one of the top three criteria for selecting a site for such establishments.

Forms of tourism outside cities (for example, green tourism or mountain tourism) often benefit less from HSR, except where intermodality issues are managed to allow tourists to reach their destinations without significant time losses.

2.2 Dynamism in terms of visitor numbers in certain cities . . .

A dynamism associated with HSR is sometimes observed in the short term and under certain conditions, but the results of studies, conducted over 30 years in France and elsewhere, tell a very different story (Delaplace et al., 2014).

First, there has been no impact on winter sports activities in France except for a change in traveler profiles due to the Paris–Lyon high-speed line (HSL) (Bonnafous, 1987), and no growth in rural tourism either (Bazin-Benoit et al., 2006). In Japan, however, there seems to have been a growth in tourism in the winter sports resort of Echigo Yuzawa, but with an expansion of same-day round-trip journeys (Mizohata, 1995) and an impact on hinterland areas (Okabe, 1980).

Concerning business tourism, research by Mannone (1995) highlighted the development of exhibitions and trade fairs nationwide, and in particular in places such as Lyon, Chambéry and Grenoble, as well as in the smaller Burgundian town of Beaune, with the creation of the Palais des Congrès in 1991, some ten years after the arrival of HSR. However, she underlined the fact that there had been no development of business tourism in Dijon.

Research conducted concerning the Atlantic HSL shows an increase in the number of conferences in Le Mans between 1987 and 1993, with 70 per cent of clients coming from the Île-de-France (Paris) region and 70 per cent of attendees coming by HSR in 1993 (Amiard, 1997). In addition, there has been some development of business tourism in Tours (Faye, 1998), also related to the opening of the city's international congress center.

Following the opening of the Mediterranean HSL, there was also a growth in the number of congress days hosted in Marseille (Ville de Marseille, 2011). By contrast, not all expectations in terms of tourism have been fulfilled in Avignon (Feliu, 2012).

According to the regional council for tourism in the Alsace region,[1] with regard to the East European HSL (inaugurated in June 2007), Strasbourg saw an increase in the number of domestic overnight stays between 2007 and 2009, as well as an increase in the number of "business" events, national and international events, seminar days and sales meetings. There was also a growth in the number of congress days—and international congress days in particular—in Reims between 2005 and 2010 (Agence d'Urbanisme Région de Reims, 2012).

Concerning tourism in general, the number of hotel rooms increased in the center of Nantes between 1988 and 1993, but occupancy rates have not matched expectations (Vickerman and Ulied, 2006). In small cities such as Beaune and Montbard (85 and 130 miles north of Lyon, respectively), there has been a growth in the number of overnight stays, but a decrease of the same in places such as Dijon, Valence and in the neighborhoods around Perrache station in Lyon. Following the opening of the North HSL, a growth has been observed in the number of hotels—and more particularly in the number of three- and four-star hotel rooms—in Lille. Growth in tourism has also been observed by Urena et al. (2009), along with an increase in overall visitor numbers between 1990 and 1995, and in foreign visitor numbers between 1990 and 2003 (CSEF, 2005).

Overnight stays are also on the increase in intermediate cities such as Nancy and Metz. However, two years after the opening of the East European HSL, the only city served by the line to show real dynamism seems to be Strasbourg (INSEE Lorraine, 2009).

In addition, the analysis conducted in France by Bazin-Benoit et al. (2013a) in certain small and medium-sized cities served by the North, Atlantic and East European HSLs shows that, despite an improvement in accessibility, increases in tourist numbers due to HSR are not systematic, even in cities with a tourist heritage.

In other countries, the effects are equally mixed. In Spain, Urena et al. (2009) argued that large intermediate cities served by HSR such as Zaragoza and in particular Córdoba would see growth in urban and business tourism. This is confirmed by Alonso and Bellet (2009) in the case of Zaragoza. Similarly, Todorovitch et al. (2011) reported that tourism had grown by 15 per cent annually in Lleida (20 per cent for business conventions). Guirao and Campa (2015) also reported how HSR is important for tourism in Toledo: over 30 per cent of weekday HSR ridership is linked to tourism mobility. A recent report in Spain suggested that "the positive effects of HSR on the number of visitors, the number of nights spent at destination and/or hotel occupancy rates are mostly restricted, at best, to larger cities, but in most cases the effects are minimal or even negative" (Albalate et al., 2015, p. 16).

The study by DB International GmbH (2011) on pairs of relatively similar cities—one served by HSR, the other not—in France, Germany and Spain shows how difficult it is to generalize with regard to the dynamic evolution of overnight stays in the cities served by HSR. In Spain, it was also shown that the dynamism of the number of overnight stays is strongly correlated to all cities regardless of whether they are served by HSR. Finally, the study led by the South East England Development Agency (2008) in thirteen cities in Germany, the Netherlands, the UK and France shows that few cities seem to have experienced a revitalization of tourism.

An increase in tourist movements is, however, reported for big cities in Taiwan (Cheng, 2009) as well as in Chinese cities such as Wuhan (Wang et al., 2012), Qufu (People's Republic of China, 2014), and Ningbo (Zhao, 2012). Provinces served by HSR in China "are likely to have approximately 20% more foreign arrivals and 25% more in tourism revenue than provinces without such systems" (Chen and Haynes, 2012, p. 1). In Japan, Okabe (1980) described an increase in tourist visits to large cities served by HSR such as Hiroshima and Fukuoka, to intermediate cities such as Mihara and Tsuyazaki, and even to small cities such as Amagi, while the number of visits decreased in cities not served by HSR. However, he also underlined the fact that smaller places could not always provide accommodation for all their visitors. In addition, he showed that, in Fukuoka City, hotel construction boomed as the arrival of tourists and businessmen was anticipated: the number of hotel rooms doubled between 1964 and 1975. Kurihara and Wu (2015) show that, in Japan, there has been a growth in tourist numbers in certain HSR-served cities and a decrease of the same in others. Growth has also been observed in Tokyo, Osaka and Kobe (reported by Albalate and Bel, 2012), as well as in London (Sen, 2004). Finally, an increase in the number of hotel rooms has also been observed in Sendai in Japan (Mizohata, 1995).

Another important point is that there has been no systematic impact on destination choice. For example, a survey carried out in 2012 in Paris, at certain key sites in the French capital and at the Gare de Lyon (one of the main railway stations in Paris) showed that, for visitors to Paris, HSR is the third most important element in the choice of destination after historical and cultural heritage, and architecture (Delaplace et al., 2014). Moreover, the modeling of results shows that the HSR variable is highly significant when it comes to the probability of returning to Paris for tourism purposes. The presence of HSR influences the choice of young tourists in particular, because it allows for faster travel (thus reducing journey time), because HSR stations are easy to access, and because young people have a good knowledge of promotional offers for HSR travel, increasing the likelihood of a return visit in the future. There has also been an impact on Disneyland Paris (Delaplace et al., 2014; 2015). Indeed, some tourists declared that HSR was so crucial in their choice of destination that they would not have come without the presence of a HSR service.

By contrast, HSR does not seem to affect people's decision to revisit Rome (Valeri et al., 2012), but does influence the probability of visiting other cities connected to Rome by HSR. The analysis conducted in Madrid showed similar results: no impact on Madrid itself, but an impact on cities linked to Madrid by HSR (Pagliara et al., 2015).

Another survey, conducted in Naples, showed that there was an effect with regard to visits to Naples and the intention to visit other cities nearby by HSR (Pagliara, 2014).

Finally, HSR does not appear to have an impact on destination choice for visitors to the Futuroscope multimedia theme park near Poitiers in western France (Delaplace et al., 2015).

Bearing in mind the above, we can conclude that the link between HSR and destination choice is not systematic; it depends on the destination in question.

Here, the extreme heterogeneity of situations comes to the fore, often with reference to specific cases and underlining the need for contextualization (Delaplace, 2012a). The effects of HSR cannot be understood without considering the socio-economic characteristics of the areas it serves, in tourism as in other fields (Bazin-Benoit et al., 2013b).

Moreover, while the number of tourists might increase, the average duration of their stays may in some cases decrease.

2.3 . . . but sometimes accompanied by a reduction in the length of stay

A reduction in the average length of stay and in the number of nights spent in a city is likely to occur because HSR opens up the possibility of same-day round trips. A survey conducted between 1980 and 1985 on the Paris–Lyon HSL (inaugurated in 1981) (Bonnafous, 1987) showed a decrease in the average length of stay in Dijon, Lyon and Valence, as well as in the hotel district around Perrache station in Lyon, while this was not the case in Beaune and Montbard. Indeed, in Dijon, the HSR service has helped reduce the proportion of business travelers who spend the night there. In Lyon, increased accessibility has also induced a reduction in the average length of stay (Mannone 1995, p. 280).

In Le Mans, the arrival of HSR has contributed to reducing the duration of events for residents and, conversely, to promoting non-residential events, i.e. fewer events lasting several days but more one-day events. In this city, the average length of stay decreased a few years after the arrival of HSR. Furthermore, events had an average duration of one day less than that generally encountered for national conferences in France in the mid 1990s (Amiard, 1997). This reduction in the duration of events was due in part to HSR, but also to the strategy adopted by the Palais des Congrès et de la Culture (the city's main convention center), which focused on one-day events in order to get around the problem of the city's limited three-star hotel capacity. Similarly, according to an analysis by the French statistics office, INSEE, between 2007 and 2008, the average stay in tourist accommodation declined in almost all areas in 2007, as well as in Reims (INSEE Lorraine, 2009). In 2009, in the area around Reims in the Champagne region, the number of overnight stays fell below 2006 levels. Equally, the average length of events held at the city's convention center decreased from 3.81 days in 2005 to 2.68 days in 2010 (Agence d'Urbanisme Région de Reims, 2012). This reduction also reflects the strategies of companies which, in order to reduce budgets, are increasingly moving towards one-day conferences.

In other countries, the same phenomena have been recorded. In Japan, Okabe (1980) observed a reduction in overnight stays in cities served by HSR such as Tokyo, Osaka, Fukuoka and Soeda. And in China, the HSR service from Hangzhou is likely to have a negative impact on the hotel industry now that it is possible to make the round trip between Hangzhou and Shanghai on the same day (Chen, 2013).

Furthermore, while the number of visitors participating in urban tourism might well grow with the arrival of HSR, a significant reduction in the length of stay can lead to an overall reduction in spending by tourists (Levinson, 2012). This trend reveals the contradictory effects of HSR on tourism (Albalate and Bel, 2012).

This raises a further question, however: what are the key elements that can explain this heterogeneity?

3. Key elements in the promotion of tourism due to the arrival of HSR: The case of France

3.1 The numerous determinants of heterogeneity in the link between HSR and tourism

First, as for other activities, the expansion of tourism depends on the economic situation, and also the political situation of a given city. The impact of HSR on tourism can be affected by an unfavorable economic climate or by a tragic event that causes tourists to postpone their visit to cities served by HSR.

Second, city size is a factor to be taken into account when considering the connection between HSR and the dynamism of tourism (Delaplace, 2012b). In particular, HSR typically promotes well-known places with numerous specific resources likely to attract tourists. This offer can be linked to historical, cultural or gastronomic heritage, the importance of which often depends on the size of the city. For cities of intermediate size, positive effects can be observed provided that they already offer tourist amenities, corresponding to a "basket of goods" that enables tourists to diversify their visits (Bazin-Benoit et al., 2014). City size is also a key element in terms of hotel capacity and the range of restaurants on offer.

Third, the location of cities in relation to other cities is important in terms of the possibility of using HSR to promote tourism, as this relative location affects the market area of a given city. Being a capital served by HSR is not important when tourists are mainly foreigners who travel by air. But, being a city with HSR close to the capital, enabling international clients to make a round trip in a single day or over two days, can be a precious asset. This relative location must also be compared with other cities served by HSR and the location of potential clients. For instance, the market for clients coming from the Île-de-France (Paris) region is a target for intermediate cities close to Paris that benefit from good weekend accessibility and, more specifically, frequent services at times suited to arrivals at the beginning of the weekend and late returns on Sunday evenings (Delaplace and Perrin, 2013).

Finally, in addition to city size and location, networking and cooperation among stakeholders is also a key element in the relationship between HSR and tourism.

3.2 The issue of cooperation in the tourism sector

Richardson shows that production can be achieved through cooperation between different firms when their activities are closely complementary but non-similar (Richardson, 1972, pp. 884–885). This analysis would appear to be useful in showing the importance of cooperation in the field of tourism.

First of all, tourism includes different but complementary services: hotels, other forms of accommodation, restaurants, leisure activities, places to visit, local food or wine specialties, and so forth.

All these activities help to produce the tourism destination that tourists are looking for. In some cases, these activities can be internalized within a single entity, as in the case of all-inclusive resorts. But, more frequently, they are produced by different organizations (hotels, restaurants, museums, theme parks, local producers, etc.). In these cases, they must be coordinated within the destination.

Moreover, a destination is not only made up of private resources. For instance, the landscape can be considered a public resource that is produced and maintained collectively by different stakeholders. Its conservation depends on the joint action of all stakeholders.

More broadly speaking, tourism often involves public actors (tourist offices at different scales, for example) and non-profit actors (site conservation associations, sport and leisure clubs, etc.). Partnerships between all these actors (private and public) are thus required in the production of the destination. This cooperation within a given field (for example, culture) or between two different sectors (culture and restaurants) is thus one of the conditions that enables a tourist region to develop a competitive advantage (Czernek, 2013). The fragmented nature of the tourism industry calls for a substantial degree of coordination and collaboration among the destination's various stakeholders in order to make the destination successful (Wang and Fesenmaier, 2007; Jones et al., 2015). Finally, the sustainability of a tourist destination depends on the sustainability of the cooperation. This is to prevent free riders whose only aim is to sell a product or a service without consideration for its quality. This is an important point, as tourists may come back again, and may also encourage other tourists to visit. This kind of cooperation can be fostered during the commissioning of a HSR service.

3.3 The different kinds of cooperation linked to HSR

Places with specific assets (Colletis and Pecqueur, 2004), whatever their nature (heritage-related, memorial, natural, cultural, etc.), can promote them to best advantage with HSR by implementing complementary policies and specific strategies (Bazin-Benoit et al., 2010). This promotion depends on communication policies, intermodality policies and a renewed offer of tourist products.

In terms of communications, local stakeholders can use HSR to modify the image of their city. HSR can give rise to a reputation or image effect, that is to say a distinction from which the cities served—and their tourism industries in particular—can benefit (Mignerey, 2013). This has been the case in Le Mans, Lille, Arras, and Reims (Menerault, 1997; Bazin-Benoit et al., 2013a; 2014), as well as in cities served by the Rhine–Rhône HSR (Carrouet, 2013).This image effect can be used by tourism stakeholders at local, departmental or regional level.

HSR operators sometimes cooperate with cities in order to promote special events and make the line as profitable as possible at weekends. This has been the case in France for the Strasbourg Christmas market. So, in cooperation with SNCF (the French national rail company), the cities served by HSR often use these rail services to get people talking about them, and vice versa. Festive events are also organized when new lines are opened, and sometimes tickets are sold at a reduced price. In France, SNCF pursued such strategies when the East European HSL was inaugurated. In the short term, this led to an expansion of tourism in the newly served cities. HSR operators might also offer additional services for occasional major events in certain destinations. For example, when the "Braderie de Lille" (a sort of huge, citywide garage sale) is held in early September each year, the capacity of certain high-speed services between Lille and Paris is increased. And in Belfort, during the "Eurockéennes" music festival, two high-speed trains with discounted tickets only (non-refundable, non-exchangeable tickets known as "Prem's", sold at very low prices), were set up. Local actors in cities served by HSR typically join forces and produce advertising campaigns that allow them to take ownership of the image associated with HSR. Since business activities can be impacted by HSR, private actors may also be interested in coordinating their action with that of public or semi-public actors in terms of communication. This is the case for conference centers (attendance at which can grow as a result), hotel resorts or companies that wish to be associated with the local area from a marketing point of view.

In terms of intermodality, if a HSR service allows for faster travel times, the time saved during the journey should not be lost upon arrival by inadequate connections with local public transportation. The opening of a new HSR service is thus frequently accompanied by a revision of interconnections in terms of rail transportation (regional trains in particular), urban public transportation, special shuttle services and even pedestrian routes (Coronado et al., 2014) in order to bring tourists to their final destination. Accordingly, when a HSR service opens, the local authority often redefines the urban integration of the station, which constitutes one of the gateways into the city. In Reims, for instance, the public transportation network has been reorganized, taking the central railway station as one of its hubs. But, in other cases, intermodal issues have not been adequately considered, as in the case of Tours, where there was no coordination between the arrival of the HSR service and the departure of organized trips to the châteaux of the Loire Valley (Troin, 2012). During specific events, the coordination of transportation modes that depart from the railway station is of great importance. Intermodality can also be improved by ensuring good connections between freeways and/or the road network and stations located on HSLs by introducing self-service bike hire services, and by ensuring there is direct access to taxis, streetcars and buses at the station exit.

Finally, as one of the main negative effects associated with HSR is the reduction of the average length of visitor stays, everything possible must be done to keep tourists in the city. Efforts must be made to maximize the products offered by the destination by strengthening the local "basket of goods and services" (Pecqueur, 2001; Mollard and Pecqueur, 2007). Producing an inventory of the existing assets in a city and reflecting upon new, complementary goods that could be offered makes it possible to enrich this "basket of goods" available to tourists, who are looking for a variety of products that enable them to make the most of their journey to the destination in question, and also to widen the range of places they visit and the types of visit they undertake (museums, themed urban pedestrian circuits, special events, excursions to nearby natural sites, etc.). They can then choose items from this "basket" in order to build their own personalized stay. Night-time products (illuminations, night-time visits, etc.) can be developed to encourage the tourist to stay the night. When the "basket of goods" is expanded by integrating secondary cities, improvements in terms of interchanges must also be extended to transportation towards these cities (see above).

All these policies require coordination between public and private actors (travel agencies, cultural event planners, tourist information offices, rail companies, public transportation operators, hotel and restaurant owners, etc.) in the destination city (Bazin-Benoit and Delaplace, 2015). Furthermore, they must produce packages (incorporating train tickets, accommodation, museum visits or a concert, a pass to visit all or a number of the city's attractions, etc.). The tourist offices of other nearby cities can offer round trips to encourage tourists to visit other places (Bazin-Benoit et al., 2011b). Collective communication on the scale of the wider area around the destination city, as well as appropriate targeting of clientele and judicious choices of places and means of dissemination, make it possible to optimize the change in image of these cities that often occurs when a HSR service opens.

So, coordination must occur:

- between competing territories (to obtain a joint offer and joint communication);
- between communities and rail companies (for the location of stations and for new modes of co-financing these stations—in order to try to maintain the service frequency and not reduce service levels and in order to adapt schedules to urban and business tourism—or in terms of communication), as well as with other transportation operators;
- between the tourist office and private firms offering innovative products;
- between the tourist office and hotels, in order to offer enticing "baskets of goods";
- between conference centers and hotels to ensure there is sufficient accommodation for all conference and trade fair participants.

4. Conclusion

Tourism is an activity that can be impacted by the opening of a HSR service, particularly for urban and business tourism in cities with specific assets. A certain dynamism associated with HSR is sometimes observed in the short term and under certain conditions. But this is not always the case; there is frequently a decrease in the length of visitor stays.

Numerous stakeholders become mobilized when a new HSR service arrives. Sometimes, this leads to new forms of cooperation among them. Concerning the French case, communication policies, intermodality improvements and new "baskets of goods and services" adapted to HSR travel have been implemented in certain places. Nevertheless, the power of these policies is greater in large and intermediate cities with high and diversified tourism potential. Cooperation between cities aiming to jointly broaden their "baskets of goods" sometimes makes it possible to avoid reductions in length of stay. However, these policies are not always effective in small- and medium-sized cities characterized by limited tourism amenities. In the field of tourism, as in other domains, HSR often seems to be most profitable for the largest cities.

Note

1 See www.clicalsace.com/fr/thematique/offre-et-frequentation/impact-du-tgv-est-sur-les-activites-touristique-apres-2-ans [accessed 15 January 2016].

References

Agence d'Urbanisme Région de Reims (2012). *"Paroles d'acteurs. TGV Est. Approche des impacts socio- économiques sur Reims et sa région"*, available at www.audrr.fr/centre_ressources/publication/paroles-d-acteurs-tgv-est.html [accessed 15 February 2016].

Albalate, D., Bel, G. (2012). *"High-speed rail: Lessons for policy makers from experiences abroad"*, Public Administration Review, 72(3), pp. 336–349.

Albalate, D., Campos, J., Jimenez, J-L. (2015). *"Tourism and high speed rail in Spain: Does the AVE increase local visitors?"*, Working Paper 2015/27, Barcelona: Universitat de Barcelona, Research Institute of Applied Economics, available at www.researchgate.net/publication/288604283 [accessed 24 April 2016].

Alonso, M., Bellet, C. (2009). *"El tren de alta velocidad y el proyecto urbano. Un nuevo ferrocarril para la Zaragoza del tercer milenio"*, in *"Scripta nova. Revista electrónica de geografía y ciencias sociales"*, Barcelona: Universidad de Barcelona, vol. XIII, no. 281.

Amiard, D. (1997). *"Le tourisme d'affaire et de Congrès dans l'agglomération mancelle"*, in Chevalier, J., *"Le Mans 6 ans après l'arrivée du TGV, groupe de recherche en géographie sociale"*, Le Mans: Université du Maine, Espaces et Sociétés, pp. 51–56.

Bazin-Benoit, S., Delaplace, M. (2015). *"Mise en service des dessertes TGV et gouvernance dans le domaine du tourisme: le cas de villes françaises"*, Revue Géographique de l'Est, 55(3–4), available at http://rge.revues.org/5614 [accessed 29 October 2015].

Bazin-Benoit, S., Beckerich, C., Delaplace, M., Masson, S. (2006). *"L'arrivée de la LGV en Champagne-Ardenne et la nécessaire réorganisation des rapports de proximité"*, Les Cahiers Scientifiques du transport, 49, pp. 51–76.

Bazin-Benoit, S., Beckerich, C., Delaplace, M. (2010). *"Grande vitesse, activation des ressources spécifiques et développement du tourisme urbain: Le cas de l'agglomération rémoise"*, Belgeo, 1–2, pp. 65–78.

Bazin-Benoit, S., Beckerich, C., Delaplace, M. (2011). *"High speed railway, service innovations and urban and business tourisms development"*, Chapter 4 in Sarmento, M.,

Alvaro, M., *"Economics and Management of Tourism: Trends and Recent Developments"*, Lisbon: Universidade Luisiada Editora, Coleção Manuais, pp. 115–141.

Bazin-Benoit, S., Beckerich, C., Delaplace, M. (2013a). *"Desserte TGV et villes petites et moyennes, une illustration par le cas du tourisme à Arras, Auray, Charleville-Mézières et Saverne"*, Les Cahiers Scientifiques du Transport, 63, pp. 33–62.

Bazin-Benoit, S., Beckerich, C., Blanquart, C., Delaplace, M. (2013b). *"Les enjeux et opportunités des dessertes ferroviaires à grande vitesse en matière de développement local et de développement durable"*, rapport final, Reims: Universite de Reims Champagne-Ardenne, available at https://hal-upec-upem.archives-ouvertes.fr/hal-01098691 [accessed 25 April 2016].

Bazin-Benoit, S., Beckerich, C., Delaplace, M. (2014). *"Valorisation touristique du patrimoine et dessertes TGV dans les villes intermédiaires à moins d'1h30 de Paris: Les cas de Reims, Metz, Le Mans et Tours"*, Revue d'économie Régionale et Urbaine, 5, pp. 5–23.

Bonnafous, A. (1987) *"The regional impact of the TGV"*, Transportation, 14(2), pp. 127–137.

Carrouet, G. (2013). *"Du TGV Rhin-Rhône au territoire Rhin-Rhône: Réticularité, mobilité et territorialité dans un espace intermédiaire"*, Thèse de doctorat en géographie-aménagement, Université de Dijon.

Chen, X. (2013). *"Assessing the impacts of high speed rail development in China's Yangtze River Delta Megaregion"*, Journal of Transportation Technologies, 3 pp. 113–122.

Chen, Z., Haynes, K. (2012). *"Tourism industry and high speed rail, is there a linkage: Evidence from China's high speed rail development"*, Paper presented at the ASRDLF 2012 conference special session on High Speed Rail, Tourism and Territories, 9–11 July, Belfort, France.

Cheng, Yung-Hsiang (2009). *"High-speed rail in Taiwan: New experience and issues for future development"*, Transport Policy, 17(2), pp. 51–63.

Colletis, G., Pecqueur, B. (2004). *"Révélation des ressources spécifiques et coordination située"*, Economies et Institutions, 6–7, pp. 51–74.

Coronado, J-M., Garmendia, M., Moyano, A. (2014). *"HSR stations' missing link: Assessing the quality of pedestrian routes for tourism trips"*, Paper presented at the second international seminar in the series "High Speed Rail Service and Urban Dynamics: Case studies in Europe", Naples, 3–4 March 2014.

CSEF (2005). *"La gare TGV: quels impacts sur l'emploi à Liège?"*, Compte-rendu d'une table ronde organisée par le CSEF de Liège, Liège: CSEF.

Czernek, K. (2013). *"Determinants of cooperation in a tourist region"*, Annals of Tourism Research, 40, pp. 83–104.

DB International GmbH (2011). *"High speed rail as a tool for regional development: In-depth study"*, Paris: UIC, available at www.shop-etf.com/en/high-speed-rail-as-a-tool-for-regional-development.html [accessed 25 April 2016].

Delaplace, M. (2012a). *"Pourquoi les 'effets' TGV sont-ils différents selon les territoires? L'hétérogénéité au cœur du triptyque 'innovations, territoires et stratégies'"*, Recherche Transports et Sécurité, 28, pp. 290–302.

Delaplace, M. (2012b). *"TGV, développement local et taille des villes: Une analyse en termes d'innovation de services"*, Revue D'économie Régionale et Urbaine, 2, pp. 265–292.

Delaplace, M., Perrin, J. (2013). *"Multiplication des dessertes TGV et tourismes urbains et d'affaires, regards croisés sur la Province et l'Île de France"*, Recherche Transport et Sécurité, 29, pp. 177–191.

Delaplace, M., Pagliara, F., Perrin, J., Mermet, S. (2014). *"Can high speed rail foster the choice of destination for tourism purpose?"*, Procedia – Social and Behavioral Sciences, 111, pp. 166–175.

Delaplace, M., Pagliara, F., La Pietra, A. (2015). *"High speed rail service and theme park: The case of Futuroscope and Disneyland Paris?"*, Paper presented at the international conference "High Speed Rail and the City", Urban Futures Labex week 21–23 January 2015.

Faye, M. (1998). *"Tours à la conquête du tourisme d'affaires"*, Norois, 178, pp. 293–300.

Feliu, J. (2012). *"High-speed rail in European medium-sized cities: Stakeholders and urban development"*, Journal of Urban Planning and Development, 138, pp. 293–302.

Guirao, B., Campa, J-L. (2015). *"The effects of tourism on HSR: Spanish empirical evidence derived from a multi-criteria corridor selection methodology"*, Journal of Transport Geography, 47, pp. 37–46.

INSEE Lorraine (2009). *"La Ligne à Grande Vitesse Est Européenne: Une évaluation de l'impact sur le tourisme"*, 163, Nancy: INSEE Lorraine.

Jones, M. F., Singh, N., Hsiung, Y. (2015). *"Determining the critical success factors of the wine tourism region of Napa from a supply perspective"*, International Journal of Tourism Research, 17(3), pp. 261–271.

Kamel, K., Matthewman, R. (2008). *"The non-transport impacts of high-speed trains on regional economic development: A review of the literature"*, West Malling, UK: Locate in Kent, available at www.locateinkent.com/images/assets/High%20Speed%20 Train%20Report%202008.pdf [accessed 15 February 2016].

Kurihara, T., Wu, L. (2015). *"The impact of high speed rail on tourism development: A case study of Japan"*, Paper presented at the international conference "High Speed rail and the City", Urban Futures Labex week 21–23 January 2015.

Levinson, David M. (2012). *"Accessibility impacts of high-speed rail"*, Journal of Transport Geography, 22, pp. 288–291.

Mannone, V. (1995). *"L'impact régional du TGV sud-est"*, Thèse pour l'obtention du doctorat de géographie, 2 tomes, Université de Provence Aix-Marseille-I.

Masson, S., Petiot, R. (2009). *"Can the high speed rail reinforce tourism attractiveness? The case of the high speed rail between Perpignan (France) and Barcelona (Spain)"*, Technovation, 29(9), pp. 611–617.

Menerault, P. (1997). *"Processus de territorialisation de la grande vitesse ferroviaire: Le TGV et les régions: Le cas du Nord – Pas de Calais"*, Bron, France: INRETS report.

Mignerey, P. (2013). *"Les effets territoriaux de la grande vitesse"*, Paris: La Documentation Française/Datur.

Mizohata, Y. (1995). *"L'impact du Shinkansen sur les villes: Le cas du Shinkansen du Tohoku"*, in Centre Jacques Cartier, Patier, D. (Eds), *"Villes et TGV: Actes des sixièmes Entretiens Jacques Cartier 8–10 Décembre 1993, Lyon, France"*, Études et Recherches 6, Lyon: University of Lyon, Laboratoire D'economie des Transports, pp. 277–280.

Mollard, A., Pecqueur, B. (2007). *"De l'hypothèse au modèle du panier de biens et de service: Histoire succincte d'une recherche"*, Economie Rurale, 300, pp. 110–114.

Okabe, S. (1980). *"Impact of the Sanyo Shinkansen on local communities"*, in Straszak, A. and Tuch, R. (Eds), *"The Shinkansen high-speed rail network of Japan"*, London: Pergamon Press, pp. 105–129.

Pagliara, F. (2014). *"High speed rail systems: Impacts on mobility, on tourism and on mobile workers"*, Saarbrücken: Lambert Academic Publishing.

Pagliara, F., Delaplace, M., Vassallo, J. M. (2014). *"High speed trains and tourists: What is the link? Evidence from the French and the Spanish capitals"*, WIT Transactions on the Built Environment, 138, pp. 17–27.

Pagliara, F., La Pietra, A., Gómez, J., Vassallo, J. M. (2015). *"High-speed rail and the tourism market: Evidence from the Madrid case study"*, Transport Policy, 37, pp. 187–194.

Pecqueur, B., (2001). *"Qualité et développement territorial: L'hypothèse du panier de biens et de services territorialises"*, Economie Rurale, 261, pp. 37–49.

People's Republic of China, (2014). *"Regional economic impact analysis of high speed rail in China: Main report"*, Washington, DC: The World Bank.

Richardson, G. B. (1972). *"The organization of industry"*, The Economic Journal, 82(327), pp. 883–896.

Sen, S. (2004). *"The Channel Tunnel and its impact on tourism in the United Kingdom"*, Geographical Paper no. 172, Reading: University of Reading.

South East England Development Agency (2008). *"HST impact study: Final report pour la Commission Européenne"*, available at www.ttr-ltd.com/downloads/pdf/HSTImpactStudyFinalReportES.doc.pdf [accessed 25 April 2016].

Todorovich, P., Schned, D., Lane, R. (2011). *"High-speed rail: International lessons for U.S. policy makers"*, Policy Focus Report Series, Cambridge, MA: Lincoln Institute of Land Policy.

Tourisme-Alsace (2008). *"Bilan 2008 de l'année touristique en Alsace"*, Alsace: Tourisme-Alsace.

Troin, J-F. (2012). *"TGV et fréquentation touristique: Une image contrastée en Val de Loire"*, Paper presented at the Colloque de l'ASRDLF 2012, special session on "High Speed Rail, Tourism and Territories", 9–11 July 2012, Belfort, France.

Urena, J., Menerault, P., Garmendia, M., (2009). *"The high-speed rail challenge for big inter-mediate cities: A national, regional and local perspective"*, Cities, 26(5), pp. 266–279.

Valeri, E., Pagliara, F., Marcucci, E. (2012). *"A destination choice model for tourism pur-pose"*, Paper presented at the Colloque de l'ASRDLF 2012 special session on "High Speed Rail, Tourism and Territories", 9–11 July 2012, Belfort, France.

Vickerman, R., Ulied, A., (2006). *"Indirect and wider economic impacts of high-speed rail"*, available at www.researchgate.net/publication/228882631_Indirect_and_wider_economic_impacts_of_high_speed_rail [accessed 15 February 2016].

Ville de Marseille (2011). *"Le tourisme made in Marseille"*, Marseille: Direction de la Communication.

Wang, X., Huang, S., Zou, T., Yan, H. (2012). *"Effects of the high speed rail network on China's regional tourism development"*, Tourism Management Perspectives, 1, pp. 34–38.

Wang, Y., Fesenmaier, D. R. (2007). *"Collaborative destination marketing: A case study of Elkhart county"*, Tourism Management, 28, pp. 863–875.

Zhao, D. (2012). *"The high-speed railway network in Yangtze River Delta: An analy-sis of the accessibility impact"*, available at www.regionalstudies.org/conferences/presentations/european-conference-2012-best-international-paper-early-career [accessed 15 February 2016].

6 HSR and the city

Accessibility to stations and intermodality

Jordi Martí-Henneberg and Eduard J. Alvarez-Palau

Constructing railway infrastructure on land near cities has never been easy. It has been a source of social, economic and environmental tension and has required careful handling. Good initial planning, appropriate design and carefully selected methods of construction are required to ensure that stations equipped with high-speed rail (HSR) services have the maximum impact possible.

This work analyses the impact that these stations have had on the geography of Europe and aims to measure and compare their accessibility. It examines such varied aspects as station location and typology, their distance from the nearest urban centre and the potential demand from users. It also looks at the availability of complementary transport services for travel to these stations and alternatives for travelling to neighbouring airports. All of these factors are examined to assess whether the transport policies applied have been appropriate.

We analysed Europe's HSR stations with reference to individual countries given the existence of different national models for their management and planning, which could explain the idiosyncrasies of some specific stations. Despite the existence of a European transport policy, which destines important subsidies for regional development and cohesion, each EU country maintains its own basic capability in transport planning. As a result, France and Spain opted to construct an exclusive and independent network for their HSR services, resulting in a large number of new stations, many of which are located outside their main urban nuclei. Italy and Germany, on the other hand, decided to selectively upgrade some stretches of track so that they could also carry HSR traffic, thereby increasing the quality of their whole rail networks. This second model has also, quite logically, helped to strengthen the position of traditional railway stations within their urban nuclei. Both policies have advantages and also present problems. We shall analyse these in the main text, with reference to an original database[1] that was created specifically for this study.

Studies of intermodality at HSR stations must contemplate the very different situations and station environments: metropolitan areas, intermediary cities and rural environments. In the first two cases, the access requirements will depend on whether the station studied is centrally, peripherally or externally located. There is, however, unanimity about the fact that well-managed intermodality improves the accessibility of stations. In the case of HSR stations, this is particularly important because, almost by definition, they tend to have only a limited number of stops. As a result, the network is polarised around just a few points of access. To reduce the tunnel effect that this can cause within a territory, it is therefore necessary to integrate the railway network within the wider transport system as efficiently as possible.

The intermodal management of stations has evolved in parallel with changes in the nature and objectives of HSR in both Europe and the world. The initial objective of HSR was to connect the centres of major urban areas located at intermediate distances from each other. This was the logic behind the following rail connections: Tokyo–Osaka (1968), Rome–Florence (1977), Paris–Lyon (1982) and Mannheim–Stuttgart (1991). The unquestionable success of HSR, in terms of the number of passengers carried, promoted its expansion to other relatively nearby urban areas: to Aomori and Kagoshima in Japan; from Paris to London and Brussels; from Mannheim to Frankfurt and Cologne; and from Rome to Naples.

The first HSR lines were mainly constructed in the most densely populated areas in order to reduce congestion in corridors already saturated with traffic. By the 1990s, some non-metropolitan areas were also benefiting from stations within the HSR network. In some countries, the main aim then became that of promoting greater national cohesion. This tendency increased in the first decade of the twenty-first century, with numerous peripheral and external areas also receiving the benefits of new HSR stations. This has been particularly evident in France and Spain, no doubt influenced by their decisions to construct exclusive HSR networks. It has, however, proved a failure in terms of attracting users. In Spain,

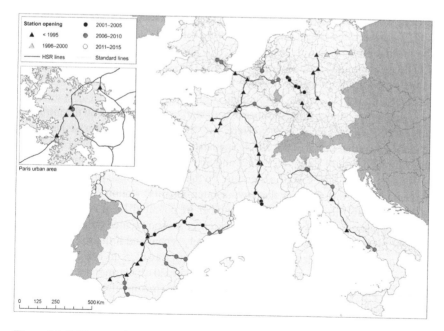

Figure 6.1 HSR network and connection to agglomerations in Europe.

a further aggravating condition has been the fact that some of these lines have ended in sparsely populated cul-de-sacs.

State of the art

The literature on the development and influence of HSR is abundant. The most recent studies include works by Campos & de Rus (2009), Albalate & Bel (2012a; 2012b) and Banister & Givoni (2013). Surprisingly, those works that have taken the station as their main focus tend to be less well known. Studies of intermodal characteristics at stations are even rarer, perhaps due to the lack of both an empirical base for comparison and an evaluation of their main features.

However, a number of more generic works relating to HSR stations (Bertolini & Spit, 1998) have been produced. The most recent of these include the work of Menéndez et al. (2006), which includes the results of an exhaustive field study into the services provided by a large number of HSR stations located in medium-sized cities in Europe. Other studies have analysed the ways in which good accessibility has improved the potential of stations (Brons et al., 2009; Chen & Hall, 2012; Garmendia et al., 2012; Martí-Henneberg, 2015; Vickerman, 2015). Perhaps unsurprisingly, studies of the accessibility of HSR stations have tended to consider their locations (Gutiérrez, 2001; Banister & Givoni, 2013); they have not, however, shown much interest in the organisational characteristics of these stations, such as their management of intermodality.

A large number of complementary works refer to methodological advances that have been used to improve our understanding of the impact of HSR on accessibility and which measures of intermodality are most relevant. De Rus & Nombela (2007) analysed the return on investment in HSR, which has a direct bearing on the profitability of stations. Reusser et al. (2008) have examined the station as a node of communication. Zemp et al. (2011) have classified stations according to their capacity to influence regional planning. Chorus & Bertolini (2011) have studied stations in the wider Tokyo area.

On the other hand, a large number of case studies have focused on the introduction of HSR in specific countries. Here, the interest in stations per se has again tended to be rather minor. The case of Spain has been studied by Ureña (2012) and the combined case of Belgium, France and Spain by Facchinetti-Mannone (2010).

Finally, we must refer to the literature on the element which presents the most evident challenge to policies that favour intermodality: stations located in areas of low intensity. In these cases, the number of potential local users is low, so attracting passengers is key to their subsistence. As commented on, the expansion of HSR into areas of low demand is a relatively recent and hitherto little-studied phenomenon. The challenge implicit in attracting travellers to non-metropolitan stations has also been analysed (Ureña et al., 2009; 2012; Garmendia et al., 2011; Ortega et al., 2012). It is, however, somewhat surprising that the problem of stations with very limited potential had not received much attention until relatively recently given that similar findings have been reported since the 1980s. The Paris–Lyon line, which opened in 1982, was given two intermediate stations

(Mâcon and Le Creusot) in order to test the potential of a project for regional development based around new HSR stations. However, the predicted relocation of numerous activities did not materialise. This problem was particularly studied by Facchinetti-Mannone (2011) and has also received attention, from a wider perspective, within the calculations of the cost/efficiency of public infrastructure undertaken by de Rus (2010). On the other hand, few works have attempted to quantify and compare the intermodal facilities of HSR stations (Brons et al., 2009; Tapiador et al., 2009).

In contrast with stances previously cited, several more optimistic works have underlined the beneficial effects of HSR, largely based on the need to achieve a better territorial balance (Bröcker et al., 2010). If we base our analysis on the added value offered by HSR projects, rather than exclusively on their profitability, it is possible to justify such investment in the same way as in EU TEN-T projects (Banister & Givoni, 2013). In fact, such policies have received the support of the EU in order to promote the cohesion of peripheral areas. In short, if it had been a question of prioritising public investment according to social and economic benefits, it is certain that HSR would not have obtained the financial support that it received for two decades.

Other studies have specifically analysed the benefits associated with HSR services in urban centres. Recent works along these lines have suggested that although HSR is capable of stimulating certain tertiary sector activities, which are already present locally, it does not have the capacity to encourage new dynamics (Bellet & Gutiérrez, 2001; Givoni & Banister, 2012). If the aim is to extend the impact of HSR to cover a wider territory in the future, both the regional transport system and intermodality of HSR stations will have a crucial role to play.

Main focus of the research

The main focus of this work is the priorities for investment in HSR. Have different states behaved logically when investing in HSR?

To answer this question, we shall examine the potential demand from users at each station and in the year of their construction. It would seem reasonable to assume that the stations with the greatest potential for attracting passengers should have been built first, followed by those with less potential.

A station-by-station analysis would allow us to go a step beyond this. If decisions concerning priority corridors depend on state administrations, it would seem natural that decisions concerning stations could be strongly influenced by local and regional political power. Provincial administrative capability in the areas of transport and urban planning could have conditioned the plans of the state and even forced it to adopt consensus solutions.

The second question raised concerns the location of the stations. Have different countries followed the same policies?

HSR is a means of transport for medium and long distances; its area of action is, therefore, predominantly transnational. A large number of these journeys could have their origins and destinations in different countries. This observation, which seems reasonable, should be accompanied by a coordination of the policies undertaken in the different countries at the moment of designing their railway networks. Without a doubt, the empirical evidence relating to this phenomenon presents certain contradictions that could complicate further decisions.

This reflection seems to prompt a third set of questions: is the accessibility to the stations guaranteed? Are there any differences between the stations that have been remodelled in line with new plans?

To answer these questions, we have correlated previous variables with variables relating to the accessibility and intermodality of the transport network. A priori, it seems that centrally located stations should have better connectivity with their cities, but it is necessary to check whether this hypothesis is supported by empirical results.

Results

In line with the approach proposed here and the different variables analysed, it was possible to obtain the following results for HSR stations.

Prioritising the construction of HSR stations

Given the lack of disaggregated data about the number of people using the system, it was decided to use Martí-Henneberg's (2015) indicator of potential passenger demand between stations.[2]

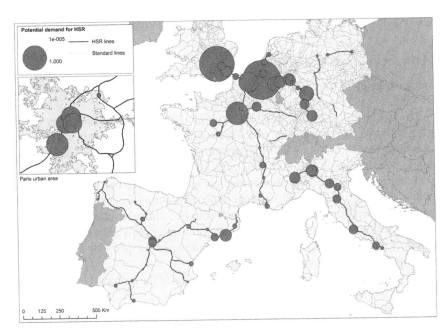

Figure 6.2 Potential user demand for HSR between stations.

Table 6.1 Potential user demand for the main stations in each state.

Rank	German stations	Potential demand	Rank	French stations	Potential demand
9	Frankfurt	371.17	3	Massy	880.08
12	Aachen	243.55	4	Lille	685.44
13	Cologne	239.88	5	Paris-Est	636.75
17	Stuttgart	206.48	6	Paris-Montparnasse	636.75
19	Cologne airport	183.61	7	Paris-Nord	636.75

Rank	Spanish stations	Potential demand	Rank	Italian stations	Potential demand
11	Barcelona	245.10	14	Milan	231.08
26	Madrid-Chamartin	119.60	15	Turin	214.49
27	Madrid-Atocha	119.60	16	Milan-Rho Expo	207.51
31	Camp de Tarragona	99.82	22	Reggio Emilia	142.09
41	Valencia	36.13	23	Rome-Tiburtina	130.12

Source: own research, based on Martí-Henneberg, 2015.

The results of this indicator of potential demand for the five highest ranking stations in each of the major countries studied are presented in Table 6.1. It is possible to note the great potential of the cities in the north of France. This is only exceeded by Brussels-Zuid (2,575.31) and London (2,121.22), which would occupy the first and second positions in the overall ranking, respectively.

The data presented above (together with Figure 6.1) are sufficiently significant to draw some initial conclusions. In the case of France, the calculation of the indicator suggests that the first connections should have been projected northwards from Paris, seeking links with Belgium. However, the first line was projected towards Lyon. In the case of Spain, the indicator clearly shows the potential of the corridor between Madrid and Barcelona. However, the first line projected was between Madrid and Seville. In fact, a reading of this indicator underlines the need to construct the Mediterranean corridor. Barcelona and Valencia are two of the places with the greatest potential demand. Even Camp de Tarragona station (fourth in the ranking) is also located in the previously cited corridor. However, Spain's central government refuses to construct this route, instead continuing to open stretches of track in regions with very low population densities.

The Italian and German cases are notably different, given that they have based their HSR construction on the upgrading of stretches of existing track. In this way, the infrastructure was improved, attending to the potential demand and the possibilities of construction. Even so, although the greatest potential demand in Italy was between Milan and Turin, the first HSR line projected was between Rome and Florence. In the case of Germany, where the greatest demand was between

Frankfurt and Cologne, construction began in the corridor between Würzburg and Kassel, where it was much lower.

It could be logically argued that the first lines to be constructed do not necessarily need to be the most significant. Branch lines offering greater potential have still to be completed. Furthermore, a simple analysis of the stations with the greatest demand does not necessarily provide a global vision at the national scale.

Whatever the case, an analysis of the previous indicator should be able to clarify this question. Figure 6.3 shows the evolution of the indicator of average potential demand in cities connected to the HSR network over the whole period studied. If a logical order of construction had been followed,[3] the resulting indicator should have been high in the initial period and then gradually fallen as places with lower potential became connected.

The French case is the only one that has followed the expected evolution. The connection between Paris and Lyon and then with Lille connected the places with the greatest demand. From this moment on, the expansion of the network connected smaller cities, so the indictor would have gradually declined.

In the case of Italy, the curve is not significant. Although the locations with the most potential were not the first to be connected, the difference between them was not great and constant values were observed from the beginning.

In the German case, the policy of remodelling lines resulted in a continual increase in the indicator. The locations with the greatest demand had gradually become connected to the network.

Finally, the Spanish case shows a relatively flat evolution in potential demand from 1992 to 2009. It then began to decline. We should consider that the network did not provide services to the places with most demand until 2009. From then on, the rest of the connections were with places that had lower expected demands. Whatever the case, the low potential demand for the whole set of Spanish stations is surprising and places the country at the bottom of the European table in terms of potential users.

Taking everything together, it is evident that assigning priority to HSR lines at the European level has not been approached in line with the expected potential

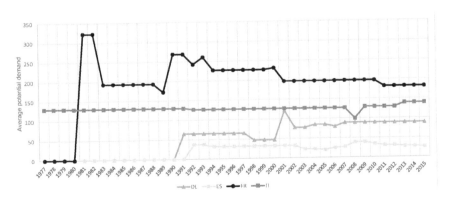

Figure 6.3 Average accumulated potential user demand at connected stations.

demand from passengers. Planning at the national scale, the previous existence of other transport networks, the network system chosen and, above all, the policies followed could all have played key roles in this.

Policies for locating HSR stations

Following the approach proposed by Menéndez et al. (2006) and applied in Spain by Bellet & Jurado (2014), Europe's HSR stations have been classified into three different groups according to their location with respect to the city: central, fringe and exterior (Figure 6.4).

Of the 95 HSR stations considered in the present work, 60 correspond to central (63 per cent), 9 to fringe (10 per cent) and 26 to exterior (27 per cent) locations. In other words, the most common preference has been to locate HSR stations in city centres rather than on their peripheries or outside of them.

Examining the classification by country, it is possible to observe that Belgium, Italy, Germany, the Netherlands and England all have more centrally located HSR stations than the global average (63 per cent). In Spain, the percentage is just on the average (63.5 per cent), while France is the country that has opted for this type of location least of all (42 per cent). The majority of the fringe stations can be found in Spain (6 out of 9), while France has the most exterior stations (15 out of 26), followed by Spain (6 out of 26).

The previous analysis was complemented by taking into account the process of either constructing a new station or modifying an existing one. An analysis

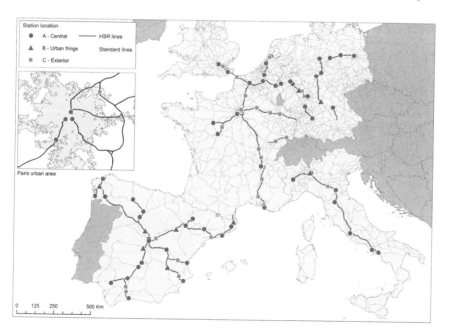

Figure 6.4 Classification of HSR stations in relation to their cities, by location.

of the results obtained shows two very different cases. France and Spain mainly opted for the construction of new stations, in 62 per cent and 55 per cent of cases, respectively. Germany and Italy, on the other hand, chose to take advantage of existing stations and to adapt them for the arrival of the new mode of transport. In these countries, it is possible to observe percentages of new construction of only 29 per cent and 20 per cent, respectively.

It is, therefore, possible to observe a clear tendency to modify central stations in Italy and Germany. France seems to be the country with the least tendency to modify central stations and the greatest to opt for new constructions at more peripheral locations. Finally, Spain has a significant number of centrally located stations, but has not made a clear choice between constructing stations on the urban fringe and outside of cities as an alternative to a central location.

The station location indicator gives us a good idea of a station's position in relation to the continuous urban area of the connected city. However, it does not explain this position with respect to a station's administrative centre or specialised sub-centres. It does not provide information either about a station's real proximity in terms of accessibility.

In order to give the previous indicator a more complementary focus, we calculated the distances between HSR stations and the administrative centre (Figure 6.5).

The interpretation of these results is complex as it shows certain deviations from the expected result. A priori, it would seem normal to expect that centrally located stations (A) should be nearer to the administrative centre than other station locations. In fact, this is so in the majority of cases, but only if we focus on the average value of each of the boxes. It seems that stations located on the urban fringe (B) tend to have very similar locations with respect to the administrative centres of cities to centrally located stations. Exterior stations (C), on the other hand, show much greater values and also a much greater degree of variability.

In an attempt to explain this phenomenon, Table 6.2 shows the four countries that have the most significant number of HSR stations.

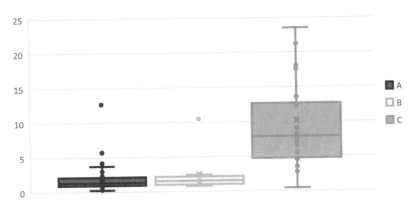

Figure 6.5 Box charts showing the average distance between HSR stations and their city halls, by location.

Table 6.2 Average access distance between HSR stations and their city halls, by station location and country (in km).

	Germany	Spain	France	Italy	Average
A	2.25	1.56	1.89	1.94	1.91
B	1.00	1.61	–	10.47	4.36
C	7.50	6.76	12.32	3.47	7.51

Reading the table country by country offers several subtle nuances. It seems that France and Spain produced the results that we would have expected: gradually growing from the central to the exterior typologies. In the case of France, as there were no stations on the urban fringe, the difference is even more pronounced.

In the case of Italy, the salient feature is the distance of the stations from the edge of the urban area. However, a detailed reading of the phenomenon suggests that this apparent discrepancy stemmed from the particular circumstances of the La Fira railway station in Milan, which is located within the continuous built up metropolitan area, but a long distance from the city centre. This could be regarded as an atypical value. If eliminate it from the analysis, the expected result would be observed.

The most curious case occurred when we analysed the German HSR stations. Those located on the edge of urban areas proved better connected to the administrative centre than the central stations themselves. This could have been due to the polynuclear nature of these cities, or to the process of metropolitan conformation, which resulted in non-symmetrical radial growth. As a result, the centres of the current metropolises could occupy positions that are more peripheral and the German HSR stations could have taken advantage of this circumstance to provide them with a better service.

It is possible to affirm that different states have pursued different policies when locating their HSR stations. France opted to give greater importance to peripheral and external stations and projected independent lines. Italy and Germany followed a very different route, banking on the modification of existing lines and central stations. Finally, Spain opted for the construction of new lines, but mainly maintaining its existing central stations. In other words, it decided to combine the new HSR infrastructure with that of conventional rail services where lines pass through cities. This was, however, an expensive approach and was only followed for the main cities.

The most significant aspect of this case study is not the assessment of the decisions taken by each of these countries. What the present analysis seeks to highlight is how the lack of a common criterion has prejudiced the integration of HSR infrastructure into the surrounding territory. The selection of different network models has reduced the possibilities of interconnecting different countries. In Italy and Germany, HSR is viewed as a form of intercity transport, but one that connects different urban centres. In other words, it makes it possible to do the whole journey without leaving the centre. In France things work rather differently, with users having to take complementary modes of transport to reach the HSR stations. This lack of uniformity is prejudicial, as it makes the railway system difficult to understand for occasional users.

Accessibility and intermodality policies

In contemporary society, the time variable has become more important than distance. It is much better for classifying the urban processes that take place in a given territory. With this in mind, a new indicator has been defined to quantify accessibility to HSR stations.

To calculate this indicator, we estimated the time required to travel between the HSR station and the administrative centre. First, we calculated the travel time on foot and then by collective public transport (Figure 6.6).[4]

To highlight the results of our calculations of accessibility to the city centre when travelling on foot, we grouped cases into 10-minute journey intervals. The greatest frequency is found in the second interval: at walking distances of between 10 and 20 minutes. From this point on, the frequency gradually decreases as the connection time increases. The unusual thing is that from 70 minutes onwards, there is another increase in the frequency of the observations, with a maximum value which groups together all of those stations located at a walking distance of over 90 minutes (see Figure 6.6). Statistically speaking, this last group is not

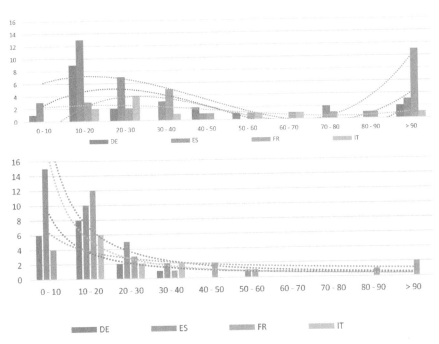

Figure 6.6 Travel time between HSR stations and their city halls, on foot (above) and by public transport (below), by country.

significant because it combines observations with different levels of accessibility. However, it does allow us to graphically represent the difficulty of access to exterior stations. It is also logical to think that no one would walk for more than 90 minutes in order to take a HSR train.

An analysis by country shows that in Spain and Germany, HSR stations are located nearer to city centres than in Italy and France. In Germany, a large percentage of the stations is concentrated near the city centre, with the curve gradually decreasing. In Spain, there are a lot of centrally located stations, but there has also been a notable increase in the number of poorly connected stations on the urban periphery. In Italy, the distribution of observations is quite homogeneous. In contrast, in France, it is possible to observe a skew towards higher values, implying worse connectivity.

On introducing motorised forms of transport, the results are very different. In the case of public transport, accessibility is not proportional to distance. Instead, the transport services offered become the most important consideration. There is, therefore, an evolution in the previous curve to a new distribution that shows a potential decrease with distance. In other words, the greatest frequencies are accumulated in the first intervals and there is a gradual fall in the number of observations with distance. The only exception is France, where it is possible to observe a slight increase with distance.

Along these lines, a reading of the results by country highlights the cases of Spain and Italy. For both countries, the observations are mainly concentrated in the first intervals, but then gradually fall off. On the other hand, the German and French cases continue to show a slight recovery between the first and second intervals; this could be due to the greater average size of the cities in question, which has made it difficult to introduce any improvements in accessibility along the urban stretch of the route.

In the light of the previous analysis, what is interesting is to know the real possibilities available to the potential users of HSR. What other modes of transport allow travellers to reach HSR stations? To answer this question, we made an inventory of the availability of different services that facilitate intermodality at each station (Table 6.3).

First of all, we have documented the availability of parking services at the different stations (park and ride). This makes it possible to attract users from the surrounding area and to channel long-distance movements by rail. Second, we have identified the different urban public transport services, whether collective, as in the case of underground train and urban bus services, or individual, as in the case of taxi services. Finally, we have also made a separate inventory of intercity coach services, as these would not form part of the urban transport network, but rather the regional transport network.

Ease of access to HSR stations using individual transport is a relevant consideration; 92 per cent of stations provide parking for private vehicles and 93 per cent offer taxi services. In the first case, this is understandable at peripheral and external stations, but not so understandable at central stations, which do not require such services as they have plenty of urban transport alternatives. In the

Table 6.3 Percentage of intermodal transport services available in relation to the location of HSR stations.

	Parking facilities	Underground	Local bus	Taxi	Coach	Number of stations
A	92%	45%	95%	93%	78%	60
B	89%	11%	78%	89%	56%	9
C	92%	4%	27%	88%	69%	26
Average	92%	31%	75%	92%	74%	95

second case, the logic could be the opposite. It is reasonable to expect good taxi services at urban HSR stations, but at those on the periphery and outside the city, the taxi could constitute an elitist mode of transport. Whatever the case, the results show excellent levels of availability for both private vehicle parking and taxi services.

With respect to collective modes of transport, the situation is notably different. Providing public transport services comes at a high cost to the public purse, particularly when their level of use does not justify this. Local administrations have therefore opted to offer citizens only certain specific transport services to access HSR.

The underground train is the most evident example of this. Only centrally located stations exhibit reasonable levels of connectivity with the underground system. In fact, this is reasonable considering the high cost involved in constructing a new stretch of underground track. It is only in very special cases that this expense can be considered.

In contrast, urban bus services are available at 75 per cent of HSR stations. However, the disaggregated result shows 95 per cent coverage for central stations, 78 per cent for those on the urban fringe and only 27 per cent for those located externally. In other words, municipal authorities have only opted to provide services to HSR users when stations are located within their urban area. This does have its logic. In Spain, for example, urban public transport is partially subsidised by local administrations. Intercity transport, on the other hand, tends to be initially contracted out at the risk of the operator.[5]

The interpretation of the indicator with respect to intercity transport reveals an interesting result. The three typologies are reasonably balanced, at between 56–78 per cent. In fact, the central stations also exhibit higher values than those on the periphery in this case. This seems to indicate that the central station has become an intermodal communications hub at the regional scale. It appears to act as a distribution node for HSR users until they reach their definitive destination.

The previous analysis gives us an idea of the utility of HSR over intermediate distances. The urban journey constitutes the access part of a trip, with the main trajectory being done by HSR. However, the HSR can also perform other roles. For instance, it can carry passengers on local trips, establishing intermodal relationships with aeroplanes for long-distance and intercontinental journeys. In these cases, the role of HSR is to attract users of air services, which would acquire a higher rank.

We have grouped together the relationships between HSR and airport services as follows:

- stations providing HSR services at airports (1)
- direct connection via a conventional rail service (2)
- direct connection via other forms of transport (3)
- without a direct connection (4)

The first group contains all of the relations that allow the HSR to act as a mode of direct intermodal recruitment for air services. Based on the work carried out, it is evident that only 4.2 per cent of the stations can be included in this group (Figure 6.7), one in Germany and two in France.

This relationship notably increases for the second group: 34 per cent of HSR stations have train services that provide direct connections to the nearest airport. This is the predominant case in Germany, with 10 stations. There are also good levels of connectivity in France and Italy, with over 30 per cent in both cases. The case of Spain, on the other hand, shows a great degree of disconnection in this respect, with only five connections.

If we add direct connections via other modes of transport to the previous case, we will see that the situation does not change very much. With only 8 per cent of the total, it is evident that the majority of HSR stations lack bus connections to nearby airports. Only the Italian case stands out, with three stations offering direct coach services to the nearest airport.

Finally, there are stations that do not have any type of direct connection with an airport. This case includes 54 per cent of the total number of stations, which shows a clear intention to minimise the possibilities of interconnection. All the countries considered have various stations without any type of direct connection. However, it is the Spanish case, with 26, and the French, with 12 that stand out as providing the least connectivity.

Although brief, this analysis makes it possible to understand the policies followed by different administrations in relation to transport infrastructure and, more specifically, their perception of the intermodality and complementarity of the networks.

The connection between different modes of transport guarantees users the greatest number of alternatives when it comes to planning a trip. However, it seems that some governments do not think it opportune for HSR to be connected to airports and use them as a way to attract regional business. The Spanish case is paradigmatic in this respect. There are two main reasons for this. The first is that the transport networks were independently planned by unconnected administrative departments. The second would answer to a declared intention to keep the two modes of transport independent in order to prevent the flow of potential users from one to the other.

Summary of the results

In conclusion, we shall now highlight the main arguments presented in this chapter.

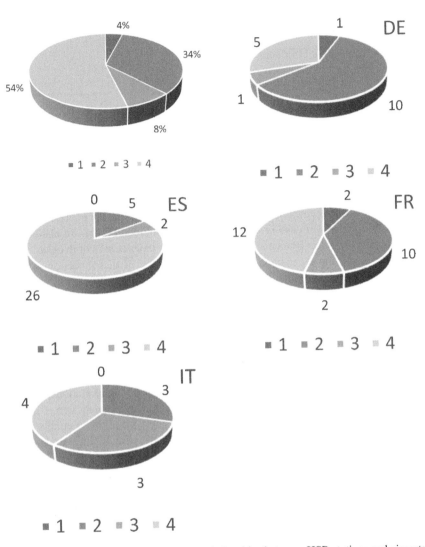

Figure 6.7 Classification of intermodal relationships between HSR stations and airports. Global pie chart on the left and pie charts for individual countries (DE, ES, FR and IT) on the right.

First of all, the validity of the main criteria used when constructing the stations has been called into question. The analysis of the indicator of potential demand and of its evolution over time shows that none of the countries began the construction of their HSR lines following the expected criteria. Only France showed reasonable values, from the construction of its second and third HSR lines. Spain and Germany are the cases in which the extension of their networks differed most from what would have initially been considered desirable. In Germany, this was due to the policy of taking advantage of existing lines, which could have limited the possibilities of launching new projects. In Spain, the country with the most HSR stations, the expected demand is extremely poor. In addition, the order of construction followed has also differed considerably from what would have been desirable.

Second, the chapter contemplates an analysis of the policies followed for the location of HSR stations in each of the different countries. This exercise shows the existence of two opposing logics. France and Spain opted for network models based on newly constructed lines, while Italy and Germany preferred to take advantage of their conventional rail infrastructure. These different stances carried with them clear differences in preferences for the location of HSR stations in these countries. France opted for newly built stations located or outside of its cities. Italy and Germany opted for the remodelling of existing central stations. Spain also opted for a network of newly constructed HSR lines, but interconnected with conventional rail stations in order to maintain urban accessibility.

Finally, the present work shows how transport policies have allowed different cities to integrate their HSR stations into their daily dynamics. New transport services have been studied considering the different modes of transport available. This allows acceptable levels of accessibility at HSR stations, whether linked to public or private transport. Something that offers less reason for hope is the lack of connectivity between HSR stations and airports; this limits the stations' intermodal potential for journeys over medium and long distances. In Germany and Italy this has been resolved reasonably well via complementary modes of transport. However, in Spain and France, it seems that this possibility was not taken into consideration at the moment of planning the HSR lines.

Notes

1 The GIS database created for the current work contains detailed information about the following station attributes: country, year of opening, location, typology, distance from the city centre, intermodality, access time and potential demand.
2 The indicator is calculated using a gravitational model weighted with a coefficient of distance between the station and city, and its regional GDP.
3 In other words, first connecting the places with the greatest potential and then extending the network into other regions.
4 This calculation is not exhaustive; information is also required about travel times by bicycle and private car. However, these times could be proportionally estimated based on the data presented here. Pedestrian transport is usually calculated using an average walking speed of around 4 km/h, while journeys by bicycle can be calculated at three times this value (Márquez et al., 2015). Car journey times could be based on those of collective public transport, but slightly improving the values for longer trips. In urban areas, traffic congestion could be considered to act as a limiting factor, but this would not be the case for trips to peripherally located stations.
5 Although in recent years it has begun to receive subsidies from supra-municipal levels of the administration.

Acknowledgement

This research has been funded by EU, Jean Monnet (562390-EPP-1-2015-1-ES-EPPJMO), ICREA-Academia Generalitat de Catalunya and Ministerio de Economía (CSO2015-65733-P).

References

Albalate, D. & Bel, G. (2012a). *"The economics and politics of high speed rail: Lessons from experiences abroad"*, Plymouth: Lexington Books.

Albalate, D. & Bel, G. (2012b). *"High-speed rail: Lessons for policy makers from experiences abroad"*, Public Administration Review, 72(3), pp. 336–349.

Banister, D. & Givoni, M. (2013). *"High-speed rail in the EU27: Trends, time, accessibility and principles"*, Built Environment, 39(3), pp. 324–338.

Bellet, C. & Gutiérrez, A. (2011). *"Ciudad y ferrocarril en la España del siglo XXI"*, Boletín de la Asociación de Geógrafos Españoles, 55, pp. 251–279.

Bellet, C. & Jurado, J. (2014). *"La localización de las estaciones de Alta Velocidad en España"*, Anales de Geografía de la Universidad Complutense, 34(2), pp. 9–24.

Bertolini, L. & Spit, T. (1998). *"Cities on rails: The redevelopment of railway stations and their surroundings"*, London: Routledge.

Bröcker, J., Korzhenevych, A. & Schürmann, C. (2010). *"Assessing spatial equity and efficiency impacts of transport infrastructure projects"*, Transportation Research Part B: Methodological, 7, pp. 795–811.

Brons, M., Givoni, M. & Rietveld, P. (2009). *"Access to railway stations and its potential in increasing rail use"*, Transportation Research Part A: Policy and Practice, 43, pp. 136–149.

Campos, J. & de Rus, G. (2009). *"Some stylized facts about high-speed rail: A review of HSR experiences around the world"*, Transport Policy, 16, pp. 19–28.

Chen, C.L. & Hall, P. (2012). *"The wider spatial-economic impacts of high-speed trains: A comparative case study of Manchester and Lille sub-regions"*, Journal of Transport Geography, 24, pp. 89–110.

Chorus, P. & Bertolini, L. (2011). *"An application of the node place model to explore the spatial development dynamics of station areas in Tokyo"*, The Journal of Transport and Land Use, 4(1), pp. 45–58.

de Rus, G. (2010). *"Introduction to cost–benefit analysis: Looking for reasonable shortcuts"*, Cheltenham, UK: Edward Elgar.

de Rus, G. & Nombela, G. (2007). *"Is investment in high speed rail socially profitable?"*, Journal of Transport Economics and Policy, 41, pp. 3–23.

Facchinetti-Mannone, V. (2010). *"L'implantation des gares de la grande vitesse. Analyse comparée des implantations belges, françaises et espagnoles"*, SNCF: Paris. [not published].

Facchinetti-Mannone, V. (2011). *"Quels effets territoriaux pour les nouvelles gares de la LGV Rhin-Rhône?"*, Images de Franche-Comté, 43, pp. 16–19.

Garmendia, M., Ureña, J.M. & Coronado, J.M. (2011). *"Long-distance trips in a sparsely populated region: The impact of high-speed infrastructures"*, Journal of Transport Geography, 19(4), pp. 537–551.

Garmendia, M., Ribalaygua, C. & Ureña, J.M. (2012). *"High speed rail: implication for cities"*, Cities, 29, S26–S31.

Givoni, M. & Banister, D. (2012). *"Speed: The less important element of the high-speed train"*, Journal of Transport Geography, 22, pp. 306–307.

Gutiérrez, J. (2001). *"Location, economic potential and daily accessibility: An analysis of the accessibility impact of the high-speed line Madrid–Barcelona–French border"*, Journal of Transport Geography, 9(4), pp. 229–242.

Márquez, J., Vallejo, I. & Álvarez, J.I. (2015). *"Estimación del tiempo de demora en rutas pedestres: comparación de algoritmos"*, GeoFocus, 15, pp. 47–74.

Martí-Henneberg, J. (2015). *"Attracting travellers to the high-speed train: A methodology for comparing potential demand between stations"*, Journal of Transport Geography, 42, pp. 145–156.

Menéndez, J.M., Coronado, J.M., Guirao, B., Rodríguez, F.J., Ribalaygua, C., Rivas, A. & Ureña, J.M. (2006). *"Diseño, dimensión óptima y emplazamiento de estaciones de alta velocidad en ciudades de tamaño pequeño"*, Working Paper, Cuadernos de Ingeniería y Territorio 7, Ciudad Real, Spain: ETSICCP/UCLM.

Ortega, E., López, E. & Monzón, A. (2012). *"Territorial cohesion impacts of high-speed rail at different planning levels"*, Journal of Transport Geography, 24, pp. 130–141.

Reusser, D.E., Loukopoulos, P., Stauffacher, M. & Scholz, R.W. (2008). *"Classifying railway stations for sustainable transitions – balancing node and place functions"*, Journal of Transport Geography, 16(3), pp. 191–202.

Tapiador, F.J., Burckhart, K. & Martí-Henneberg, J. (2009). *"Characterizing European high-speed stations using international time and entropy metrics"*, Transportation Research Part A: Policy and Practice, 43(2), pp. 197–208.

Ureña, J.M. (2012). *"Territorial implications of high speed rail: A Spanish perspective"*, e-book, Ashgate Publishing.

Ureña, J.M., Menerault, P. & Garmendia, M. (2009). *"The high-speed rail challenge for big intermediate cities: A national, regional and local perspective"*, Cities, 26, pp. 266–279.

Vickerman, R. (2015). *"High-speed rail and regional development: The case of intermediate stations"*, Journal of Transport Geography, 42, pp. 157–165.

Zemp, S., Stauffacher, M., Lang, D.J. & Scholz, R.W. (2011). *"Classifying railway stations for strategic transport and land use planning: Context matters!"*, Journal of Transport Geography, 19(4), pp. 670–679.

7 Environmental performance and implications of high-speed rail

Torben Holvad, Amandine Craps and Javier Campos

1. Introduction

The relationship between transportation and the environment is paradoxical in essence. On the one hand, the provision of transport infrastructure and services supports the ever increasing mobility demands from passenger and freight flows and simultaneously conveys substantial short- and medium-term benefits both from a social and economic viewpoint. But, on the other hand, the same transportation activities have also become a major source of environmental externalities, whose negative effects could jeopardize the sustainability of those social and economic benefits in the long term. The complexities embedded in this relationship and their undisputable consequences in terms of efficiency and equity have made environmental concerns a critical issue in current transport policies and also help explain part of the relative success and public support enjoyed by high-speed rail (HSR) in recent years around the world.

In Europe, for example, although the movement towards a more sustainable transport system had started at least a decade earlier, it was not until 2008 when a specific 'greening transport package' was introduced by the European Commission (EC). It contained several provisions aimed at internalizing external costs that were later developed in more detail in the 2011 White Paper (European Commission, 2011).[1] Many of these initiatives were implicitly based on the idea that a 'modal shift' was needed to displace passengers and freight flows from less 'environmentally friendly' modes (road and air) towards 'greener' ones (rail and maritime transport). To achieve this goal the EC has renewed its interest in the restructuring of the European rail markets in order to strengthen its position vis-à-vis other modes. Recent figures (Eurostat, 2015) suggest that the rail freight market is still stagnant (its EU-28 share has remained at 18 per cent since 2002) but efforts are paying out in passenger traffic, where the aggregate share increased to 7.5 per cent in 2012 as compared to 6.8 per cent in 2002. Most of this success is explained by the development of HSR which, according to International Union of Railways (UIC) statistics (www.uic.org/highspeed), has consistently increased the number of passengers in France, Germany and Spain, and gained market share from airlines over medium-distance routes.

The reasons that justify this decisive support of the EC (and, by extension, of national governments) for passenger rail transport – and, particularly, for HSR – as a more 'environmentally friendly' mode of transport were first numerically provided by the IWW/INFRAS (2000) report on the external costs of transport in Europe (later updated in IWW/INFRAS, 2004), which argued that, excluding congestion costs, road transport was responsible for nearly 84 per cent of total external costs, and air transport for 13 per cent, whereas rail passenger transport accounted for less than 1.5 per cent. In terms of euros per 1,000 pkm, the differences were also significant: private cars represented €76 whereas rail costs were only €23. In 2008, a handbook on estimation procedures for external costs in the transport sector that included internalization measures (Maibach et al., 2008) updated some of these numerical results but also provided some additional reference values that essentially maintained and reinforced the relative environmental advantages of passenger rail transport over other modes, as discussed later in this chapter.[2]

Outside the European Union (EU), other countries have also showed decisive support for HSR, appealing to environmental reasons to justify the social and economic interest of the projects. Japan, which in 1964 inaugurated the world's first high-speed train from Tokyo to Osaka, has continued to expand services (reaching over 350 million passengers per year), arguing that HSR has lower land occupation effects and less emissions than alternative modes (see Ha et al., 2011). Similarly, in China, where more than 8,000 kilometres of HSR lines have been built in recent years and a record of 800 million passengers was achieved in 2014, the concern about the carbon footprint of road transport has convinced authorities to embark on an ambitious HSR expansion plan over the next decade (IFEU/ICT, 2008).

In the United States, both federal and state governments have generally exhibited a more limited enthusiasm about HSR undertakings. Although plans to invest $53 billion on railways over the next 25 years, connecting major cities through high-speed corridors, are still on the agenda, the potential environmental advantages are still exhaustively evaluated against the high construction and operating costs, as done by Levinson et al. (1999) with respect to an HSR line in California using an engineering perspective. Although the conclusions of the California High-Speed Rail Authority (California High-Speed Rail Authority, 2005) were positive, other studies suggest that the environmental benefits of HSR in the United States could be less relevant than in Europe.[3] Additional performance analyses using a life cycle perspective (Chester and Horvath, 2010; Chang and Kendall, 2011) have specifically attempted to capture the energy inputs and emission outputs for vehicle, infrastructure and fuel production components, including all the associated supply chains for railways and competing modes.[4]

The only country where a similar debate has emerged in Europe is the United Kingdom, which is contemplating plans to extend its more modest HSR network. Kemp (2004a; 2004b), for example, argues that some of the reference values from EU studies are not suitable for very sensitive areas and the average impact of car usage as compared to railways in the United Kingdom is not so favourable to the latter on many older lines, an idea also defended in Givoni et al. (2009). Although the report by Network Rail (2009) comparing the environmental impact of conventional and high-speed lines clarified the issue by providing a detailed impact analysis, some controversy remains (Miyoshi and Givoni, 2014).

Other papers in the economic literature have also contributed to identifying and measuring the environmental effects of HSR from different perspectives and provided additional issues to be discussed in this chapter. Thus, the seminal paper by Janic (2003) was the first one comparing the environmental performance of HSR and air transport, which again favoured the first one. Marsden (2003) argued that this was mostly due to lower CO_2 emissions and considered that the factors that determined these were related to energy consumption (either directly associated with the operation of the infrastructure and rolling stock or indirectly resulting from their construction and maintenance).[5] A more exhaustive analysis in García (2010a; 2010b) makes it even clearer that the relative better performance of HSR and its carbon footprint critically depended on the source of electricity generation, as confirmed by Wang and Sanders (2011) or the IER (2014) report.

Givoni (2006) accomplished a broader analysis of HSR environmental performance including additional external effects, such as noise of land impacts, but most of the literature has insisted on searching for the comparative advantages of HSR as compared to conventional rail or air transport, implicitly supporting the 'modal shift' towards greener transport advocated by the EC. This is, for example, the conclusion of van Essen et al. (2003), who calculated the energy consumption/emissions savings resulting from changes in modal choice and demand generation. This view is shared by Givoni (2007), who updates Janic's initial perspective, by Givoni et al. (2012) and, more recently, by D'Alfonso et al. (2015), who explicitly considered the effects of intermodal competition over environment and social welfare. Finally, a similar reasoning underlies other studies that have attempted to quantify the environmental cost advantages of HSR against road or air travel from the perspective of investment appraisal. They usually include detailed numerical estimates of these costs for facilities (as in Goodenough and Page, 1994, for the Channel Tunnel), corridors (de Rus and Inglada, 1997 or van Wee et al., 2003, for Spain and the Netherlands, respectively) or simulate more general intercity passenger routes (see Kageson, 2009 or Westin and Kageson, 2012).

After introducing the context and relevance of the environmental externalities associated with HSR, the remainder of the chapter will be organized as follows. Section 2 will provide specific figures about the HSR environmental performance, both as compared to other modes of transport and in comparison with conventional rail. A more detailed study of the life cycle perspective is also addressed in this section, and it also includes a discussion of the main trends in HSR environmental performance. Section 3 will be devoted to the analysis of the HSR environmental balance sheet, not only discussing the current total environmental impacts but also the overall impacts of HSR on the transport system environmental costs. Finally, section 4 will be devoted to discussing some future perspectives and will provide a summary of our main conclusions.

2. HSR environmental performance

It is a well-established fact that most transport activities contribute – among other anthropogenic and natural causes – to relevant environmental problems. This contribution may be directly related to the provision of infrastructure and services, indirectly related to them via secondary industries and/or produce cumulative impacts through the additive, multiplicative or synergetic consequences of transport activities as a system. All these effects differ in geographical scale (ranging from local to global effects) and across time (due to technological changes) and are mainly determined by the characteristics of each transport mode (Rodrigue, 2013). In the case of railways, and particularly HSR, the four more relevant environmental effects are related to climate change, air pollution, noise and other effects related to the territory (CER/UIC, 2015). These effects can be first analysed within an operational comparison of rail transport versus other modes.

2.1. Rail vs other modes: Operation

The transport sector is the biggest energy consumer as it represents one third of EU-28's final energy consumption in 2012. However, rail is one of the smallest consumers, along with inland waterways and pipelines. Indeed, it only represents 2 per cent of the transport sector's final energy consumption compared to road, which accounts for 82 per cent (Figure 7.1). In relation to energy consumption

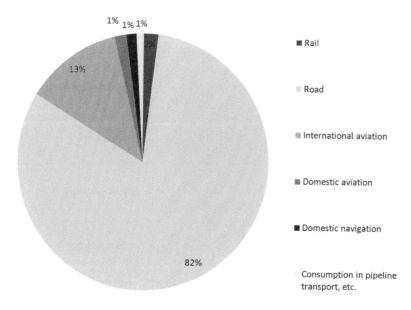

Figure 7.1 EU-28 final energy consumption share by mode in 2013 (%) – Total = 348.5 Mtoe.

Source: European Commission, 2015a.

being linked to emissions of greenhouse gases (GHG) and air pollutants, we will examine how each mode impacts climate change and the environment. However, because rail primarily uses electricity, most of its environmental impact is indirect. It is thus important to consider the energy mix, which differs from one country to another. Since this section focuses on operations we will cover this in section 2.3, which is about up/downstream impacts.

The overall context for climate change is raised in the IPCC report (Myhre et al., 2013) where the link between GHG emissions and a rise in temperature is demonstrated. Transport emits about one fifth of the total GHG emissions in EU-28 and thus plays a major role in climate change (European Commission, 2015a). Furthermore, while other economic activities have reduced CO_2 emissions, transport's emissions have remained at the same level. However, all transport modes do not contribute to the same extent. As illustrated in Figure 7.2, rail has the smallest share of GHG emissions, with only 0.6 per cent of the total emissions from transport. The biggest contributor to GHG emissions is road transportation, which represents about 72 per cent of the total emissions. While ground and sea modes have stayed relatively stable since 1990, civil aviation showed a significant increase (8.7 per cent in 1990 against 12.8 per cent in 2012). The European Environment Agency (2008) estimated CO_2 equivalent emissions for each mode as illustrated in Figure 7.2:

This shows that rail has lower emissions than air transport and cars. Emission data for the United Kingdom showed that conventional diesel trains emit

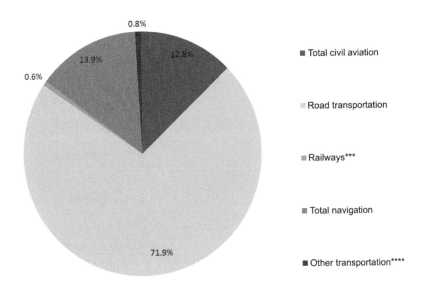

Figure 7.2 EU-28 greenhouse gas emissions share by mode in 2012 (%) – Total = 1173.2 MteCO$_2$.

Source: European Commission, 2015a.

*** Excluding indirect emissions from electricity consumption.
**** Combustion emissions from all remaining transport activities including pipeline transportation, ground activities in airports and harbours and off-road activities.

Table 7.1 Average CO_2 emissions per pkm for different modes.

	Average CO_2 emission per pkm (g/pkm)
Air – short-haul	77–240
Air – long-haul	118–153
Car – 1.1 passenger	100–500
Bus or coach	45–80
Rail – conventional	45–130
Rail – high-speed	80–165

Source: European Environment Agency, 2008, pp. 34–35.

69 gCO_2/pkm and conventional electric trains emit 60 gCO_2/pkm (Givoni et al., 2009). Givoni et al. (2009) suggest, however, that HSR has lower CO_2 emissions than conventional trains and they give figures such as 11 gCO_2/pkm and 25 gCO_2/pkm for the case of Eurostar. This is much smaller than figures from the European Environment Agency (2008) exposed above. According to Givoni et al. (2009), the number of stops and distance between them has a substantial impact on emissions, as the amount of energy required to reach high speeds is high too.

However, this table only takes CO_2 emissions into account. Drawing on figures available in Maibach et al. (2008) and assuming that the actual load of a car, conventional train and high-speed train is 1.5, 120 and 270 persons respectively, we can compare marginal costs of all modes of transport. As can be seen in Table 7.2, HSR's costs are the lowest with 0.82 €/1,000 pkm while air transport's costs are the highest with between 35 and 371,000 €/1,000 pkm. The difference between conventional rail (electric and diesel) and HSR is very small for climate change costs.

The main air pollutants produced by the transport sector are nitrogen oxides (NO_x), carbon monoxide (CO), primary particulate matter ($PM_{2.5}$), particulate matter (PM_{10}), sulphur oxide (SO_x) and non-methane volatile organic compounds (NMVOC). These substances can harm human health as well as ecosystems and buildings. Despite the different norms put in place by the EU (e.g. Euronorm), these pollutants are still present in significant quantities. The following graphs show on

Table 7.2 Marginal costs from climate change, air pollution and up/downstream processes for passenger transport (€/1,000 pkm)

Vehicle type	Climate change	Air pollution	Up/downstream
Car: petrol, average size (1.4–2L), EURO-0	4.2	11.2	6.16
Car: diesel, average size (1.4–2L), EURO-0	2.8	16.8	3.36
Rail: electric	1.172	1.04536	0.48
Rail: diesel	0.9312	13.904	0.7856
HSR	0.824	0.368	0.368
Air : <500km	62–13000	21	71
Air : >2000km	35–371000	3	40

Source: Maibach et al., (2008).

the one hand, the share of the transport sector in these emissions and, on the other hand, the share of each mode in the transport sector (Figure 7.3). We can see that railways play a minor role in emitting these pollutants and that road transport and short sea maritime transport are the main emitters. This is also what is observed by van Wee et al. (2003) when comparing NO_x and SO_x emissions from conventional rail and HSR to those of cars and buses. Janic (2003) compared HSR and air transport and also found that HSR had lower emissions of air pollutants than air transport.

Drawing on figures from Maibach et al. (2008) (Table 7.2), we can clearly see that the cost of air pollution from rail is almost always lower than for other modes

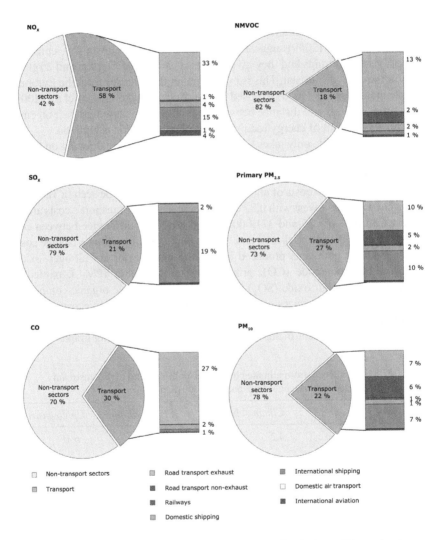

Figure 7.3 The contributors of the transport sector to total emissions of the main air pollutants in 2010 (EEA-32).

Source: EEA, 2012: 34.

of transport. Diesel rail's performance is, however, not as good as electric rail or HSR that use exclusively electricity as their energy source. Indeed, it shows a cost of 13.9 €/1,000 pkm when electric rail's cost is 1.05 €/1,000 pkm and HSR's cost is 0.37 €/1,000 pkm. Diesel rail's cost is actually even higher than for average petrol cars. HSR has the lowest cost in the case of air pollution with only 0.37 €/1,000 pkm. Obviously, these values are estimates of the marginal costs and therefore can only be considered as indicative. Indeed, Maibach et al. (2008) also provide upper and lower values in addition to the central estimates used in this chapter.

Moreover, transportation also has an impact on the environment in terms of noise (Campos and de Rus, 2009). It is, however, a difficult externality to measure; even though it can be measured on a physical level, it can be perceived differently by different people and at different times of the day. This is why different levels of noise are measured according to the time of the day (day, evening and night).

Figure 7.4 shows the number of people exposed to the noise of airports, railways and roads according to the different levels of noise. Looking at this figure, we can see that road traffic is by far the main contributor to noise externalities. Moreover, compared to conventional rail, Korzhenevych et al. (2014) estimate that a rural environment where less people live mostly determines HSR lines. This is indeed how they differentiate the impact of HSR from conventional rail for air pollution. We can thus suggest that the impact of HSR in terms of noise should be lower than conventional rail which passes through more populated areas. According to Campos and de Rus (2009), in order to keep a reasonable noise level (55 dB(A)) at 280 km/h, it is necessary for the tracks to be situated in a 150 m wide corridor. This leads to a net increase in land take and thus in the

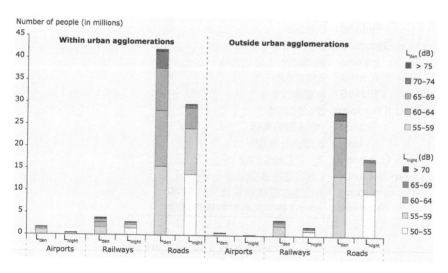

Figure 7.4 Exposure to transport noise in Europe based upon the common indicators for Lden and Lnight.

Source: EEA, 2014: 22.

increase of the impact explained below. Compared to air transport, Janic (2003) assumes that HSR should have an advantage at departure and arrival since it has lower speeds. However, air transport has an advantage for the cruising part, especially if HSR has to go through heavily populated areas (Janic, 2003). We can see here that there is no consensus yet to what extent rail has a lower or higher impact on the environment in terms of noise. This is particularly difficult since the impact largely depends on local specificities.

Finally, transport may also have other impacts such as land take and fragmentation. This creates barriers for animals and can lead to the disappearance of species that need large spaces to survive. The EEA estimated the average size of non-fragmented land in the EU-15 was slightly over 100 km^2 in 1998 (EEA, 2002, p. 23). The issue of increasing consumption of land was also raised by the EEA and Figure 8.5 shows the share of the country's surface that is being used for roads in the EU-15. On the other hand, the share of rail is very small. In 2004, the EEA estimated that roads occupied 93 per cent of the land used by transportation in EU-15 while rail occupied only 4 per cent. The remaining 3 per cent was used by pipelines, access roads, forestry tracks, harbours and canals (European Environment Agency, 2004). Finally, on this point, air transport has a special advantage since aircraft do not need any infrastructure other than airports and most of these are already built. HSR, however, needs new lines to be built (Janic, 2003).

Member states

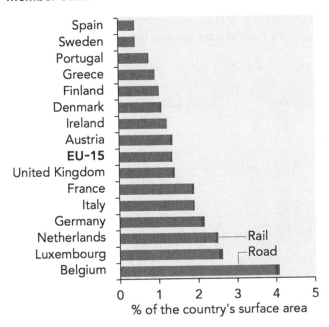

Figure 7.5 Share of the country's surface area used by roads and rail, EU-15, 1998.

Source: EEA, 2002: 22.

2.2. HSR life cycle perspective on environmental implications

As mentioned in the above section, when assessing the environmental impact of the railway sector, it is important to take the production of electricity into account. Indeed, the environmental impact, rather than being located through the railway network, is concentrated where the electricity is produced. Moreover, there are different ways of producing this electricity and they do not all have the same impact on the environment. We thus need to focus on the electricity mix of the EU in order to have an idea of the impact. The electricity mix is defined as the proportion of different sources in electricity production: electricity produced from coal shows higher emissions than electricity produced with renewable or nuclear energy. As shown in Table 8.3, in EU-28, electricity is mainly produced from renewables, nuclear and solid fuels (European Commission, 2015a). According to Givoni et al. (2009), the CO_2 intensity (kgCO_2/kWh) of the different primary energy sources is as follow: 0.876 for coal, 0.59 for oil, 0.37 for gas, 0.016 for nuclear fuel and 0 for renewables. These observations are very favourable for conventional or HSR transport that uses electricity. On the contrary, it is less favourable to transportation using solid fuels since in order to produce the same amount of energy, they will produce more CO_2.

Table 7.2 shows that up/downstream process costs are the lowest for rail and the highest for air transport (40–71 €/1,000 pkm) and cars (3.36–6.16 €/1,000 pkm). As far as rail transport is concerned, diesel has again the highest cost with 0.78 €/1,000 pkm compared to 0.48 and 0.37 €/1,000 pkm for electric rail and HSR respectively.

Finally, there are other impacts linked to vehicle production and maintenance, and infrastructure production and maintenance that are not taken into account in the figures given above.

2.3. Trends in HSR environmental performance

According to Givoni et al. (2009), the environmental performance of rail depends on the number of stops, the distance between them, the load factor and the electricity mix. Indeed, they have shown that the fewer stops there were and the longer the distance between them, the lower the impact on the environment. Since HSR usually has fewer stops and longer distances between them, new operations on new lines should thus have a relatively good environmental performance.

Table 7.3 EU-28 gross electricity generation by fuel in 2013 (total electricity generation: 3261.5 TWh).

TWh	Gross electricity generation	Solid fuels	Nuclear fuel	Renewables	Gases	Petroleum and products	Wastes, non-RES
EU-28	3261.5	871.8	876.8	886.0	540.4	61.3	20.7
Share (%)	100%	26.7%	26.9%	27.2%	16.6%	1.9%	0.6%

Source: European Commission, 2015a, p. 91.

Load factor is also an important criterion as the impact per pkm will be lower if the train is completely filled. According to Smith (2012), this increasing load factor is the best way for railways to improve their energy efficiency. They even put forward the fact that, for long distance travel, the performance of a car that has a high load factor does not have such a high impact as some trains. Rail thus needs to attract people from other modes of transport rather than create new demand, as this will help increase the load factor and therefore decrease the environmental impact. According to Eurostat data (2015), the share of car and bus travel remained quite stable between 2004 and 2013 while the share of rail travel gained 1 per cent in the same period. We thus see a slight increase in rail's share of the total inland pkm. However, even if the traffic increases, this will only have a positive impact if it is done by increasing the load factor rather than adding vehicles to the rail network. For example, van Essen et al. (2003) show that energy consumption per pkm for HSR with a 49 per cent load factor is 1.08 MJ per pkm, while with a 70 per cent load factor it is 0.76 MJ per pkm. These figures should be contrasted with the corresponding ones for a diesel car of 0.94 MJ per pkm (assumed load factor of 36 per cent).

Finally, as explained above, since most of the energy used by rail is electricity, the source of this energy is also a crucial criterion for rail to have the highest environmental performance. For road transport, it is expected that technologies will improve towards those that are more energy efficient (European Commission, 2013a), making the competition harder. However, the electricity generation will also be more efficient and the share of renewable energy sources should increase, while generation from solid fuel decreases (European Commission, 2013b). This means that environmental performances of transportation using electricity should improve over time.

The trend in HSR performance is thus determined by numerous factors. Generally, HSR uses electricity, has high load factors, fewer stops and longer distances between stops. This would contribute to obtaining a relatively good environmental performance. However, the critical aspects would concern the extent to which construction and maintenance of HSR rolling stock and infrastructure can be improved in terms of (embedded) emissions. Moreover, the particular factor of nuclear fuel is not considered here.

3. HSR environmental balance sheet

3.1. Current total environmental impact of HSR

Based on the identified unit values in the previous section we will here take a more aggregated view on the environmental impacts of HSR. The approach used will involve the following steps. First, available data on HSR passenger usage for EU-28 (pkm) will be multiplied with the marginal costs estimates put forward in Table 7.2. This will give an estimate of total environmental costs for HSR covering climate change, local air pollution and up/downstream processes. In order to get a more comprehensive estimate we will incorporate estimates for noise-related costs. Overall, this will provide indications of the HSR-related environmental costs from an operational perspective in Europe (among those EU member states with HSR). The estimates will be discussed both in terms of the total impact and category of impact, as well as how all these effects differ by country. The estimated costs for HSR will be compared to the ones for the transport system as a whole in order to highlight the importance of HSR environmental costs in this context. Subsequently, the aggregated analysis will seek to address issues beyond the operational perspective by looking into a life cycle context with a particular focus on the environmental impacts linked to the construction and maintenance of HSR lines.

Table 7.4 shows total environmental costs linked to HSR operation by category of impact (climate change, air pollution, up/downstream processes, noise) and per country. The estimate for noise-related costs is also based on Maibach et al. (2008), suggesting a marginal cost per passenger trip of €ct5.93 as reported in Petrazzuolo et al. (2013) with specific reference to the Madrid–Barcelona link. Assuming an average trip length of 500 km would imply a marginal cost for noise per pkm of €ct0.012 which is used as the basis for calculating the total noise costs for HSR. An order of magnitude estimate of total environmental costs associated with the four categories is around €190 million per annum (at current, 2013, levels of pkm). Furthermore, the biggest contributor is climate change with almost 50 per cent of the total costs, followed by air pollution and up/downstream processes with about 20 per cent each, while noise appears to generate less than 10 per cent. The table also shows from which countries the environmental costs are generated. With France having the highest number of HSR pkm it follows that the biggest share of environmental costs are produced here (close to 50 per cent). Other big contributors are Germany (about 20 per cent), Italy (about 10 per cent) and Spain (around 10 per cent). It should be mentioned that these indications of total costs and their distribution on environmental impact category and country should be considered in order of magnitude, given that there is variation in marginal costs values as highlighted in Maibach et al. (2008), who reported upper and lower values along with the central estimates. Furthermore, the top-down approach used provides an overall indication without consideration for local or regional issues, such as the environmental implications of HSR in sensitive areas.

Using the same approach, the HSR environmental costs will be compared to the ones generated by car travel to put these in context. On the basis of the marginal costs values for climate, air pollution and up/downstream processes given in Table 7.2 for car travel (diesel and petrol) and marginal costs for noise in Maibach et al. (2008) we have estimated the total marginal costs for car travel per 1,000 pkm to be around €22. As the latest available figures for car travel in Europe (EU-28) from 2013 show a total of around 4,700 billion pkm (European Commission, 2015b) this would imply total environmental costs for car travel of more than €100 billion. This demonstrates that the HSR environmental costs amount to at most 0.2 per cent of the ones produced from car travel.

Apart from the environmental impacts associated with operating HSR (including those linked to energy production and distribution) examined above there

Table 7.4 Estimated total cost from climate change, air pollution, up/downstream processes and noise for HSR passenger transport (million €).

	Climate change	Air pollution	Up/downstream processes	Noise	Total
BE	0.7	0.3	0.3	0.1	**1.5**
CZ	0.2	0.1	0.1	0.0	**0.4**
DE	20.7	9.3	9.3	3.0	**42.3**
ES	10.5	4.7	4.7	1.5	**21.4**
FR	41.8	18.7	18.7	6.0	**85.2**
IT	10.5	4.7	4.7	1.5	**21.5**
NL	0.3	0.1	0.1	0.0	**0.6**
PT	0.4	0.2	0.2	0.1	**0.8**
SI	0.0	0.0	0.0	0.0	**0.0**
FI	0.6	0.3	0.3	0.1	**1.3**
SE	2.5	1.1	1.1	0.4	**5.1**
UK	3.6	1.6	1.6	0.5	**7.3**
Total	**92.0**	**41.1**	**41.1**	**13.2**	**187.4**

Source: Maibach et al., 2008.

are other important elements to consider. These include the indirect emissions of construction, maintenance and decommissioning of HSR rolling stock, the embedded emissions from construction and maintenance of HSR infrastructure, along with implications such as land take, fragmentation and visual intrusion. Particular attention will be given to the emission impacts from construction and maintenance of HSR links due to their likely magnitude. In Network Rail (2009) the embedded emissions for the construction and maintenance of HSR infrastructure were estimated to be in the range of 140–230 tonnes CO_2 eq. per rail track km per year (where the variation reflects type of track and recycling rate). On this basis, with specific assumptions with regard to a recycling rate of 50 per cent and the proportion of line (tunnels are 10 per cent) it was estimated that the construction and maintenance of a 500 km double track HSR line would result in annualized emissions of 118,000 tonnes CO_2 eq. For an HSR project of such a length this would imply a cost in monetary terms of about €3.8 million per annum (using a unit value of €32.5 per tonne of CO_2 eq. in accordance with Maibach et al. (2008)). Assuming that the estimated annualized emissions would be valid for the entire HSR network in Europe this would then translate into an annual overall European value of embedded emissions of 1,726,576 tonnes CO_2 eq. (length of HSR lines in 2014 is 7,316 km (European Commission, 2015b)). This would translate in monetary terms to a cost of about €56 million per annum.

3.2. Overall impact of HSR on transport system environmental costs

The earlier estimates of HSR environmental impacts were determined from a partial approach by considering this mode of transport in isolation from the rest of the transport system. As such, it would be important to complement these estimates by considering any relevant interactions between HSR and other modes of transport. In the following section this aspect will be examined with particular reference to the modal shift effects of HSR compared to any generation of entirely new traffic. If a significant number of HSR passengers have, in fact, changed mode then it is possible that for the transport system as a whole the environmental costs would be reduced if the transfer is from modes with higher environmental costs. On the other hand, if HSR passengers largely consist of new traffic then this would imply that, overall, HSR would increase the adverse environmental impacts of the transport system. Available evidence on the importance of modal shift compared to induced traffic will be discussed.

A comprehensive review of evidence on modal shift and HSR is provided in Haas (2014). The evidence presented covers secondary analysis of aggregated existing data as well as recent results using original data. From the secondary analysis evidence, Haas (2014) concludes that in each country that has introduced HSR, modal shift has occurred in particular from air transport (as well as from conventional rail where applicable); for other modes (bus and car) it would appear that there is also transfer but there is less information available. Overall, Haas (2014) stresses that precise indications about the impact of HSR on modal shares is not possible given the lack of systematic intermodal data collection and analysis for implemented HSR schemes. From the recent evidence of modal shift using original data a similar conclusion is drawn: that there is significant shift to HSR from other modes.

Preston (2010) shows the generation of passengers for five HSR links in Europe, distinguishing between induced (new) traffic and that transferred from other modes (road, conventional rail, air transport)[6]. The evidence suggests that induced traffic ranges between 11 per cent (Thalys) and 50 per cent (Madrid–Seville) with a simple average of 26 per cent. Although this is a relatively small sample it does highlight both that significant modal shift occurs but also that the extent of induced traffic is subject to significant variation and, hence, can be an important determinant of the environmental impacts of HSR. On this basis, it is likely that the estimated total environmental costs given in section 3.1 should be adjusted down, assuming that the modal shift is from modes with higher environmental costs. As highlighted earlier, this would be dependent on several factors, including load factor for HSR and the electricity mix.

4. Future perspectives and conclusions

A recent view of the future is provided in (European Commission, 2013a) in terms of expected trends with regard to energy, transport and GHG emissions until 2050. According to the report, the transport sector will follow the GDP trend and will grow steadily until 2040 after which the growth will slightly decrease. Road transport will keep its dominant role even though it will grow less than other modes and thus lose shares in the modal split. The share of road transport is expected to go down from 84 per cent in 2010 to 76 per cent by 2050. Air transport, on the other hand, will experience the highest growth – 133 per cent between 2010 and 2050. Air transport is expected to be the second mode after road for passenger transport. Rail transport will also gain from road transport due to the expected increase in fossil fuel prices and due to the competition of HSR with short-haul air transport.

Against this background, it is foreseen that there will be significant expansion of the HSR network in Europe and beyond over this period (e.g. in Europe the completion of the high-speed TEN-T by 2030). This is considered one of the main instruments in ensuring a rebalancing of modes through modal shift towards rail and thereby a way of reducing the environmental impacts of transport. However, as highlighted in this chapter, several caveats for this to be achieved are of importance. In particular, the issue of the load factor achieved for HSR links can influence the extent to which it performs better than other modes (notably car and conventional rail). Provided the load factor is optimized it would also be important that HSR traffic generation is through modal shift rather than new traffic in order to avoid HSR leading to additional emissions. As there are important embedded emissions from construction and maintenance of HSR lines where these can only be offset through substantial modal shift, this implies that the introduction of HSR would normally require catchment areas with large populations in order to ensure sufficient numbers of transferred trips. Therefore, the decision to build HSR needs to be considered carefully in order to ensure economic and environmental feasibility. Subsequently, there would be important additional environmental concerns to consider in terms of routing and technical solutions in order to minimize local environmental impacts such as land take and visual intrusion.

Notes

1 Updated methodologies and stricter targets have been outlined in two more recent documents (European Commission, 2013a; 2013b), as well as in a transport-specific report by the European Environmental Agency (European Environmental Agency, 2014).
2 Updates of this handbook did not change these relative values. See van Essen et al. (2011) and Korzhenevych et al. (2014) for details.
3 See, for example, Chester and Horvath (2010), Deakin (2010) and Chester and Ryerson (2014). A recent report (Airport Cooperative Research Program, 2013) assessing air and high-speed rail corridors confirms lower environmental impacts of the railways.
4 This life cycle approach was also used by Akerman (2011) for Sweden, and Song et al. (2014) and Yue et al. (2015) for China. See also Kamga and Yazici (2014) for the United States.
5 The relative size and empirical relevance of these factors were later compared between the United Kingdom and Spain in Gonzalez et al. (2010).
6 The five HSR links included are Paris–Lyon, Madrid–Seville, Madrid–Barcelona, Thalys and Eurostar.

References

Airport Cooperative Research Program (2013). "*Environmental assessment of air and high-speed rail corridors*", Washington, DC: Transportation Research Board. Available at http://onlinepubs.trb.org/onlinepubs/acrp/acrp_syn_043.pdf [accessed 1 February 2016].

Akerman, J. (2011). *"The role of high-speed rail in mitigating climate change – the Swedish case Europabanan from a life cycle perspective"*, Transportation Research Part D: Transport and Environment, 16(3), pp. 208–217.

California High-Speed Rail Authority (2005). *"Final program environmental impact report/environmental impact statement for the proposed California high-speed train system"*, Sacramento, CA: CAHSRA.

Campos, J. and G. de Rus (2009). *"Some stylized facts about high-speed rail: A review of HSR experiences around the world"*, Transport Policy, 16(1), pp. 19–28.

CER/UIC (2015). *"Rail transport and environment. Facts and figures"*, Paris: CER/UIC.

Chang, B. and A. Kendall (2011). *"Life cycle greenhouse gas assessment of infrastructure construction for California's high-speed rail system"*, Transportation Research Part D: Transport and Environment, 16, pp. 429–434.

Chester, M. and A. Horvath (2010). *"Life-cycle assessment of high-speed rail: The case of California"*, Environmental Research Letters, 5, pp. 1–8.

Chester, M. and M.S. Ryerson (2014). *"Grand challenges for high-speed rail environmental assessment in the United States"*, Transportation Research Part A: Policy and Practice, 61, pp. 15–26.

European Commission (2011). *"White Paper. Roadmap to a single European transport area – towards a competitive and resource efficient transport system"*, COM(2011) 144 final, Brussels: EC.

European Commission (2013a). *"EU energy, transport and GHG emissions – trends to 2050: Reference scenario 2013"*, Luxembourg: EC.

European Commission (2013b). *"Summary of measures that internalize or reduce transport externalities"*, Commission Staff Working Document, Report in accordance with Art. 11(4) of Directive 1999/62/EC, SWD(2013) 269 final, Brussels: EC.

European Commission (2015a). *"EU energy in figures. Statistical pocketbook 2015"*, Brussels: EC.

European Commission (2015b). *"EU transport in figures. Statistical pocketbook 2015"*, Luxembourg: EC.

D'Alfonso, T., C. Jiang and V. Bracaglia (2015). *"Would competition between air transport and high-speed rail benefit environment and social welfare?"*, Transportation Research Part B: Methodological, 74, pp. 118–137.

Deakin, E. (2010). *"Environmental and other co-benefits of developing a high speed rail system in California: A prospective vision 2010–2050"*, Working Paper No. CEPP001, Berkeley, CA: UCB, Center for Environmental Public Policy.

de Rus, G. and V. Inglada (1997). *"Cost–benefit analysis of the high-speed train in Spain"*, Annals of Regional Science, 31, pp. 175–188.

European Environment Agency (2002). *"Paving the way for EU enlargement: TERM 2002: Indicators of transport and environment integration"*, Environmental Issue Report No. 32, Luxembourg: EEA.

European Environment Agency (2004). *"Ten key transport and environment issues for policy-makers. TERM 2004: Indicators tracking transport and environment integration in the European Union"*, Report No. 3/2004, Luxembourg: EEA.

European Environment Agency (2008). *"Climate for a transport change. TERM 2007: Indicators tracking transport and environment in the European Union"*, Report No. 1/2008, Luxembourg: EEA.

European Environment Agency (2012). *"The contribution of transport to air quality. TERM 2012: Transport indicators tracking progress towards environmental targets in Europe"*, Report No. 10/2012, Luxembourg: EEA.

European Environment Agency (2014). *"Focusing on environmental pressures from long-distance transport. TERM 2014: Transport indicators tracking progress towards environmental targets in Europe"*, Report No. 7/2014, Luxembourg: EEA.

Eurostat (2015). *"Energy, transport and environment indicators"*, Luxembourg: EC.

García, A. (2010a). *"High speed, energy consumption and emissions"*, Paris: UIC, Study and Research Group for Railway Energy and Emissions.

García, A. (2010b). *"Energy consumption and emissions of high-speed trains"*, Transportation Research, 2159(1), pp. 27–35.

Givoni, M. (2006). *"Development and impact of the modern high-speed train: A review"*, Transport Reviews, 26(5), pp. 593–611.

Givoni, M. (2007). *"Environmental benefits from mode substitution: Comparison of the environmental impact from aircraft and high-speed train operations"*, International Journal of Sustainable Transportation, 1(4), pp. 209–230.

Givoni, M., C. Brand and P. Watkiss (2009). *"Are railways climate friendly?"*, Built Environment, 35(1), pp. 70–86.

Givoni, M., F. Dobruszkes and I. Lugo (2012). *"Uncovering the real potential for air–rail substitution: An exploratory analysis"*, in Inderwildi, O. and D.A. King, *"Energy, transport and the environment: Assessing the sustainable mobility paradigm"*, London: Springer, pp. 495–512.

Goodenough, R.A. and S.J. Page (1994). *"Evaluating the environmental impact of a major transport infrastructure project: the Channel Tunnel high-speed rail link"*, Applied Geography, 14, pp. 26–50.

Ha, H.K., Y. Yoshida and A. Zhang (2011). *"Social efficiency benchmarking of Japanese domestic transport services: A comparison of rail and air"*, Transportation Research Part D: Transport and Environment, 16(7), pp. 554–561.

Haas, P.J. (2014). *"Modal shift and high-speed rail: A review of the current literature"*, Report No. 12-35, San José, CA: San José State University, Mineta Transportation Institute.

IER (2014). *"ExternE. External costs of energy"*, Stuttgart: University of Stuttgart, IER. Available at www.externe.info/externe_d7/?q=node/46 [accessed 1 February 2016].

IFEU/ICT (2008). *"Transport in China: Energy consumption and emissions of different transport modes"*, Final Report, Heidelberg: IFEU.

IWW/INFRAS (2000). *"External costs of transport. Accident, environmental and congestion costs in Western Europe"*, Paris: UIC.

IWW/INFRAS (2004). *"External costs of transport. Update study"*, Paris: UIC.

Janic, M. (2003). *"High-speed rail and air passenger transport: a comparison of the operational and environmental performance"*, Proceedings of the Institution of Mechanical Engineers Part F: Journal of Rail and Rapid Transit, 217, pp. 259–269.

Kageson, P. (2009). *"Environmental aspects of inter-city passenger"*, Discussion Paper No. 2009–28, Paris: OECD/ITF Joint Transport Research Centre.

Kamga, C. and M.A. Yazici (2014). *"Achieving environmental sustainability beyond technological improvements: Potential role of high-speed rail in the United States of America"*, Transportation Research Part D: Transport and Environment, 31, pp. 148–164.

Kemp, R. (2004a). *"Environmental impact of high- speed rail"*, Paper presented at the IMechE seminar on High-Speed Rail Developments, London, 21 April 2004.

Kemp, R. (2004b). *"Take the car and save the planet? The environmental impact of rail transport"*, Power Engineering, 18(5), pp. 12–17.

Korzhenevych, A., N. Dehnen, J. Bröcker, M. Holtkamp, H. Meier, G. Gibson, A. Varma and V. Cox (2014). *"Update of the handbook on external costs of transport: Final report"*, London: Ricardo-AEA.

Levinson, D., A. Kanafani and D. Gillen (1999). *"Air, high speed rail or highway: A cost comparison in the California corridor"*, Transportation Quarterly, 53(1), pp. 123–132.

Maibach, M., C. Schreyer, D. Sutter, H.P. van Essen, B.H. Boon, R. Smokers, A. Schroten, C. Doll, B. Pawlowska and M. Bak (2008). *"Handbook on estimation of external costs in the transport sector: Produced within the study Internalisation Measures and Policies for all External Cost of Transport (IMPACT)"*, Delft: CE Delft.

Marsden, G. (2003). *"Review of CO2 emission studies of high-speed rail in Europe"*, Leeds: University of Leeds, ITS.

Miyoshi, C. and M. Givoni (2014). *"The environmental case for the high-speed train in the UK: Examining the London–Manchester route"*, International Journal of Sustainable Transportation, 8, pp. 107–126.

Myhre, G., D. Shindell, F.-M. Bréon, W. Collins, J. Fuglestvedt, J. Huang, D. Koch, J.-F. Lamarque, D. Lee, B. Mendoza, T. Nakajima, A. Robock, G. Stephens, T. Takemura and H. Zhang (2013). *"Anthropogenic and natural radiative forcing"*, Chapter 8 in Stocker, T.F., D. Qin, G.-K. Plattner, M. Tignor, S.K. Allen, J. Boschung, A. Nauels, Y. Xia, V. Bex and P.M. Midgley (eds), *"Climate change 2013: The physical science basis"*, Contribution of Working Group I to the Fifth Assessment Report of the Intergovernmental Panel on Climate Change, Cambridge, UK and New York: Cambridge University Press, pp. 659–740.

Network Rail (2009). *"Comparing environmental impact of conventional and high speed rail"*, London: Network Rail.

Petrazzuolo, M., A. Ortega, F. Pagliara and J.M. Vassallo (2013). *"Does high speed rail compete fairly with other transportation modes? Madrid–Barcelona case study"*, 13th World Conference on Transport Research Selected Proceedings, Brazil: WCTR.

Preston, J.M. (2010). *"The case for high-speed rail: An update"*, London: RAC Foundation.

Rodrigue, J-P. (2013). *"The geography of transport systems"*, 3rd edn, New York: Routledge.

Smith, R.A. (2012). *"Energy for railways"*, in Inderwildi, O. and D.A. King, *"Energy, transport and the environment: Addressing the sustainable mobility paradigm"*, London: Springer, pp. 561–575.

Song, X., Y. Fu, Z. Chen and H. Liu (2014). *"Environmental impact evaluation for high-speed railway"*, Journal of Central South University, 21, pp. 2366–2371.

van Essen, H., A. Schroten, M. Otten, D. Sutter, C. Schreyer, M. Zandonella, M. Maibach and C. Doll (2011). *"External costs of transport in Europe: Update study for 2008"*, Delft: CE Delft.

van Essen, H., O. Bello, J. Dings and R. van den Brink (2003). *"To shift or not to shift, that's the question. The environmental performance of the principal modes of freight and passenger transport in the policymaking context"*, Delft: CE Delft.

van Wee, B., R. van den Brink and H. Nijland (2003). *"Environmental impacts of high-speed rail links in cost–benefit analyses: A case study of the Dutch Zuider Zee line"*, Transportation Research Part D: Transport and Environment, 8, pp. 299–314.

Wang, X.C. and L. Sanders (2011). *"Energy consumption and carbon footprint of high-speed rail projects: Using cahsr and fhsr as examples"*, Proceedings of the Institution of Mechanical Engineers Part F: Journal of Rail and Rapid Transit, 226, pp. 26–35.

Westin, J. and P. Kageson (2012). *"Can high speed rail offset its embedded emissions?"*, Transportation Research Part D: Transport and Environment, 17, pp. 1–7.

Yue, Y., T. Wang, S. Liang, J. Yang, P. Hou, S. Qua, J. Zhou, X. Jia, H. Wang and M. Xu (2015). *"Life cycle assessment of high speed rail in China"*, Transportation Research Part D: Transport and Environment, 41, pp. 367–376.

8 Environmental assessment of high-speed rail

David Hoyos, Gorka Bueno and
Iñigo Capellán-Pérez

1. Introduction

Transport policy faces, at the beginning of the twenty-first century, an unresolved dilemma: how to reconcile an apparently unstoppable growth of passenger and freight traffic with its undesirable harmful effects, both socially and environmentally. The concept of sustainable mobility has been proposed as a solution to this dilemma, but it struggles to become an operational concept. Policy makers are thus faced with a complex decision, as there is an urgent need to reconcile economic development and environmental protection, while considering different social priorities and distributional consequences (Akerman et al., 2000).

Transport policy has traditionally focused on the offer of new infrastructures as the only instrument to cope with a continuously growing demand for transport, under the assumption that mobility and speed are good for the economy and even for their own sake (i.e. progress). Transport growth was enormous at the end of the twentieth century (+107 per cent increase between 1970 and 1995) and is expected to rise by 1.7 per cent each year from 2004 to 2030 (+63 per cent in the period) if current trends continue and economic growth expectations are attained (Jehanno et al., 2011). However, this view was increasingly challenged at the end of the twentieth century as traffic congestion was aggravated rather than resolved, and public awareness regarding the environmental and social effects of transport policies was raised. It is widely accepted today that current global transport trends are unsustainable (Banister et al., 2011) and, perhaps more worrisome, transport seems unable to lower its emissions (IPCC, 2014).

The European Union (EU) constitutes a paradigmatic example: transport currently accounts for about a third of its energy consumption and a quarter of greenhouse gas (GHG) emissions and, whereas in other sectors GHG emissions have been decreasing, in transport they have grown by 29 per cent between 1990 and 2009. Moreover, transport activity is expected to double by 2050 (European Commission, 2011a). That is the main reason why European commitment to reduce GHG emissions is a considerable challenge, especially to the transport sector. The European Commission has gone even further in previous emissions reduction targets. In presenting its roadmap aimed at a low carbon economy by 2050, it undertakes to reduce its emissions to at least 80 per cent below 1990 levels (40 per cent by 2030 and 60 per cent by 2040), in order to be consistent with a +2°C temperature stabilisation in comparison to pre-industrial levels (European Commission, 2011a). These targets have been accompanied by others, such as reducing European energy dependency and reducing the use of critical resources such as energy, raw materials, soil and water (European Commission, 2010; 2011b).

As a consequence, the development of sustainable forms of transport has been one of the key priorities of the European transport policy. The European Commission has repeatedly stressed the need to pursue a series of measures to limit the contribution of transport activity to climate change, calling for a strengthening of environmental assessments of policy initiatives with important environmental effects (European Commission, 1998). However, current European practices do not seem to implement adequately the level of sustainability that one would assume when looking at current legislation (Humphreys, 2010). In this context, high-speed rail (HSR) is sometimes proposed as a means to reconcile the dilemma between growth and sustainability—i.e. as a sustainable transport mode. However, after massive investments in different European countries, the environmental arguments favouring investments in HSR are far from clear.

This chapter aims to assess the environmental contribution of HSR, ultimately evaluating whether it can be included in the set of policies towards sustainable mobility.[1] The rest of the chapter is structured as follows: section 2 establishes the basis of how to operationalise the concept of sustainable mobility; section 3 discusses, under the previous framework, the potential of HSR to reverse the current unsustainability of the transport system; section 4 illustrates the discussion with a case study—the project of HSR for the Basque Country, Spain; and, finally, section 5 provides the main conclusions and policy implications.

2. Operationalising the concept of sustainable mobility

There is an increasing awareness that continuing on the current path of intensive mobility may contribute to surpassing the limits of a sustainable society. There are not only limits on the capacity of infrastructures, causing increasing congestion, but, more importantly, on the carrying capacity of natural ecosystems to deal with contaminating emissions, land use changes, availability of natural resources, and so on (Rockström et al., 2009; Steffen et al., 2015), and limits on the social boundaries too (Leach et al., 2013). Sustainable transport emerges as a concept requiring transport to be brought back in balance with the natural and social environment, now and in the future—a concept that, far from having a common definition or operational framework, is continually evolving (Gudmundsson et al., 2015).

Given its operational difficulties and profound implications, the concept of sustainable mobility has become blurred in recent European legislative developments. After 20 years of debate, there is still no politically agreed definition of sustainable transport in the EU. Europe's political dilemma between growth and sustainability seems to be at the centre of transport policy. Sustainable mobility is defined, in practical terms, as

> a transport system and transport patterns that can provide the means and opportunities to meet economic, environmental and social needs efficiently and equitably, while minimising avoidable or unnecessary adverse impacts and their associated costs, over relevant space and time scales.
>
> (European Commission, 2001)

The definition lacks a clear hierarchy of objectives, although it highlights the need to decouple economic growth from transport growth. In this sense, Akerman et al. (2000) redefine the objectives of sustainable mobility as technological improvement and the decoupling of transport from economic growth (i.e. a decrease in transport intensity in terms of GDP). The focus is, as a consequence, placed on all the driving forces behind decoupling, including land use policy as well as behavioural and lifestyle changes. The authors also stress the importance of technology in moving policy in the direction of sustainable mobility, especially in the long term.

In another attempt to operationalise the concept of sustainable mobility, Hoyos (2009) defines sustainable mobility as a process that tends to reduce the irreversible environmental degradation of the current transport model while it satisfies the social need of accessibility. This definition encompasses several key issues surrounding the concept of sustainable mobility: (1) environment is an essential element of the development process; (2) sustainable mobility, more than being a static representation, is a process (i.e. it requires permanent actions and not single solutions); (3) sustainable mobility can only be defined within a broader framework of sustainable development; (4) reducing irreversible environmental degradation requires giving priority to the use of renewable resources; (5) transport is a means (and not an end) to meet needs (and not wishes); and, finally, (6) political action must insist on providing accessibility and not transport, i.e. pursuing the satisfaction of necessities favouring their proximity, instead of feeding the number and length of movements.

In addition, Hoyos (2009) argues that in order to ensure that the social access demand does not exceed the environmental limits, a turnaround is required concerning public policies directed towards the achievement of three hierarchical goals: (1) reducing the need for transport; (2) rebalancing the modal allocation in favour of more environmentally friendly modes of transport; and (3) improving the eco-efficiency of trips. The accomplishment of these goals requires a systemic approach, capable of designing strategies conceived from a holistic and cross-disciplinary viewpoint, in which all policies with effects on mobility (land and urban planning, industrial and energy policy, etc.) participate integrally with special attention to the source of problems. Additionally, an awareness on the part of citizens, enterprises and institutions is necessary in order to change their behaviour regarding transport and lifestyle, as well as encourage active social participation in the design of policies. In sum, the sustainable mobility approach requires actions to reduce the need to travel, to encourage modal shift, to reduce the length of trips and to encourage greater efficiency of the transport system (Banister, 2008).

In this vein, the use of hierarchies has been proposed to guide prioritisation in complex policy areas such as waste management, energy or, more recently, transportation. In fact, some examples of these approaches can already be found in the transport policy literature. For example, it is not uncommon to find in transport assessment guidance the recommendation to always start by reducing the need to travel, especially by car, or the assertion that building new infrastructures should always be a last resort. In this sense, Dalkmann and Brannigan (2007) recommend a three-level "avoid-shift-improve" model to classify (and prioritise) carbon reduction measures. More recently, a transport hierarchy (TH) approach has been proposed by the Sustainable Development Commission (2011) in the United Kingdom. Rather than trying to meet all the (sometimes contradictory) objectives, previous approaches provide a decision-making tool for transport policy aimed at ensuring that most sustainable transport solutions are prioritised. The TH provides a general framework for the assessment of transport systems from a sustainability perspective. As shown in Table 8.1, the TH establishes a priority order for the design and management of transport systems, differentiating four levels of priority: (1) demand minimisation; (2) modal shift and intermodality; (3) efficiency optimisation; and (4) capacity increase.

For the main purpose of this chapter—i.e. evaluating the environmental contribution of HSR—the TH approach may be considered a useful starting point. This operational framework is coherent with the approaches proposed by Akerman et al. (2000), Banister (2008) and Hoyos (2009) and, as a consequence, it will be the basis for evaluating the environmental contribution of HSR in the next section, where it will be further developed.

3. A transport hierarchy approach to evaluating the contribution of HSR to sustainable mobility

The TH approach provides a general framework for transport assessment by establishing a priority order in transport systems' design and management. The priority order that it establishes is based on the application of lifecycle assessment (LCA), and any departure from this hierarchy should be properly justified in the framework provided by lifecycle thinking (JRC/IES, 2010). Consequently, the TH is found to be a valuable tool for making decisions and for testing proposals.

LCA is a technique that calculates the environmental impact of a product or service (e.g. the provision of transport) from a holistic perspective, considering its complete lifecycle from the extraction of its raw materials through to its eventual disposal, re-use or recycling. In a LCA, inputs and outputs of energy, materials, resources and waste are systematically quantified at every lifecycle stage, allowing an overall assessment of different specific environmental impacts[2] based

Table 8.1 Transport hierarchy approach.

		Best sustainability options
Priority 1	Demand reduction for powered transport	Reduce the need for powered transport. This can be achieved through a wide range of measures from good spatial planning through to technological solutions such as telecommuting. If some of these measures result in increased demand for walking and cycling this should be viewed positively.
Priority 2	Modal shift to more sustainable and space-efficient modes	Modal shift to more sustainable and space-efficient modes: a shifting away from motorised modes to cycling and walking; b shifting from private motor vehicles to public transport. Includes better integration between different public transport systems, walking and cycling.
Priority 3	Efficiency improvements of existing modes	Efficiency improvements to existing modes: a behavioural changes, including: encouraging higher occupancy rates for both private vehicles (e.g. lift sharing) and public transport; promotion of car clubs; promotion of eco-driving techniques; incentives to spread demand peaks on public transport, etc; b technical interventions to improve vehicle efficiency – prioritising public transport efficiency improvements over private vehicles; c technical interventions to promote more efficient use of transport infrastructure and networks.
Priority 4	Capacity increases for powered transport	Capacity increases should only be considered once the first three steps have been fully explored. Any capacity increases that are required should be prioritised to the most efficient and sustainable modes.
		Worst sustainability options

Source: Sustainable Development Commission, 2011.

on available lifecycle databases such as Ecoinvent[3] or the European Life Cycle Database,[4] which include transport data sections.

In general terms, the impact in a specific environmental category can be expressed as the product of the transport serviced (measured in terms of passenger-kilometre (pkm) or tonnes-kilometre (tkm)) and a factor that relates to the characteristics of that specific transport mode, such as vehicle capacity and occupancy, and the proportionality factor between the vehicle movement and the impact category under assessment. For example, when evaluating the climate change potential of transport, GHG emissions can be calculated by formula (1) when a vehicle transports people:

$$\text{Emissions}\big[\text{kg CO}_{2e}\big] = \text{Passengers}\big[\text{p}\big] \times \text{Journey}\big[\text{km}\big]$$
$$\times \frac{\text{VehicleEmissions}\big[\text{gCO}_{2e}\,/\,\text{km}\big]}{\text{VehicleCapacity}\big[\text{p}\big] \times \text{Occupancy}\big[\%\big]} \qquad (1)$$

And by (2) when it transports freight:

$$\text{Emissions}\big[\text{kg CO}_{2e}\big] = \text{Freight}\big[\text{t}\big] \times \text{Journey}\big[\text{km}\big]$$
$$\times \frac{\text{VehicleEmissions}\big[\text{gCO}_{2e}\,/\,\text{km}\big]}{\text{VehicleCapacity}\big[\text{t}\big] \times \text{Loading}\big[\%\big]} \qquad (2)$$

Actually, formulae (1) and (2) give direct clues of the available paths to reduce impacts in transportation: reducing transport (measured in terms of pkm, tkm); reducing impacts by changing from one transport mode to a different one characterised by lower impacts; or reducing impacts associated with a specific vehicle by improving its efficiency (for example, reducing vehicle emissions), or increasing its capacity and its occupancy (or loading, in the case of freight transport) (Bueno, 2012). Once more, these paths are practically coincident with the priority options of the TH. In the following, we aim to analyse the conditions and requirements that the TH imposes on new HSR lines. For simplicity, we will base our discussion on the environmental category of global warming potential (GWP), measured in terms of kgCO_2e of GHG emissions.

When evaluating the contribution of HSR to sustainability using the TH approach, it is important to note that constructing a new HSR line goes directly to the last option (capacity increase), which makes it a difficult starting point from which to obtain a "positive" environmental assessment. A first conclusion that can be drawn from the above is that building a new HSR as a means to achieve sustainable mobility patterns would seem to have doubtful results. However, it is compulsory to evaluate its contribution to sustainable mobility according to the first three steps of the TH ladder, especially, if rather than a new HSR, we aim to assess transport policies that intend to modernise conventional railway lines into HSR lines. More specifically, some important questions need to be answered: (1) will the new HSR line reduce demand for transport? (Priority 1); (2) will the new HSR line enable a shift from other transport modes with a higher environmental impact? (Priority 2); and (3) will the new HSR line increase the efficiency of transport? (Priority 3).

3.1 Priority 1: Minimising demand

In accordance with the concept of sustainable mobility (see e.g. Hoyos, 2009), the first priority, following the TH, underlines the need to focus on accessibility as opposed to mobility. This step is about engineering whole systems so that goods and services that meet the needs of society can be better accessed with less need for motorised transport. However, the problem of new infrastructures is that due to the effect of induced demand, overall transport demand increases when supply increases. There are different estimations of induced transport, but most authors have found that developing new HSR induces a latent demand in the range of 20 per cent, from the quite modest in lines like Madrid–Barcelona (around 9 per cent) to the very high in Paris–Lyon (49 per cent) or Wuhan–Guangzhou (45 per cent) (Givoni and Dobruszkes, 2013).

Figure 8.1 shows graphically the methodology for the calculation of the environmental impact reduction in a specific category for a simplified generic case where a new HSR line is put into service complementary to two other generic transport modes, MODE1 and MODE2, already in operation.

On the one hand, HSR infrastructure start-up leads to transport movements from other modes; on the other hand, it leads to new induced traffic on the HSR line which is non-existent in the transport system without HSR. The environmental impact per transport system is calculated multiplying the transport per mode

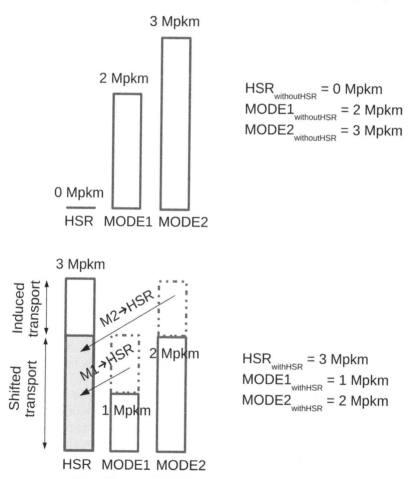

Figure 8.1 Graphic representation of transport in MODE1, MODE2 and HSR in two alternative transport systems, one without HSR (above), and another one in which an HSR line is put in service (below).

(e.g. $MODE1_{withoutHSR}$ is the annual transport serviced in MODE1 expressed in pkm in the system without HSR) by the environmental impact coefficients per mode (e.g. in the GHG emissions calculation, c_{MODE1} is the GHG emissions factor in gCO_2e/pkm in MODE1). The reduction associated with the infrastructure start-up is the subtraction of the impacts without and with the HSR in service.

$$REDUCTION = MODE1_{withoutHSR} \cdot c_{MODE1} + MODE2_{withoutHSR} \cdot c_{MODE2}$$
$$- \left\{ \begin{array}{l} HSR_{withHSR} \cdot c_{HSR} + MODE1_{withHSR} \cdot c_{MODE1} \\ + MODE2_{withHSR} \cdot c_{MODE2} \end{array} \right\} \quad (3)$$

If we suppose that environmental impact coefficients per mode are identical in both scenarios, with/without HSR, then (3) can be rewritten:

$$REDUCTION = \left(MODE1_{withoutHSR} - MODE1_{withHSR} \right) \cdot c_{MODE1} +$$
$$\left(MODE2_{withoutHSR} - MODE2_{withHSR} \right) \cdot c_{MODE2}$$
$$- HSR_{withHSR} \cdot c_{HSR} \quad (4)$$

However, the HSR line transport is the sum of transports shifted from the other modes plus the induced transport:

$$HSR_{withHSR} = \left(MODE1_{withoutHSR} - MODE1_{withHSR} \right) +$$
$$\left(MODE2_{withoutHSR} - MODE2_{withHSR} \right)$$
$$+ HSR_{induced} = \left(M1 \rightarrow HSR \right) + \left(M2 \rightarrow HSR \right) + HSR_{induced} \quad (5)$$

The environmental impact reduction can be rewritten as:

$$REDUCTION = \left(M1 \rightarrow HSR \right) \left(c_{MODE1} - c_{HSR} \right) + \left(M2 \rightarrow HSR \right) \cdot$$
$$\left(c_{MODE2} - c_{HSR} \right) - HSR_{induced} \cdot c_{HSR} \quad (6)$$

The environmental impact reduction derived from the HSR line start-up can therefore be calculated as the sum of transports derived from other modes to the HSR line multiplied by the difference of the transport environmental impact factors (gCO_2e/pkm) in the transport mode of origin of the diverted transport and in the HSR line, subtracting the new transport induced in the HSR line multiplied by the environmental impact factor of transport in the HSR line.

This latter formula is very important because it shows not only the potential of HSR lines to reduce certain environmental impacts but also the limits of said reduction. HSR lines can reduce impact in certain environmental categories provided the HSR transport presents impact coefficients below those of other modes. However, this requires traffic diverted from other modes to present sufficient volume, once the effect of the new traffic is discounted. Actually, it could be the case that the environmental impact linked to the induced transport in the new line might overwhelm the benefits of shifting transport from other modes. In that case, putting the new HSR line into service would not provide a net reduction of overall environmental impacts.

3.2 Priority 2: Enabling modal shift

The second priority of the TH approach is modal shift and intermodality. This priority step seeks to enable delivery of a higher proportion of the demand for transport by more sustainable modes. In this sense, the commissioning of a new HSR line may imply a modal shift from other modes with a higher environmental impact of transport (i.e. short-haul flights, long-distance car journeys). At this point it must be remembered that lifecycle thinking requires that not only operation, but also construction, maintenance and disposal of the transport systems are considered. Therefore, when comparing two alternative transport systems in which the difference between them is the construction and putting into service of a new HSR line, the environmental burdens of the new line need to be considered. Construction and maintenance burdens of the other transport modes cancel out, as they are more or less similar in both scenarios.

Burdens linked to construction and maintenance of transport infrastructure, especially HSR lines, are not negligible. Table 8.2 shows data taken from the bibliography for some HSR lines, most of them already in service.

Table 8.2 GHG emissions linked to construction and maintenance of some lines – emissions expressed in terms per pkm assuming a lifetime of 60 years.

		km	*Millions annual passengers*	*$MtCO_2$*	*tCO_2/km per year*	*gCO_2/pkm*
Basque Y	(Bueno et al., 2016)	180	2.45	2.71	251	102.6
LGV Méditerranée	(Baron et al., 2011)	250	15.8	1.44	96	6.1
South Europe Atlantic HSR	(Baron et al., 2011)	302	15.5	1.43	79	5.1
Taipei–Kaohsiung	(Baron et al., 2011)	345	19.9	5.59	270	13.6
Beijing–Tianjin	(Baron et al., 2011)	117	23.0	1.46	208	9.1
California HSR	(Chester and Horvath, 2010)	1,100	24.2	9.7	147	6.1
Beijing–Shanghai	(Yue et al., 2015)	1,318	47.1	37.2	470	6.0
Hanover–Würzburg	(Von Rozycki et al., 2003)	325	15.5	2.9	149	9.7
Madrid–Barcelona	(Sanz et al., 2014)	621	4	6.9	185	46.5
Europabanan	(Akerman, 2011)	740		4.0		
San Francisco–Anaheim	(Chang and Kendall, 2011)	725		2.4		

When considering a lifetime of 60 years, GHG emissions burdens linked to construction and maintenance of HSR lines covered in Table 8.2 range from 79 tonnes CO_2e/km per year for the South Europe Atlantic HSR up to 470 tonnes CO_2e/km per year for the Beijing–Shanghai line, in carbon-intensive China. When annual passengers using these lines are taken into account, most of these burdens average in the range of 5–15 gCO_2e/pkm. These burdens linked to construction and maintenance are not negligible, and have to be added to the emissions linked to movement of vehicles, which may average 20 gCO_2e/pkm, depending on occupancy (see Figure 8.2). Anyway, these burdens may imply a net reduction when transport is shifted to HSR lines from other modes with a higher emissions factor of transport, such as short-haul flights (127.1 gCO_2e/pkm; see Figure 8.2), or long-distance car journeys (101.6 gCO_2e/pkm). But an important requisite is needed for a modal shift to HSR in order for the previous to be true: total usage of the HSR line (measured in terms of passengers per year, for the whole length of the line) has to be sufficiently high in order to minimise the impact associated with infrastructure construction and maintenance burdens. Data from Spanish lines clearly show this important aspect. A quite modest usage of the Madrid–Barcelona line of just 4 million annual passengers would maintain emissions linked to construction and maintenance over 46 gCO_2e/pkm, deeply curtailing any important cut in emissions due to transport shifting. Potential reduction would be almost cancelled in the case of the Basque Y line, still under construction, for which usage projections do not surpass 2.5 million passengers a year, as we shall show later (see section 4).

Thus, Priority 2 of the TH requires that this modal shift ensures a minimum usage of the new HSR line, sufficient to guarantee that environmental burdens linked to construction and maintenance (measured in pkm terms) are well below the direct impact reduction derived from modal shift.

3.3 Priority 3: Optimising system efficiency

The third step of the TH approach is efficiency optimisation. The focus in this step is on engineering transport systems such that the residual demand for each transport mode is delivered with the smallest negative environmental impact possible, in our case in terms of GHG emissions.

Transport by HSR is considered very efficient when compared to other transport modes (Jehanno et al., 2011). Although total energy consumption by HSR trains is high, other factors compensate in terms of overall consumption when measured in terms of per pkm: HSR lines tend to present higher load factors than other modes (i.e. cars); HSR routes are shorter and more direct than those using conventional railway lines or road; energy consumed in auxiliary services is reduced too, as it depends on journey time and reduces with speed; and higher speeds also allow for lighter breaking in downhill phases, significantly alleviating breaking losses. Actually, HSR trains are considered to provide a net energy consumption reduction when compared to improved conventional trains (García Álvarez, 2010). Although aerodynamic drag is much higher in HSR units (over 70 per cent), they consume less in all other aspects. The energy needed to overcome mechanical resistance, losses in auxiliary systems, and losses in the network and in the locomotive may be reduced by a third, and energy dissipated by the brake may be reduced by more than a half. Also, more energy can be recovered by regenerative braking in HSR trains than in conventional units. However, efficiency optimisation is also possible in all other transport systems. In this subsection, we will focus on one aspect of efficiency optimisation—increasing vehicle occupancy—which is critical in every transport mode. The potential for improvement of vehicle occupancy is not generally limited by technological conditions, and may be very significant in some transport modes, such as movement in private cars, which show average occupancies well below 50 per cent.

Figure 8.2 shows GHG emissions calculations provided by García Álvarez (2007), linked to vehicle movement in five different transport modes (aeroplane, conventional train, car, bus and HSR) for a Madrid–Barcelona journey. Figure 8.2 shows emissions when average occupancy is assumed in each transport mode: 127.1 gCO_2e/pkm by aeroplane with an occupation of 75 per cent; 101.6 gCO_2e/pkm by car with an occupation of 30 per cent; 23.2 gCO_2e/pkm by conventional train where average occupation is 64 per cent; 22.9 gCO_2e/pkm by bus with an average occupation of 61 per cent; and 20.89 gCO_2e/pkm by HSR, where the estimated average occupation is 70 per cent.

If high utilisation of the HSR line is ensured (and provided by shifted transport from other modes), then HSR transport is found to be more efficient than competing transport modes, such as short-haul flights (20.9 vs 127.1 gCO_2e/pm). But Figure 8.2 shows clearly that this relative advantage of HSR transport requires constantly high occupancies in HSR vehicles and low occupancy rates in other transport modes. Emissions in cars with high occupancies (greater than 80 per cent) are comparable to those in HSR with modest occupancies (50 per cent), especially if burdens from construction are also considered. This high sensitivity to occupancy is also stressed by other authors (Chester and Horvath, 2009; Chester and Horvath, 2010; Westin and Kågeson, 2012). Other technological factors, such as aerodynamic improvements, weight reduction, engine optimisation and electrification of traction, present a great potential for efficiency improvements in road transport. That means, clearly, that construction of new HSR lines is not the only way, and probably not even the best way to optimise transport system efficiency in general.

4. Lifecycle assessment of a new HSR in Spain: The Basque Y

This section is based on the results of a simplified LCA of a new HSR line projected in the Basque Autonomous Community (BAC), Spain, known as the Basque Y (for details, see Bueno et al., 2016).

The mountainous Basque topography is highly complicated for railways in general, and for HSR in particular, due to the strict design required to ensure high speeds (e.g. minimum railway curve radius). The Basque Y is part of an administrative plan to improve regional communications and promote the transition to sustainable transport in the region in the coming decades, explicitly

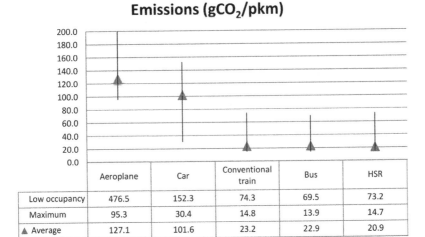

Figure 8.2 GHG emissions linked to vehicle movement for a Madrid–Barcelona journey in five different transport modes (528 km by aeroplane, 708 km by conventional train, 621 km by car, 632 km by bus and 627 km by HSR). Low occupancy is 20 per cent in all modes, maximum is 100 per cent, and average occupancy is 75 per cent in aeroplane, 30 per cent in car, 64 per cent in conventional train, 61 per cent in bus and 70 per cent in HSR.

aimed at mitigating climate change and reducing energy consumption (Basque Government, 2012; 2015; Ente Vasco de la Energía, 2012). The projected infrastructure is a star-shaped European gauge (International Union of Railways (UIC)) HSR covering 180 km, connecting the region's three capitals and characterised by the enormous technical complexity imposed by the topography (60 per cent of the layout is through tunnels and 10 per cent over viaducts), translating into a vast budget (6,000 million euros). It is planned that the line will be connected to the Spanish and French HSR networks in an undefined future. Its construction began in 2006 and its start-up is expected after 2020. The network is built to support a combined traffic of passengers and freight. In fact, the scenarios from the Basque Government (2012) attribute the greatest emissions and energy savings potential to freight transport.

However, LCA studies of the HSR Spanish network in general (García Álvarez, 2010) and specific studies for the Basque Y (Basque Government, 2012) do not include in the assessment the emissions and energy involved in the construction of the infrastructure, despite the scientific consensus on its importance (Baron et al., 2011; Cour des Comptes, 2014; Sims et al., 2014). Thus, although the Basque administration publicly insists on a potential emissions savings of approximately 425 tonnes of CO_2 per day, this analysis has yet to be performed on the entire infrastructure lifecycle. Therefore, the main objective of this simplified LCA was to consistently assess the potential contribution of this new infrastructure to GHG emissions and energy consumption in the BAC.[5]

Additionally, in order to gain a more realistic picture, we decided to model future scenarios in a dynamic way. While the demand scenarios from the Basque Government report (2012) are considered according to 2010 levels of the value of critical parameters, such as the characteristics of the electric mix (i.e. renewables share) or the electrification of road transport, we estimated them dynamically using as a reference the Basque government's own reports, complemented by EU roadmaps.

Our calculation of the loads associated with the construction of the Basque Y is based on the lifecycle inventory of the HSR infrastructure construction and maintenance included in the *Carbon Footprint of High Speed Rail* report (Baron et al., 2011). The calculations provide a carbon footprint of 251 tCO$_2$/km (see Table 8.3), on the upper end of the 96–270 tCO$_2$/km curve provided by Baron et al. (2011). This means a total carbon footprint of 2.71 MtCO$_2$, or 251 tCO$_2$/km yearly over a 60-year lifetime.

To calculate the energy consumption burdens associated with the Basque Y construction, we assumed an emissions factor of 4.7 CO$_2$/toe, coherent with the calculations of reports which have estimated both the carbon footprint and energy consumption in the construction of other large infrastructures (Botniabanan AB, 2010; Acciona Infraestructuras, 2015). This factor provides an annual consumption burden of 9.6 ktoe over all its lifetime (53.4 toe/km).

The Basque Y project considers, in its optimistic scenario, traffic of 4.94 million passengers in 2020 (Basque Government, 2012), which corresponds to 2.45 million travellers per annum over the entire infrastructure layout, since due to its star shape no passenger ever travels the entire 180 km of network. The emissions burden associated with the construction of 251 tCO$_2$ per layout kilometre and year, distributed among 2.45 million passengers, is equal to a footprint of 102.6 gCO$_2$/pkm (see Table 8.2). This burden on the Basque Y is of a higher order magnitude than on other HSR lines, essentially due to the very scarce provision of passenger transport demand—i.e. under 2.5 million per annum. With such low usage, the supposed benefit of 80.7 gCO$_2$/pkm of moving a car

Table 8.3 Annual carbon footprint of elements and components linked to the construction and maintenance of the Basque Y.

Basque Y (60-year lifetime)	tCO$_2$/km, tCO$_2$/station	Units	Lifetime	Total
Conception	0.45	180 km		81
Earthwork	37	54 km	60 years	1,998
Building roads	31.6	180 km	30 years	5,688
Large viaducts	305	18 km	60 years	5,490
Tunnels	285	108 km	60 years	30,780
Railway equipment	3.5	180 km	50 years	630
Secondary stations	55	2 stations	60 years	110
Main stations	136.7	3 stations	60 years	410
Basque Y (per year)	251 tCO$_2$/km	180 km		45,187 tCO$_2$

passenger ($101.6\,gCO_2$/pkm) to HSR ($20.9\,gCO_2$/pkm) is virtually null due to the burden associated with the infrastructure construction ($102.6\,gCO_2$/pkm), as shown in Figure 8.2. Burdens associated with infrastructure construction can never be ignored; however, as they imply a fixed burden, their weight can be significantly reduced in pkm terms if a sufficient number of annual passengers can be guaranteed.

The results for our central scenario[6] are displayed in Figure 8.3. For comparison purposes, results from a static scenario (regarding road electrification and renewables penetration) are represented by dashed lines. Figure 8.3 shows how progressive road transport electrification fed with renewable electricity softens the sloping curve, particularly after 30 years' operation, whereby at the end of the useful infrastructure lifetime the carbon footprint associated with construction is still far from full amortisation, with a final deficit of $0.9\,MtCO_2$. As to energy savings, electrification with renewables means that compensation of the environmental burdens linked to construction is delayed by 15 years, leaving a final net positive balance of only 39 ktoe. Even non-compliance of transport electrification and renewability targets (static scenario—i.e. the most optimistic scenario) would not guarantee the achievement of any net emissions reduction at the end of lifetime, and the final energy balance (297 ktoe) would be less than 5 per cent of the primary energy supply in the Basque Country in 2010 (Ente Vasco de la Energía, 2012). Similar balances would be achieved on extending the infrastructure lifetime to 100 years.

To improve its environmental balance, the Basque Y would have to considerably increase passenger transport diverted from other modes. However, the potential of passenger transport increase on the Basque Y at the expense of long-haul transport (air and rail) is very limited. The greatest potential comes from car journeys, but 73 per cent of those made in the BAC in 2014 were short haul (OTEUS, 2015). In addition, sensitivity analysis indicates the great importance of freight traffic in amending the environmental balance in the case of the Basque Y, as already noted by Akerman (2011) for the Europabanan line in Sweden. This is due to the negligible passenger transport prevision, a mere 2.45 million per annum over the entire layout, against a minimum threshold of 10 million passengers proposed by Westin and Kågeson (2012) for a line with much less constructive complexity. However, it is also important to bear in mind that HSR lines may not be compatible for passenger and freight transport for both technical and economic reasons (Ekai Center, 2013; Bermejo and Hoyos, 2016).

To conclude this section, the unfavourable environmental assessment of the Basque Y in terms of GHG emissions and energy consumption reductions must be contextualised within the bubble of Spanish infrastructure (and construction in general) during the last 20 years. In fact, Spain is currently the second country in the world in terms of kilometres of HSR (after China), having created a huge oversupply (and debt) due to a combination of bad governance, capture and political interests (Aguilera Klink and Naredo Pérez, 2009; Bel et al., 2013).

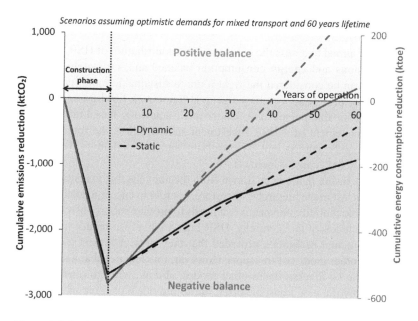

Figure 8.3 Environmental balance of Basque Y CO_2 emissions and energy consumption (central dynamic and static scenarios).

5. Conclusions

After massive investment in transport infrastructures over the past half a century, traditional supply-side policies (i.e. dealing with increasing transport demand by providing new infrastructures) have promoted economic growth and better transport infrastructures, but they have failed to provide net benefits to society due to a series of environmentally and socially undesirable effects: congestion, GHG emissions, etc. As a consequence, transport policy in the EU has struggled between growth as the centrepiece of European treaties and environmental and social protection commitments. However, the indefinite continuation of current trends in transport would be unsustainable in relation to the environmental impact, in particular with regard to global warming, as transport is one of the most polluting sectors and its ability to lower its emissions has been somewhat limited.

Sustainable mobility requires both transport and land use planning to promote actions to reduce the demand and journey length for motorised transport, to encourage modal shift and to increase the efficiency of the transport system. Given its environmental performance, the promotion of rail transport has become an important element in achieving more sustainable paths of mobility. However, HSR appears to be in a rather uncomfortable position—it uses more energy than conventional rail, but less than road and air transport—and its overall efficiency is dependent upon high occupancy factors. Furthermore, promoting HSR will be counterproductive for sustainable mobility if it induces a demand for transport and increases the length of trips, and if it favours urban sprawl processes (Givoni and Banister, 2012a).

This chapter aimed to assess the environmental contribution of HSR, focusing on GHG emissions and energy consumption balance and, ultimately, evaluating whether it can be considered the right route to sustainable mobility. For this purpose, we used the TH approach as a general framework for the assessment of HSR from a sustainable perspective. Under this framework, based on LCA, the design and management of a HSR investment should follow the four levels of priority: (1) demand minimisation; (2) modal shift and intermodality; (3) efficiency optimisation; and (4) capacity increase.

The first conclusion that can be drawn from the above is that investing in new HSR lines ranks last in the hierarchy; therefore, in order to ensure a positive effect from a sustainable mobility perspective, it needs to provide robust positive results in the first three levels of the hierarchy. HSR lines are likely to reduce impacts on certain environmental categories provided that they present impact coefficients below those of other modes of transport. However, this requires that a significant volume of traffic be diverted from other modes, able not only to overcome the traffic induced by the new transport offer, but to provide a positive net effect. If this is not the case, new investments in HSR would result in an increase in overall environmental impact.

Regarding the second level of the TH, in order to evaluate whether a significant shift from modes with a higher environmental impact is achieved, it is important to conduct a proper LCA to consider not only the operation, but also the construction, maintenance and disposal of the new HSR line. In this sense, these additional burdens derived from adding new infrastructure to the transport system may overwhelm or significantly reduce benefits derived from modal shift. In this respect too, HSR seems to have had a modest impact on modal shift: by doubling the network between 1995 and 2008, HSR increased its share in the demand for rail from 16 per cent in 2000 to 24 per cent in 2008, but there was a reduction in the rail network's modal share from 6.6 per cent to 6.3 per cent (Givoni and Banister, 2012b). Furthermore, in countries like Spain, investments in HSR are provoking a progressive abandonment of conventional lines.

Although it is true that HSR shows a remarkable level of energy efficiency, the third level of the TH highlights the fact that these efficiency improvements require the traffic to be diverted from less sustainable modes (i.e. aeroplanes and private cars with low occupation), but not from similarly efficient modes such as bus or conventional train. Furthermore, if dynamic scenarios are considered and overall demand is induced, then the energy arguments favouring investments in HSR are considerably less clear. In this context, the role of the Trans–European Network may be controversial: it may favour sustainable mobility by achieving a significant modal shift from road and air to rail, but it may increase overall mobility, so the net effect may be negative.

Taking into account the magnitude of the environmental problem, as well as the commitments already signed by the EU, the most important contribution of

HSR to sustainable mobility lies in its potential for environmental impact reductions, especially with regard to GHG emissions and energy consumption. In an illustrative example of the Basque Y project in Spain, we show that net GHG emissions reductions are not likely to exist in a time horizon below 50 years, which goes against fulfilling the European goal of reducing GHG emissions by 80 per cent by 2050.

Acknowledgements

Financial support from the University of the Basque Country (UPV/EHU) under research grants UFI11/03 and US15/11, from the Department of Education of the Basque Government through grant IT-642-13 (UPV/EHU Econometrics Research Group) and from the Spanish Ministry of Economy and Competitiveness through grant ECO2014-52587-R is gratefully acknowledged.

Notes

1 The chapter focuses on the GHG emissions and energy consumption balance; however, the reader should bear in mind that other environmental dimensions are also affected by the construction and operation of HSR lines, such as habitat fragmentation, impact on flora and fauna (affecting biodiversity), occupation of fertile land, landscape and visual impact, noise and vibrations, etc. In fact, impacts are generally similar along roads and railways (Jehanno et al., 2011; Cour des Comptes, 2014; Dorsey et al., 2015).
2 For example, the Environmental Product Declaration for the railway infrastructure on the Bothnia Line (Botniabanan AB, 2010) considers the following environmental impacts: use of non-renewable and renewable materials, non-renewable and renewable energy, recycled resources, water, land use; global warming, acidification, ozone depletion, photochemical oxidant formation, eutrophication; generation of materials for recycling, hazardous waste, excess soil and other wastes.
3 www.ecoinvent.org/database/database.html.
4 http://eplca.jrc.ec.europa.eu/ELCD3/processList.xhtml.
5 Additionally, some methodological errors from the original report (Basque Government, 2012) were detected and corrected during the analysis in relation to the consideration of journeys outside the Basque Y and the assumption of substantial improvements in conventional railway infrastructure that are not consistently considered (see Bueno et al. (2016) for details).
6 This LCA considers a main scenario with the following assumptions: (1) infrastructure lifetime is 60 years; (2) mixed passenger and freight transport; (3) constant transport demand throughout infrastructure lifecycle, based on the official estimations for 2020 (Basque Government, 2008; 2012; Adif, 2009); (4) dynamic scenario with progressive road transport electrification (+15 per cent annual growth from 2020 until reaching a 56 per cent share in 2050) and decarbonisation of the power system (+10 per cent annual reduction in the emissions factor of electricity until almost total decarbonisation by 2050, $5gCO_2/MJ$) following European Commission (2011a; 2011b), Ente Vasco de la Energía (2012) and Basque Government (2015); and (5) energy intensities from the Basque Government (2012) for passenger and freight transport. Four other complementary scenarios are considered for sensitivity analysis: static context for road electrification and renewables penetration, 100-year lifetime, passenger transport only (no freight), and realistic freight transport demand.

References

Acciona Infracstructuras (2015). "*'Arroyo Valchano' railway bridge*", Environmental Product Declaration, Reg. no. S-P-00455, Madrid: Acciona Infraestructuras, available at http://gryphon.environdec.com/data/files/6/11271/epd455%20Railway%20bridge%20 Arroyo%20Valchano.pdf [accessed 14 April 2014].

Adif (2009). "*Estudio de mercado de viajeros y rentabilidad económico-social y financiera de la Línea de Alta Velocidad Madrid-Norte y País Vasco*", Madrid: Gobierno de España, Ministerio de Fomento.

Aguilera Klink, F., Naredo Pérez, J.M. (2009). "*Economía, poder y megaproyectos*", Lanzarote: Fundación César Manrique.

Akerman, J. (2011). "*The role of high-speed rail in mitigating climate change – the Swedish case Europabanan from a life cycle perspective*", Transportation Research Part D: Transport and Environment, 16, 208–217, doi:10.1016/j.trd.2010.12.004.

Akerman, J., Banister, D., Dreborg, K., Nijkamp, P., Schleicher-Tappeser, R., Stead, D., Steen, P. (2000). "*European transport policy and sustainable mobility*", London: Routledge.

Banister, D. (2008). "*The sustainable mobility paradigm*", Transport Policy, 15, 73–80, doi:10.1016/j.tranpol.2007.10.005.

Banister, D., Anderton, K., Bonilla, D., Givoni, M., Schwanen, T. (2011). "*Transportation and the Environment*", Annual Review of Environment and Resources, 36, 247–270, doi:10.1146/annurev-environ-032310-112100.

Baron, T., Martinetti, G., Pépion, D. (2011). "*Carbon footprint of high speed rail*", Paris: International Union of Railways.

Basque Government (2008). "*El petróleo y la energía en la economía. Efectos económicos del encarecimiento del petróleo en la economía vasca*", Vitoria-Gasteiz, Spain: Basque Government, available at http://www.ogasun.ejgv.euskadi.net/r51-19220/es/contenidos/ informacion/estudios_publicaciones_dep/es_publica/adjuntos/petroleo_y_energia.pdf [accessed 4 April 2014].

Basque Government (2012). "*La y Vasca: Un proyecto de país, una conexión internacional*", Vitoria-Gasteiz, Spain: Basque Government.

Basque Government (2015). "*Estrategia de cambio climático 2050 del País Vasco*", Vitoria-Gasteiz, Spain: Basque Government.

Bel, G., Estache, A., Foucart, R. (2013). "*Transport infrastructure failures in Spain: mismanagement and incompetence, or political capture?*", in: Soreide, T., Williams, A. (Eds), "*Corruption, grabbing and development: Real world challenges*", Cheltenham, UK: Edward Elgar, p. 129.

Bermejo, R., Hoyos, D. (2016). "*Análisis del origen y desarrollo del proyecto de Y vasca en el contexto de la política europea de transporte*", Working Paper, Bilbao, Spain: University of the Basque Country, Department of Applied Economics I.

Botniabanan AB (2010). "*Environmental product declaration for the railway infrastructure on the Bothnia line*", Environmental Product Declaration Railway Infrastructure, Reg. no. S-P-0019, UN CPC 5321, Sweden: Botniabanan AB.

Bueno, G., (2012). "*Analysis of scenarios for the reduction of energy consumption and GHG emissions in transport in the Basque Country*", Renewable and Sustainable Energy Reviews, 16, 1988–1998, doi:10.1016/j.rser.2012.01.004.

Bueno, G., Hoyos, D., Capellán-Pérez, I. (2016). "*Environmental performance of high speed rail in the Basque Country*", Working Paper, Bilbao, Spain: University of the Basque Country, Department of Electronics Engineering.

Chang, B., Kendall, A. (2011). *"Life cycle greenhouse gas assessment of infrastructure construction for California's high-speed rail system"*, Transportation Research Part D: Transport and Environment, 16, 429–434. doi:10.1016/j.trd.2011.04.004.

Chester, M.V., Horvath, A. (2009). *"Environmental assessment of passenger transportation should include infrastructure and supply chains"*, Environmental Research Letters, 4(2), 024008, doi:10.1088/1748-9326/4/2/024008.

Chester, M., Horvath, A. (2010). *"Life-cycle assessment of high-speed rail: The case of California"*, Environmental Research Letters, 5 (1), 014003, doi:10.1088/1748-9326/5/1/014003.

Cour des Comptes (2014). *"La grande vitesse ferroviaire: Un modèle porté au-delà de sa pertinence"*, Paris: Cour des Comptes.

Dalkmann, H., Brannigan, C. (2007). *"Transport and climate change. Module 5e: Sustainable transport: A sourcebook for policy-makers in developing cities"*, Eschborn, Germany: GTZ, available at http://siteresources.worldbank.org/EXTAFRSUBSAHTRA/Resources/gtz-transport-and-climate-change-2007.pdf [accessed 16 May 2016].

Dorsey, B., Olsson, M., Rew, L.J. (2015). *"Ecological effects of railways on wildlife"*, in: van der Ree, R., Smith, D.J., Grilo, C. (Eds), *"Handbook of road ecology"*, Chichester, UK: John Wiley & Sons Ltd, pp. 219–227.

Ekai Center (2013). *"Evaluación económica de la Y vasca"*, Mondragón, Spain: Ekai Center.

Ente Vasco de la Energía (2012). *"Estrategia energética de Euskadi 2020"*, Bilbao: EVE.

European Commission (1998). *"The common transport policy. Sustainable mobility: Perspectives for the future"*, Communication from the Commission to the Council, the European Parliament, the Economic and Social Committee and the Committee of the Regions, (COM(98) 716 final), Brussels: European Commission.

European Commission (2001). *"Integrated policy aspects of sustainable mobility"*, EXTRA/Thematic Paper, EXTRA Project within the Transport RTD Programme, Fourth Framework Programme, Brussels: European Commission.

European Commission (2010). *"Critical raw materials for the UE"*, Report of the Ad-hoc Working Group on Defining Critical Raw Materials, Brussels: European Commission.

European Commission (2011a). *"A Roadmap for moving to a competitive low carbon economy in 2050"*, Communication from the Commission to the European Parliament, the Council, the European Economic and Social Committee and the Committee of the Regions, (COM(2011) 112 final), Brussels: European Commission.

European Commission (2011b). *"Roadmap to a resource efficient Europe"*, (COM(2011) 571 final), Brussels: European Commission.

García Álvarez, A., (2007). *"Consumo de energía y emisiones del tren de alta velocidad en comparación con otros modos de transporte"*, Anales de Mecánica y Electricidad, 84(5), 26–34.

García Álvarez, A. (2010). *"Energy consumption and emissions of high-speed trains"*, Transportation Research Record, 2159, 27–35, doi:10.3141/2159-04.

Givoni, M., Banister, D. (2012a). *"Reinventing the wheel – planning the rail network to meet mobility needs of the 21st century"*, in: Frenkel, A., Nijkamp, P., McCann, P. (Eds), *"Societies in motion innovation, migration and regional transformation: Essays in honor of Daniel Shefer"*, Cheltenham, UK: Edward Elgar, pp. 320–342.

Givoni, M., Banister, D. (2012b). *"Speed: The less important element of the high-speed train"*, Journal of Transport Geography, 22, 306–307, doi:10.1016/j.jtrangeo.2012.01.024.

Givoni, M., Dobruszkes, F. (2013). *"A review of ex-post evidence for mode substitution and induced demand following the introduction of high-speed rail"*, Transport Review 33, 720–742, doi:10.1080/01441647.2013.853707.

Gudmundsson, H., Hall, R.P., Marsden, G., Zietsman, J. (2015). *"Sustainable transportation: Indicators, frameworks, and performance management"*, Berlin and Heidelberg: Springer-Verlag.

Hoyos, D. (2009). *"Towards an operational concept of sustainable mobility"*, International Journal of Sustainable Development Planning, 4, 158–173, doi:10.2495/SDP-V4-N2-158-173.

Humphreys, M. (2010). *"Sustainability in European transport policy"*, New York: Routledge.

IPCC (2014). *"Climate change 2014. Mitigation of climate change: Working group III contribution to the fifth assessment report of the Intergovernmental Panel on Climate Change"*, New York: Cambridge University Press.

Jehanno, A., Palmer, D., James, C. (2011). *"High speed rail and sustainability"*, Paris: UIC.

JRC/IES (2010). *"ILCD handbook. General guide for life cycle assessment: Detailed guidance"*, Luxembourg: Publications Office of the European Union.

Leach, M., Raworth, K., Rockström, J. (2013). *"Between social and planetary boundaries: Navigating pathways in the safe and just space for humanity"*, in: *"World social science report 2013"*, Paris: OECD, pp. 84–89.

OTEUS (2015). *"Panorámica del transporte en Euskadi, 2014"*, Vitoria-Gasteiz, Spain: Basque Government.

Rockström, J., Steffen, W., Noone, K., Persson, Å., Chapin, F.S., Lambin, E.F., Lenton, T.M., Scheffer, M., Folke, C., Schellnhuber, H.J., Nykvist, B., de Wit, C.A., Hughes, T., van der Leeuw, S., Rodhe, H., Sörlin, S., Snyder, P.K., Costanza, R., Svedin, U., Falkenmark, M., Karlberg, L., Corell, R.W., Fabry, V.J., Hansen, J., Walker, B., Liverman, D., Richardson, K., Crutzen, P., Foley, J.A. (2009). *"A safe operating space for humanity"*, Nature, 461, 472–475, doi:10.1038/461472a.

Sanz, A., Vega, P., Mateos, M., (2014). *"Las cuentas ecológicas del transporte en España"*, Madrid: Libros en Acción.

Sims, R., Schaeffer, R., Creutzig, F., Nunez, X., D'Agosto, M., Dimitriu, D., Meza, M., Fulton, L., Kobayashi, S., Lah, O., McKinnon, A., Newman, P., Ouyang, M., Schauer, J.J., Sperling, D., Tiwari, G. (2014). *"Transport"*, in: Edenhofer, O., Pichs-Madruga, R., Sokona, Y., Farahani, E., Kadner, S., Seyboth, K., Adler, A., Baum, I., Brunner, S., Eickemeier, P., Kriemann, B., Savolainen, J., Schlömer, S., von Stechow, C., Zwickel, T., Minx, J.C. (Eds), *"Climate change 2014: Mitigation of climate change. Contribution of Working Group III to the Fifth Assessment Report of the Intergovernmental Panel on Climate Change"*, Cambridge, UK and New York: Cambridge University Press.

Steffen, W., Richardson, K., Rockström, J., Cornell, S.E., Fetzer, I., Bennett, E.M., Biggs, R., Carpenter, S.R., de Vries, W., de Wit, C.A., Folke, C., Gerten, D., Heinke, J., Mace, G.M., Persson, L.M., Ramanathan, V., Reyers, B., Sörlin, S. (2015). *"Planetary boundaries: Guiding human development on a changing planet"*, Science, 347(6223), 1259855, doi:10.1126/science.1259855.

Sustainable Development Commission (2011). *"Fairness in a car-dependent society"*, London: Sustainable Development Commission.

von Rozycki, C., Koeser, H., Schwarz, H. (2003). *"Ecology profile of the German high-speed rail passenger transport system"*, International Journal of Life Cycle Assessment, 8, 83–91, doi:10.1007/BF02978431.

Westin, J., Kågeson, P. (2012). *"Can high speed rail offset its embedded emissions?"*, Transportation Research Part D: Transport and Environment, 17, 1–7, doi:10.1016/j.trd.2011.09.006.

Yue, Y., Wang, T., Liang, S., Yang, J., Hou, P., Qu, S., Zhou, J., Jia, X., Wang, H., Xu, M. (2015). *"Life cycle assessment of high speed rail in China"*, Transportation Research Part D: Transport and Environment, 41, 367–376, doi:10.1016/j.trd.2015.10.005.

9 Reality and opportunities for on-track competition in HSR

Paolo Beria and Raffaele Grimaldi

1. Introduction: On-track competition in HSR

The very first cases of on-track competition are shyly deploying on the battlefield of the rail arena, trying to open niche long-distance markets behind the front-line of regional franchises. The high-speed (HS) segment remains untouched by competition, with the exception of Italy.

The chapter aims to introduce the main cases of on-track competition in Europe. Despite them being limited, existing experiences (Section 2) help us understand the strategies adopted and outline the possible potential for on-track competition. We provide a schematisation of existing high-speed rail (HSR) models and their implications for potential competition (Section 3) and describe the case of NTV in Italy, the only experience of on-track competition on high-speed lines (HSLs) (Section 4). Conditions for competition to take place and its effect on prices is analysed in the literature (Section 5), in particular the effect of different services operated by NTV in Italy (Section 6). The text concludes (Section 7) with an analysis of possible barriers and of the potential for open-access competition, with a focus on strategies for competitive advantage (cost leadership, product differentiation and niche market focus) and their application by recent newcomers.

2. Cases of on-track competition in the EU

With the adoption of the third rail package in 2007, the current regulation in the EU allows international services to provide "cabotage" of passengers within single member states. The general rule is that open-access services should not compromise the economic equilibrium of existing local public service contracts, but the definition of the criteria is left to local regulators (Office of Rail Regulation, 2009; CER, 2011).

The most visible effect of the rail liberalisation up to now is in regional transport, with many important cases of competition in quite a few European countries (CER, 2011; Alexandersson and Rigas, 2013; Nash et al., 2013). This competition is based on tendering procedures and often referred to as *for the market* (ECMT, 2007). To the contrary, although included in the fourth rail package proposed by the European Commission (European Commission, 2013a) and often even legally possible,[1] just a few countries actually experience competition *in the market* for long-distance services in the open-access regime, moreover with services still limited in numbers (Nash, 2011; Nash et al., 2013).

The following Figure 9.1 and Table 9.1 list and describe the existing open-access services provided by newcomers in 2016. They are present in Italy, Germany, the Czech Republic, Slovakia, Austria, Sweden and the UK. Other open-access operators exist, but operate on international routes not in competition, and are not newcomers, usually being commercial partnerships among incumbents (e.g. Eurostar, Thello, etc.).

Two of the Swedish and all the German newcomers operate in very small, niche local markets (Nash et al., 2013), where the incumbent appears not interested, or runs targeted services, but their impact on competition is barely visible.

The UK operators provide frequent intercity services from London to cities not directly connected by services operated under franchises. Despite being of

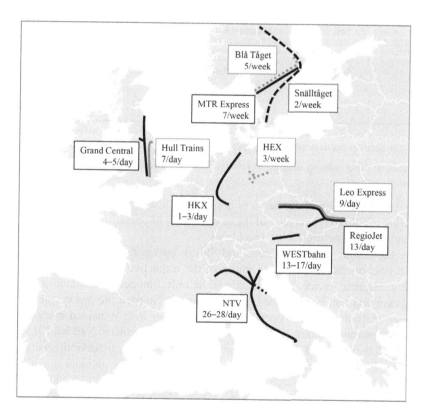

Figure 9.1 Map of open-access long-distance services in Europe operated by newcomers (incumbents' international services excluded).

Table 9.1   List of open-access long-distance services in Europe operated by newcomers in 2016.

Country	Newcomer	Route(s) 2016	Frequency (couples)	Model
Sweden	MTR Express	Gothenburg–Stockholm	7/day	intercity
	Blå Tåget	Gothenburg–Stockholm–Uppsala	5/week	quality service
	Snälltåget (Veolia)	Malmö–Stockholm–Uppsala–Are	2/week	night service
UK	Grand Central	Bradford/Sunderland–London	4–5/day	intercity
	Hull Trains	Hull–London	7/day	intercity
Germany*	HKX	Hamburg–Köln (–Frankfurt)	1–3/day	low-cost
	HEX	Goslar/Blankenburg/Thale–Berlin	3/week	weekends
Czech Rep. and Slovakia	RegioJet	Prague–Ostrava (–Košice) Bratislava–Košice	13/day 3/day	low-cost
	Leo Express	Prague–Ostrava (–Košice)	9/day	low-cost
Austria	Westbahn	Wien–Salzburg	13–17/day	intercity
Italy	NTV	Turin–Milan–Rome–Salerno Venice–Rome–Salerno Verona–Rome–Naples	26–28/day	high-speed

* An open-access service was operated by Inteconnex (Veolia) on the Warnemünde–Berlin–Leipzig route (1–2 frequencies per day), closed in October 2014.

Source: authors' elaborations on companies' websites, consulted December 2015.

some relevance locally, these services account for just 0.7 per cent of the total UK market (CER, 2011) because of the impossibility of operating services on the main routes in competition with franchisees.

Only the Italian, Austrian, Czech and Slovak operators, plus the remaining Swedish one, operate on the main routes of the respective countries offering a relatively frequent service. NTV in Italy is the only European newcomer in the HS segment and will be described later in detail. In Sweden the process of liberalisation started soon, but open-access competition long remained marginal (Alexandersson and Hulten, 2008; Nilsson et al., 2013; Fröidh and Nelldal, 2015), until in 2015 the private MTR Express started operations on the main Gothenburg–Stockholm line. The Austrian WESTbahn runs frequent conventional intercity services on the Wien–Salzburg route and is also integrated with buses to extend the catchment area. Finally, the only case of newcomers is in the Czech Republic on the Prague–Ostrava line (with extensions to Košice, in Slovakia), where both RegioJet and Leo Express face the incumbent, CD, and have adopted a low-cost model (Tomeš et al., 2014).

3. High-speed models and competition

Literature tried different classifications of HSR models according to the level of integration with the rest of the network, speed and types of services (Campos and de Rus, 2009; Perl and Goetz, 2015), and also track pricing (Sanchez-Borras et al., 2010). Table 9.2 summarises the main concepts.

Actually, each country adopted specific combinations of the characteristics in Table 9.2, resulting in quite different HSR services. For example, Japan opted for fully separated HSR corridors, connecting the main cities and using dedicated fast trains. This model foresees no integration with the rest of the network, which is consequently limited to interchange at stations. Germany, however, built selective fast doublings on key sections or where punctuality problems required local solutions. These links are usually not faster than 250 km/h, but can be used by the normal ICE trains (and in some cases even by freight trains), on the conventional network. Crucially, Germany did not build a national HSR infrastructure, but opted for a nationwide network of fast intercity services. On the other hand, Spain built a totally new nationwide infrastructure, used both by dedicated trains and by trains that can switch to the conventional network to extend the range of HSR services to unconnected cities. France and Italy built single fast lines on high-demand routes and used exclusively by fast trains[2] but, as in Spain, such trains can also run on conventional lines (Campos and de Rus, 2009; Albalate and Bel, 2012; Perl and Goetz, 2015).

Interestingly, these variants – and the consequent models – also have consequences in terms of actual or potential competition, besides the normative (Beria et al., 2012; European Commission, 2013b) and governance (Nash, 2008; Weidmann and Nash, 2008; Finger, 2014) frameworks, considered and commented on elsewhere. In particular, the need for dedicated and fast trains results on the one side in more expense and on the other introduces a degree of irreversibility in the investment choices. Both facts make actual competition more difficult.

Table 9.2 Characteristics of HSR models

	Options available
Separation HS/conventional lines	• Full separation/independent networks • Connections HS/conventional lines • Selective fast doublings
Speed	• 200 km/h–350 km/h
Trains	• Conventional trains • Dedicated HSR trains
Type of network	• Fast doublings of selected segments • Single lines/exclusive corridors • Hybrid networks • Brand new full network
Track access charging	• Mark-ups to social marginal cost (MC+) • Full financial cost minus subsidies (FC–) • Social marginal cost pricing (SMC)

A first aspect is that interoperable HSR systems, such as the French, Spanish or Italian ones, are less demanding than the Japanese one in terms of rolling stock (similar standards) and less binding.[3] However, the need for speed remains crucial and cheaper or second-hand conventional trains cannot be used. The German model, eliminating de facto the distinction between HS and conventional tracks, could be in this sense more open to competition.[4]

A second element is the type of network and, in particular, the density of demand on corridors. High-demand corridors (e.g. Tokyo–Osaka, Paris–Lyon or Milan–Rome) can adapt to competition because demand is abundant (and maybe not totally exploited by the incumbent, e.g. between Milan and Rome before the entry of NTV into the market, see below). However, a competitor aiming at a non-marginal market share must provide a level of supply comparable to the incumbent one, which requires very significant investments, particularly in specialised systems like the Japanese one.

Thirdly, infrastructure access charges are likely to have an impact on traffic levels and mode split. In particular, in the majority of cases analysed, the charges exceed even the optimal Ramsey mark-ups to social marginal cost (MC+), reducing traffic and benefits on the lines (Sanchez-Borras et al., 2010) and also limiting the conditions for financial sustainability of newcomers in head-on competition (Preston et al., 1999).

Summarising, HSR competition presents more barriers to newcomers than competition for conventional or mixed services. Not surprisingly, the cases of competition other than the Italian one show that, to date, on-track competition has been deployed more on conventional tracks than on HS ones. We may rather affirm that on-track competition on HSR routes is the exception and not the rule. This also suggests that the distinction between HSR and conventional services, when talking about competition, can be blurred, in particular in countries like Germany where such a distinction does not exist at all. It is the same with regard to NTV in Italy which extends its services out of the HSR network on conventional tracks (Bologna–Venezia, Bologna–Verona and Bologna–Ancona).

4. NTV and on-track competition in Italy

The Italian case is the only one, to date, in which the newcomer operates a large and complex nationwide long-distance network in the specialised HSR segment. Given the relative abundance of studies, we can gain deeper insights into the effects of competition in a HSR market some years after this was initiated.

4.1 Description and history

NTV is a private rail operating company; it was founded in 2007 to benefit from the early opening of the Italian long-distance rail market allowed by the *Decreto Legislativo* n.188 of 8 July 2003, implementing the European Directives on rail competition (2001/12/CE, 2001/13/CE and 2001/14/CE). According to the decree, any authorised rail company can have access to the national RFI rail network and operate both open-access or contracted services. The decree also allowed the possibility of open access for any domestic long-distance passenger service, different from the current state of affairs in the majority of EU countries.

The company now operates Italo services using 25 new Alstom AGV 575 trains. On 28 October 2015, NTV announced the purchase of eight new-generation Alstom Pendolino trains (non-tilting version), that the company wants to use for future services on the Milan–Venice conventional rail line.[5]

4.2 The market

Italian HSR services are provided by the former incumbent Trenitalia (train operating company of the national rail holding company Ferrovie dello Stato Italiane, entirely publicly owned) and by NTV.

Trenitalia had already started improving and rebranding its long-distance services before the gradual completion of the new HSR line Turin–Salerno (via Milan, Bologna, Florence, Rome and Naples) between 2006 and 2009. Long-distance fast services, operated on a market basis, were renamed "le Frecce" ("the Arrows"), including the new HSR ones. For these services, Trenitalia progressively improved rolling stock quality and, often, also commercial speed. The current commercial names of the services are:

- Frecciarossa, full HSR services (with few exceptions);
- Frecciargento, services using both HS and conventional tracks;
- Frecciabianca, fast services using conventional tracks.

NTV now operates north–south Italo services between Turin, Verona and Venice, to Rome, Naples and Salerno. A service on the (Turin)–Milan–Bologna–Ancona route was operated in 2013 and is now limited to the summer season.

In Figure 9.2 we represent fast services supplied by Trenitalia (left) and NTV (right) in 2015.

NTV announced that it had served 2.1 million passengers in 2012 (eight months) and 6.6 million in 2014; they expected to reach 9 million passengers in 2015.[6] Trenitalia declared that the Frecciarossa, Frecciargento and Frecciabianca trains had served 43 million passengers in 2013 (MIT, 2015). Of these, Cascetta and Coppola (2015) estimate 24.6 million passengers served by Frecciarossa and Frecciargento HSR services. The same source indicates an overall growth, between 2009 and 2013, from 6.1 to 12.1 billion passengers·km on HSLs. It is interesting to note that Trenitalia did not lose traffic after the entry of NTV into the market in 2012 and passengers·km rose from 6.1 to 9.5 billion (Cascetta and Coppola, 2015); it simply lost market share.

4.3 The model adopted

The vision of NTV was to provide high-quality services in opposition to the widespread low-quality perception of the public with regard to the long-term offering

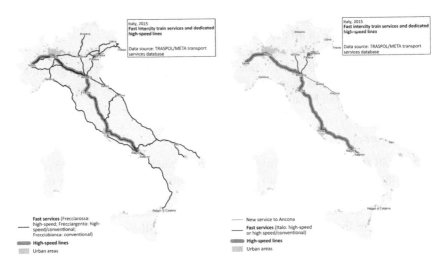

Figure 9.2 The network of Italian fast trains operated by Trenitalia on the left
(Frecciarossa, Frecciargento and Frecciabianca) and NTV on the right (Italo).
High-speed infrastructure is represented in dark grey (our elaboration).

of the incumbent. In this sense, the model the company promoted was one of "a luxury train for everyone", quite a long way from a low-cost/no-frills model.[7]

In line with this vision, they decided to buy the most advanced trains on the market at the time, the Alstom AGV 575 (with an extraordinary initial financial outlay of €900m),[8] and to equip them with high-quality interiors. In addition, they also introduced unconventional premium services (cinema coaches, on-board Wi-Fi with films and shows, refreshments provided by the top brand Eataly, etc.).

As shown in the former section, they planned the network to be quite similar to Trenitalia's Frecciarossa and Frecciargento, following the major demand routes. Apart from this, the choice of stations was different in some cities. An innovative mixed service between Milan and Ancona was introduced in 2013 (see Section 6.2).

In general, Trenitalia proved capable of reacting quickly and improving its services as soon as the competitor proved effective (and sometimes even before): they rebranded and refurbished their trains, frequencies were further increased (Bergantino et al., 2015) and average prices were also cut through yield management (see Section 6.1). Moreover, the general quality level (on-board services, reliability, etc.) improved dramatically.

NTV found itself providing luxury services with lower frequencies and (slightly) lower prices, competing with the much bigger incumbent in providing a comparable service. In other words, NTV lost its (limited) product differentiation and worked with a limited cost advantage in a huge market. Soon the financial results for NTV proved disappointing[9] and the company had to pass a €100 million budget package in mid 2015, €60 million of which was equity increase. In the initial plans, the company expected to break even in 2015, with a market share of 20 per cent.[10] While the market share was substantially met, breakeven was not, due to the need to adapt the former fare structure and radically reduce the yields.

The company then decided to redesign its offering, focusing on the most profitable routes, introducing new direct Milan–Rome services, changing stations in Milan, Torino and Rome (shifting to those already served by Trenitalia) and also providing a service on the Verona–Roma–Napoli route. Today, as a result, the new offering is very similar to the Frecciarossa and Frecciargento HSR services provided by Trenitalia.

5. Competition and prices

The literature extensively analysed the relationship between HSR and other transport modes in terms of intermodal competition (Bergantino et al., 2015, provide a review). On the other hand, few empirical analyses study intramodal competition among HSR (and/or conventional) rail services. This reflects the very limited experiences that currently exist in the field, as we showed in Section 2.

A first group of studies attempts to set the conditions for competition to take place. Preston (1999) analyses four different strategies of direct competition adopted by a new entrant in rail services and finds that conditions for financial sustainability of head-on competition are limited to a low-cost model and marginal infrastructure pricing. Ivaldi and Vibes (2005) develop a simulation model to analyse inter- and intramodal competition, suggesting that a low-cost model is the only feasible one. Otherwise, potential market shares found for newcomers remain very low, typical of niche services. In addition, Johnson and Nash (2012) find that a large cost differential with respect to the incumbent is the sole condition (together with the incumbent's inactivity) that makes on-track competition feasible.

Other studies analyses the effect of competition on prices. Bergantino et al. (2015) and Cascetta and Coppola (2015) (discussed later in more detail), analyse the Italian case where fares on the Milan–Rome route decreased by around 30 per cent after the entry of NTV into the market. Tomeš et al. (2014) describe the price war due to on-track direct competition in the Czech Republic between the three competitors providing comparable services and frequencies. They found that fares fell from CZK438 (CD pre-competition) to an average of CZK209 for the cheapest competitor (Leo Express). The lack of substantial differences among the operators translates into a predatory situation and all competitors, and especially the newcomers (as formerly suggested by Preston et al, 1999), experience unpredicted losses.

Competition may affect fares in a different way. Fröidh and Byström (2013) report that the two competitors on the international Copenhagen–Malmö route use different pricing strategies (demand dependent vs fixed with discounts for regular users) which have the effect of differentiating users.

Theoretical and empirical literature in the field thus suggests that there is limited scope for on-track competition, except in niche markets or in the presence of a clear and wide cost advantage for the newcomer. In the next section, we will discuss the Italian case of NTV, which seems to go in the different direction of a broad-scope competition with the incumbent.

6. The effect of NTV services on fares

6.1 The effect on existing rail and air services

The quantification of the intermodal effect of competition due to the opening of the Italian HSR was first studied by Cascetta et al. (2013). Using a multi-year survey, they analyse the users' behaviour, observing a significant modal shift from car (from 31 per cent to 25 per cent share of passengers km) and a slightly more stable figure for air transport (17 per cent to 15 per cent) and then calculate the elasticity of demand to the sole parameter of travel time. Looking at the effect of NTV, Cascetta and Coppola (2014), affirm that between 2011 and 2012, due to the entrance of the newcomer, fares reduced on average 31 per cent in one year. Consistent results are also in Cascetta and Coppola (2015), with a decrease in rail fares of 34 per cent in two years. When considering the whole "core area" influenced by the HSR infrastructure, including also medium- and short-haul demand, they found different and to a certain extent broader results in terms of modal shift: from 57 per cent to 44 per cent for road and from 10.5 per cent to 7.3 per cent for air transport.

Bergantino et al. (2015) study a database of fares observations on routes served by the former incumbent Trenitalia and the newcomer NTV.[11] The authors show how the arrival of the newcomer in 2012 increased the overall capacity of the Rome–Milan route by 56 per cent, but not at the expense of the incumbent's supply, which did not reduce. The authors suggest – by analysing the level of correlation among the fares – that both Trenitalia and NTV adopt strategic pricing behaviour (i.e. the fares of one company are influenced by the fares of the other). They do not find evidence of predatory pricing by the former incumbent, as Trenitalia's fares are on average 29.92–34.67 per cent higher that NTV's.

The authors also perform an intermodal analysis to understand the effect of competition among rail services on competing air services. They find that – after allowing for intertemporal price discrimination, airline market share and other flight characteristics – the presence of intermodal competition on the Rome–Milan route also reduced air fares by up to €13.26.[12] They suggest that this very significant impact is due to the limited presence of intramodal competition on the Rome–Milan air route.

6.2 The effect of the opening of a new direct high-speed route by a new entrant

The previous studies analysed the effect of a new entrant on existing routes already operated by the incumbent. A different case is analysed by Beria et al. (2014), who looked at the effect of the opening of a new direct HSR service by a new entrant, in spite of previously indirect or conventional trains. In contrast to previous studies, the fare structure is collected before and after the time of the new entrant starting operations.

In December 2013, NTV launched new direct Italo services on the (Turin)–Milan–Bologna–Ancona route, using the existing HSR infrastructure between Turin and Bologna and the conventional one south to Ancona (3 couples/day, one from Turin; travel time c. 3h15). This route was previously served by Trenitalia with Frecciabianca trains, entirely using the conventional line (9 couples/day; travel time c. 4h00); alternatively, passengers could take a Frecciarossa HSR service on the Turin–Milan–Bologna line and then interchange with a Frecciabianca conventional service to Ancona (12 couples/day; travel time c. 3h15). After the announcement of the new service by NTV, Trenitalia launched a couple of new direct Frecciarossa HSR services a day (travel time c. 3h05). Since NTV was delayed in opening its services by technical problems,[13] Trenitalia eventually opened its services shortly before NTV.

The authors monitored Trenitalia and NTV fares on the Milan–Ancona route during a time span of eight months (30 August 2013–12 April 2014), over the period of the start of the new services by NTV on 15 December 2013. The analysis suggests a stronger impact on weekly peak-time fares and a general greater reduction in first-class, non-flexible fares, with average savings around 20€ (70–80€ instead of 95€, Figure 9.3). Interestingly, in this case, NTV could particularly catch business users, thanks to the better characteristics of its services (in terms of travel time and frequency). These findings differ from what Bergantino et al. (2015) found for the rest of its network, where NTV's services are always less frequent than the ones of the existing operator, Trenitalia.

In addition, the authors show that NTV keeps lower prices than Trenitalia's only Frecciarossa, even though providing better services. Only when considering

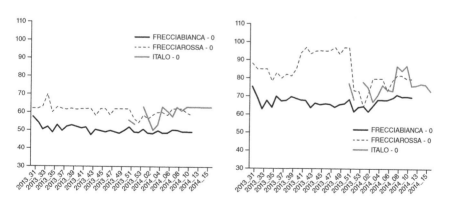

Figure 9.3 Best available fare (left) and best first-class class fare (right), weekly average, one day before departure, for different types of train – trains from Milan to Ancona.

Source: Beria et al., 2014.

the normal Frecciabianca trains is Trenitalia cheaper, on average. Moreover, the trend of fares over time of the newcomer NTV is steeper than Trenitalia's, with more expensive fares being charged only in the very last two–three days before the departure date. According to the authors, these facts suggest that the newcomer may suffer from a lack of information about the demand characteristics: in fact, the newcomer NTV seemed to replicate the strategy already adopted on the Milan–Rome route on this one. However, while NTV is likely a price taker on the Milan–Rome route, it could have aimed – following its market penetration – at being a price leader on the Milan–Ancona one, given its product advantage. Actually, this did not happen, and NTV abandoned the route about one year later, keeping it only as a summer service.

7. Barriers and potentialities of open-access competition in Europe

7.1 Barriers to open-access competition

The cases of open-access competition presented in the previous sections, and the Italian one in particular, are very interesting and promising. However, one cannot acknowledge how limited these experiences are and how only to a very slight extent this form of market is penetrating European railways. This fact suggests that a number of barriers still exist, but also some unavoidable limits.

A first set of problems lies in general discriminatory practices of the rail industry towards the newcomers. Weidmann et al. (2008) helps us in pointing out the main ones:

- *network planning and development*, without considering the needs of the newcomers;
- *network access conditions*, barriers in the form of too-high prices or too-high technical requirements;
- *path allocation process*, in which the infrastructure manager lowers its risks and efforts, damaging the newcomers (e.g. setting low capacity limits);
- *technical standards and migration*, without considering the needs of the newcomers;
- *train operations*, with discretional management of delays and ineffective services to trains (such as removal of waste) from the infrastructure manager;
- *information management*, with difficulties for newcomers in getting information useful for planning and managing their services;
- *staff-related functions*, also considering that staff with railway experience represent a natural monopoly in the short term.

As already pointed out, these technical–regulatory barriers are even worse in the most demanding segment, HSR: rolling stock standards are more demanding, timetable optimisation and access to main stations are crucial, etc.

Ex-ante barriers are not the only ones that can make newcomers' entry into the field difficult or impossible. The marketing of services is also a limit: the gap between (smaller) newcomers and already existing larger operators in terms of ticketing and information to users can harm newcomers' profitability. Nilsson et al. (2013) present a case of partial removal of such barriers in Swedish terms, which guarantee the right of newcomers to appear on the incumbent's website, but not for ticket sales.

The issue of cross-subsidies (money from profitable services used to operate other services at a loss) is also crucial in a network industry such as rail transport. Newcomers will tend to offer profitable services only, skimming the margins the incumbent uses to cross-subsidise loss-making services. More competition will thus require the public to cover the costs of services operated at a loss. This implies a trade-off between the overall socio-economic efficiency and the use of taxpayers' money (and the related opportunity vs cost equation). Actually, in most European countries, cross-subsidies between long-distance and regional market segments are already mostly absent. Cross-subsidies among trains within the long-distance market are limited and often unofficial (Beria et al., 2012). Instead, in the UK, on-track competition is de facto limited to niche markets by the fact that franchises include long-distance services (Office of Rail Regulation, 2011).[14]

Another possible issue, which does not seem to have already been studied in the literature, is the possibility that some Mohring effect (which is also present in long-distance transport (Jansson, 2001)) is lost with the fragmentation of supply among different operators.

7.2 Strategies for competitive advantage

The overcoming of normative, technical and de facto barriers is just a necessary condition. Competition, and on-track competition in HSR services in particular, necessitates that some players enjoy some form of competitive advantage over the other players in the markets they are in. Well-known literature on industrial competition identifies three generic strategies for achieving competitive advantage (Porter, 1985): cost leadership, product differentiation and product focus. In the following, we will try to explain these strategies as far as they apply to on-track competition.

Cost leadership of rail newcomers can be obtained in two ways (see Table 9.3): A) adopting a no-frills strategy or B) reducing the industrial costs with respect to the state of the art. In rail services, a newcomer cannot enjoy economies of scale in competition with the huge public providers. Consequently, the main ways to reduce industrial costs appear limited to: B1) labour cost reduction via different work contracts with respect to the public incumbents; B2) rolling stock cost reduction, for example via better contracting with suppliers or second-hand carriages; B3) saving access charges to urban nodes by serving secondary stations; B4) different (tighter) timetable/workforce organisation. The effectiveness of the B4 strategy is relatively limited and surely not comparable with

Table 9.3 Strategies for competitive advantage in the rail market.

Leadership	Strategy
Cost leadership	A No-frills strategy
	B1 Labour cost reduction/different work contracts
	B2 Rolling stock cost
	B3 Secondary stations to avoid node access charges
	B4 Timetable/workforce optimisation
Product differentiation	C1 Direct services
	C2 Extensions on conventional lines
	C3 Luxury (or no-frills) services
	C4 Innovative customer care services
	C5 Intermodal integration
Focus on niche markets	D Services in unexploited niches

what happened in the airline industry for low-cost carriers (Dobruszkes, 2006), because it is largely constrained by network operator rules. The B3 strategy can be effective in some cases and depends on track access charges rules. The B2 strategy is something that, in the medium term, can be replicated also by the incumbent and thus provides a temporary advantage. Strategy B1 is the most promising for private newcomers, but is the one that raises more difficulties with the incumbent, who may claim unfair competition due to "social dumping".[15] Due to the limits of cost reduction strategies, the "no-frills" model (A) seems the one that can be better planned and actuated by newcomers to guarantee a long-term cost leadership, while industrial costs in the long term can be lower with respect to the incumbent ones only if labour contracts are different. Interestingly, this strategy is tentatively also used by some incumbents, providing parallel low-cost services (Delaplace and Dobruszkes, 2015).

The second way to competitive advantage is *product differentiation*. Competitors try to be unique or leaders in some segments of the market, in order to enjoy a comparative advantage. Early low-cost airlines obtained this result by operating from different airports ("adjacent competition") and adopting the point-to-point low-frequency model, in opposition to the high-frequency hub-and-spokes operations of the flag carriers at main airports (Dobruszkes, 2006; Burghouwt and de Wit, 2015). Differentiation in HS products is more difficult to obtain: speed tends to be the same (both because of line capacity management and similar rolling stock), served cities too (main centres are usually the ones connected by HSLs) and the use of secondary stations does not seem to be an actual advantage in general[16]. Consequently, the strategies that can be adopted in this sense are the differentiation of the services in terms of cities directly connected, the provision of luxury (or no-frills) services in contrast to standard incumbent services and, to some extent, the introduction of innovative customer care services (dedicated app, different booking change policies, lounges, etc.). In addition, there might be a further difference in the catchment area of the services, which could go beyond the stations directly served. Typically, in fact, the incumbent has an advantage because of its feeder network (conventional trains, local services, etc.), while newcomers, especially at the beginning, must limit their supply to point-to-point routes. In this sense, newcomers could focus on intermodal integration, for example, introducing coach connections going beyond the rail network,[17] or becoming an intermediary for car rentals or air links.[18]

The third strategy is that of product *focus on niche markets* (Fröidh and Nelldal, 2015). Competitors not aiming at competing with the full range of incumbent services may focus, on a small scale, on abandoned/unserved routes or stations. We have examples of that especially with regard to international connections. For example, DB-ÖBB operates open-access EuroCity services, also on domestic pairs, between Munich and Milan/Bologna/Venice, a route abandoned by Trenitalia.[19] Similarly, Thello (a joint venture between Trenitalia and Transdev) runs a handful of trains between Milan and Marseille. The *focus strategy* could be the most interesting for small-scale entrants, thanks to its limited capital requirements. On the other hand, because HSR trains are effective in high-demand corridors, it is likely that niche operators could operate primarily on conventional tracks.

7.3 Models of competition on HSLs

Outlining the more feasible models for on-track competition, especially in the HSR segment, one must also consider the long-term sustainability of the three strategies described above. A long-lasting cost leadership of the newcomer depends mostly on the incumbent and its capability to adapt/evolve, rather than on the entrant's choices. For example, incumbents could be very quick to require more efficiency from suppliers as soon as a competitor started gaining on them, especially if they can account the sources of inefficiency to other services free of competition. In this sense, newcomers might risk a form of dumping. Product differentiation is even more volatile: a good new route can be quickly copied by the incumbent, as happened to NTV with its Italo services on the Milan–Ancona route (see Section 6.2).

On the other hand, one factor of stability is, if any, a labour cost advantage, which can hardly be tackled by the incumbent. In addition, operating on marginal routes could result in more stability, because demand is too little for two players and the incumbent's monopoly on the rest of the network cannot be jeopardised by an efficient but small-scale competitor.

On these premises, the forms of direct competition on HSR tracks which might more easily appear, are (see also Figure 9.4):

a   *mixed model networks*, with services using both HSR and conventional lines, differentiated among competitors;

b   *high-density demand corridors*, if the newcomer has the financial power to set up a service comparable to the one of the incumbent;

c   *niche markets* unexploited by the incumbent, for example unserved stations or point-to-point services on marginal routes;

d   a significant *cost advantage* in respect of the incumbent;
e   a *different product level*, typically a no-frills, low-cost model. "Luxury" services, however, could face the limits that we discussed in Section 6.

In the following paragraph, we will discuss how existing operators adopted these models.

7.4 Adopted strategies and potential markets

The analysis of existing experiences, although limited, suggests that most operators, with the relevant exception of NTV in Italy, have clearly opted (Figure 9.5) for one of the three strategies discussed in Section 7.2. HSR operators are different from the airline sector, which is more mature, and so far we cannot recognise a unique dominant strategy among the newcomers.

The UK operators have *differentiated* their supply in terms of cities served, simply filling a gap left by existing franchises. The Austrian and Czech operators, together with MTR Express in Sweden, compete on the main lines of the respective countries. Of course, they introduced some form of product differentiation, but the core of their business is the exploitation of a *cost advantage*, obtained via operational procedures, labour contracts or rolling stock. The other experiences are basically *niche products*: targeted services, cheap but not impacting on the respective incumbents either as a general alternative service or in financial terms.

Only NTV in Italy adopted a "full-range" model. This is surely not a niche service – the extension of the network, the geographical scope, the supply, the investment and also the corporate identity tell of a newcomer aiming at competing with the incumbent au pair and at the national scale. NTV tried to adopt two different strategies at the same time: *market differentiation* and *cost leadership*. Unfortunately, none of these advantages has resulted in anything significant up to now.

Some *cost leadership* exists, thanks to a different labour contract, smaller trains and a less complex company structure. However, the cost advantage is limited because of the initial choice of being a "luxury" train rather than a low-cost operator.

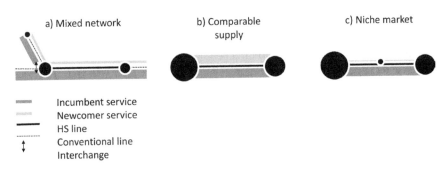

Figure 9.4 Forms of on-track competition models.

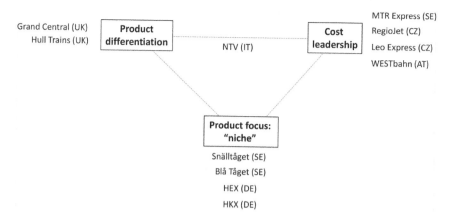

Figure 9.5 Competitive strategies adopted by open-access newcomers in Europe (our elaboration).

Also, some *differentiation* initially existed: the quality gap with respect to the incumbent, but also the use of alternative stations and routes. However, a few years later, the quality level became perfectly comparable, the routes the same (because NTV moved towards Trenitalia's supply), the stations too. Trenitalia is today almost equally good, but more frequent, more geographically spread, more known. The absence of differentiation caused a reduction of expected yields for NTV to a level still not compatible with the cost advantage. The consequence is in the financial problems of the company, whose breakeven was delayed, despite the good patronage.

In conclusion, open-access competition is possible, and in the HSR segment too. Fierce competition clearly showed the huge potential of stimulating demand on important corridors and of improving incumbents' services. However, some conditions need to be fulfilled: not only a large investment to overcome the frequency barrier on high-demand routes, but also a clear strategy. Both *cost leadership* – through a clear adoption of a low-cost model – and *product differentiation* are possible – through the supply of innovative routes and services. An ambiguous attitude seems, up to now, ineffective in guaranteeing long-term financial sustainability of the competitor itself.

The case of NTV leaves us with an open question, which challenges the need for specialisation. The growth in demand after its entry to the market was such that, if the service is to continue, it could build the field for the financial sustainability of a non-specialised model too, with a significant offering and just slightly lower prices. Only time will tell if this is going to happen.

Notes

1 Domestic market competition is currently forbidden only in Portugal, Spain, France, Belgium, Ireland, Croatia, Hungary, Greece, Finland and Norway (CER, 2011).

2 Theoretically, Italian HSLs can host freight trains, but up to now this has never happened.
3 Trains can be moved or services extended to conventional lines to reach more potential demand unexploited by the incumbent.
4 The fact that in Germany on-track competition is extremely limited could instead be explained by the market power of DB and by its extreme level of integration with local services, making point-to-point open-access operators less attractive.
5 "*Alstom and NTV unveil the design and technology of the Pendolino*", www.alstom.com, consulted in January 2016.
6 Corriere della Sera (31 May 2015), *NTV: Cattaneo, chiudiamo 2015 con 9 mln di passeggeri.*
7 "*NTV: anche l'Italia avrà i suoi treni di lusso*", www.lussuosissimo.com/*NTV*-italia-treni-lusso/.
8 Of which €650 million was for the 25 new trains, €100 million for construction of the maintenance depot and €150 million for start-up costs including staff training (Railway Gazette, "*NTV targets 20% market share by 2015*", 1 September 2008).
9 €77 million of losses on €239 million in sales in 2013 and €53.6 million of losses on €261.5 million in sales in 2014 (Bureau Van Dijk, "*AIDA – Analisi informatizzata delle Aziende Italiane*", NTV S.p.A. balance sheet, consulted on 24 December 2015.
10 Railway Gazette, "*NTV targets 20% market share by 2015*", 1 September 2008.
11 The routes analysed are Rome–Milan, Rome–Turin and Rome–Venice, in Italy.
12 As a result of reductions in fares of 15.5 per cent on the business-oriented Rome–Fiumicino–Milan–Linate route (average fare €85.59) and of 29 per cent on the leisure-oriented Rome–Fiumicino–Milan–Malpensa route (average fare €34.61).
13 NTV's AGV trains were claimed to not be completely compatible with existing platforms in Rimini and the infrastructure manager RFI had to do some remedial work.
14 New open-access services have to be "not primarily abstractive", i.e. not impacting the equilibrium of the PSO franchise contracts (Nash, 2008; CER, 2011). In a consultation document, the UK's Office of Rail Regulation (Office of Rail Regulation, 2009) recognised that greater on-track competition would benefit passengers and the economy, forcing the rail industry to provide a higher value for money as a whole. However, this would be more costly for the taxpayers, as some cross-subsidies would be lost.
15 This claim can be partially true, but can also be used strategically to hide inefficient labour conditions or privileges of public sector workers.
16 The already quoted Ouigo service in France (Delaplace and Dobruszkes, 2015), or the ceased Trenok in Italy (Sauter-Servaes and Nash, 2007), are the exceptions and their success is, in fact, limited.
17 Both operators in the Czech Republic and the Austrian WESTbahn extend their rail network with interconnected buses and in 2015 NTV in Italy started to do the same.
18 NTV signed agreements with Cathay Pacific and with some Italian ship services to Sardinia. Similarly, it has agreements with some cities to give free access to urban public transport services.
19 Initially, the Italian Ministry of Transport and Infrastructure banned the selling of some domestic OD pairs, claiming that such services were compromising the economic equilibrium of the regional services operated by Trenitalia under PSO on parts of the route.

References

Albalate, D., & Bel, G. (2012). "*High-speed rail: Lessons for policy makers from experiences abroad*", Public Administration Review, 72(3), 336–349.
Alexandersson, G., & Hultén, S. (2008). "*The Swedish railway deregulation path*", Review of Network Economics, 7(1), 18–36.

Alexandersson, G., & Rigas, K. (2013). *"Rail liberalisation in Sweden. Policy development in a European context"*, Research in Transportation Business & Management, 6, 88–98.

Bergantino, A. S., Capozza, C., & Capurso, M. (2015). *"The impact of open access on intra- and inter-modal rail competition. A national level analysis in Italy"*, Transport Policy, 39, 77–86.

Beria, P., Quinet, E., de Rus, G., & Schulz, C. (2012). *"A comparison of rail liberalisation levels across four European countries"*, Research in Transportation Economics, 36(1), 110–120.

Beria, P., Redondi, R., & Malighetti, P. (2014). *"The effect of open access rail competition on average prices. The case of Milan–Ancona"*, Paper presented at the XVI meeting of the Italian Society of Transport Economics (SIET), Florence, Italy, 8–10 October 2014.

Burghouwt, G., & de Wit, J. G. (2015). *"In the wake of liberalisation: Long-term developments in the EU air transport market"*, Transport Policy, 43, 104–113.

Campos, J., & de Rus, G. (2009). *"Some stylized facts about high-speed rail: A review of HSR experiences around the world"*, Transport Policy, 16(1), 19–28.

Cascetta, E., & Coppola, P. (2014). *"Competition on fast track: An analysis of the first competitive market for HSR services"*, Procedia – Social and Behavioral Sciences, 111, 176–185.

Cascetta, E., & Coppola, P. (2015). *"New high-speed rail lines and market competition: Short-term effects on services and demand in Italy"*, Transportation Research Record: Journal of the Transportation Research Board, (2475), 8–15.

Cascetta, E., Coppola, P., & Velardi, V. (2013). *"High-speed rail demand: Before-and-after evidence from the Italian market"*, disP – The Planning Review, 49(2), 51–59.

CER (2011). *"Public service rail transport in the European Union: An overview"*, Brussels: CER.

Delaplace, M., & Dobruszkes, F. (2015). *"From low-cost airlines to low-cost high-speed rail? The French case"*, Transport Policy, 38, 73–85.

Dobruszkes, F. (2006). *"An analysis of European low-cost airlines and their networks"*, Journal of Transport Geography, 14(4), 249–264.

ECMT (2007). *"Competitive tendering rail services"*, Paris: OECD.

European Commission (2013a). *"The fourth railway package – completing the single European railway area to foster European competitiveness and growth"*, COM(2013) 25 final, Brussels: European Commission.

European Commission (2013b). *"Executive summary of the impact assessment"*, Commission Staff Working Document, Accompanying the documents, *"Proposal for a Regulation of the European Parliament and of the Council amending Regulation (EC) No 1370/2007"* and *"Proposal for a Directive of the European Parliament and of the Council amending Directive 2012/34/EU of the European Parliament and of the Council of 21 November 2012 establishing a single European railway area, as regards the opening of the market for domestic passenger transport services by rail and the governance of the railway infrastructure"*, SWD(2013) 11 final, Brussels: European Commission.

Finger, M. (2014). *"Governance of competition and performance in European railways: An analysis of five cases"*, Utilities Policy, 31, 278–288.

Fröidh, O., & Byström, C. (2013). *"Competition on the tracks – passengers' response to deregulation of interregional rail services"*, Transportation Research Part A: Policy and Practice, 56, 1–10, doi: 10.1016/j.tra.2013.09.001.

Fröidh, O., & Nelldal, B. L. (2015). *"The impact of market opening on the supply of inter-regional train services"*, Journal of Transport Geography, 46, 189–200.

Ivaldi, M., & Vibes, C. (2005). *"Intermodal and intramodal competition in passenger rail transport"*, IDEI Working Paper no. 345, Toulouse: IDEI.

Jansson, J. O. (2001). *"UNITE, case studies 7G: The Mohring effect in inter-urban rail transport. A case study of the Swedish railways*, Leeds: University of Leeds, UNITE.

Johnson, D., & Nash, C. (2012). *"Competition and the provision of rail passenger services: A simulation exercise"*, Journal of Rail Transport Planning & Management, 2(1), 14–22.

MIT (2015). *"Conto Nazionale delle Infrastrutture e dei Trasporti"*, Rome: Ministero delle Infrastrutture e dei Trasporti.

Nash, C. (2008). *"Passenger railway reform in the last 20 years – European experience reconsidered"*, Research in Transportation Economics, 22(1), 61–70.

Nash, C. (2011). *"Developments in European railway policy"*, Network Industries Quarterly, 13(1), 11–13.

Nash, C., Nilsson, J-E., & Link, H. (2013). *"Comparing three models for introduction of competition into railways"*, Journal of Transport Economics and Policy, 47(2), 191–206.

Nilsson, J-E., Pyddoke, R., Hultén, S., & Alexandersson, G. (2013). *"The liberalisation of railway passenger transport in Sweden"*, Journal of Transport Economics and Policy, 47(2), 307–312.

Office of Rail Regulation (2009). *"Guidance on the assessment of new international passenger services"*, London: ORR.

Office of Rail Regulation (2011). *"The potential for increased on-rail competition – a consultation document"*, London: ORR.

Perl, A. D., & Goetz, A. R. (2015). *"Corridors, hybrids and networks: Three global development strategies for high speed rail"*, Journal of Transport Geography, 42, 134–144.

Porter, M. E. (1998 [1985]). *"The competitive advantage: Creating and sustaining superior performance"*, New York: Free Press.

Preston, J., Wardman, M., & Whelan, G. (1999). *"An analysis of the potential for on-track competition in the British passenger rail industry"*, Journal of Transport Economics and Policy, 33(1), 77–94.

Sanchez-Borras, M., Nash, C., Abrantes, P., & Lopez-Pita, A. (2010). *"Rail access charges and the competitiveness of high speed trains"*, Transport Policy, 17(2), 102–109.

Sauter-Servaes, T., & Nash, A. (2007). *"Applying low-cost airline pricing strategies to European railroads"*, Transportation Research Record: Journal of the Transportation Research Board, 1995, 1–8.

Tomeš, Z., Kvizda, M., Nigrin, T., & Seidenglanz, D. (2014). *"Competition in the railway passenger market in the Czech Republic"*, Research in Transportation Economics, 48, 270–276.

Weidmann, U., & Nash A. (2008). *"Open access to railway networks: Hidden discrimination potential in an integrated railway organisation"*, Paper presented at Competition and Regulation in Network Industries, Brussels, Belgium, 28 November 2008.

10 Assessing the competition between high-speed rail and airlines

A critical perspective

*Frédéric Dobruszkes, Moshe Givoni and
Catherine Dehon*

1. Introduction: The changing role of HSR

High-speed rail (HSR) has long been promoted in the name of the economic impacts it offers to cities or regions served (see other chapters in this book). Today, HSR is also often regarded as a 'green' mode of transport that should help to achieve so-called sustainable mobilities. This vision is based on some successful HSR services that have led to a dramatic decrease in the provision of air services. As a result, the supposed environmental benefit of HSR is now inevitably part of high-speed line (HSL) projects and of several (national or international) plans that aim to reduce the environmental footprint of medium-distance mobilities and especially of air travel.[1]

In this context, this chapter will first recall the move of HSR projects towards environmental rhetoric (Section 2). In Section 3, we analyse the available evidence about the intermodal impacts of HSR services, starting with common methodological misunderstandings. Section 4 will then discuss the limitations affecting the power of HSR to reduce air services. Finally, Section 5 brings some conclusions.

2. From energy and revenue concerns to environmental virtue: The changing role of HSR

At the time the first HSR projects were being developed in Japan and then in France (in the 1950s and 1970s, respectively),[2] nobody had in mind their potential advantages for the environment. Japan was facing fast-growing ridership and expected saturation on the Tokyo–Kebe Tōkaidō main line. Upgrading this narrow gauge line and speeding up trains was difficult, notably because of physical constraints imposed by the local topography, so at the end it appeared better to build a new, higher-speed line, but above all the aim was to increase capacity (Smith, 2003). In France, the principle of developing HSR self-formed within the French railway company SNCF itself (Fourniau, 1989; Klein, 2001). As in the 1960s, SNCF was facing several challenges. As in other developed countries, railways were progressively losing market share against car use and modern air travel. At best, their modernisation was restricted to the electrification of main lines, after which gains in speed ended. In contrast, the state engaged in the construction of new rapid roads and motorways, while air transport was modern by nature. Furthermore, the so-called Aérotrain emerged as a serious potential competitor for medium-distance rail services. The Aérotrain project aimed to develop a high-speed overtrain (thus not using steel tracks and wheels) propelled by a gas turbine. It received significant support from the state and went to the stage of test tracks and prototypes. All this made SNCF aware of growing intermodal competition. Following the Japanese national railways example, it was thus decided to create a transversal research department within SNCF (Fourniau, 1989). This department developed the future so-called TGV with the cooperation of the industry. Developing the HSR made it possible to demonstrate that railways fundamentally based on the steel track/steel wheel technology could also be modern. Clearly, SNCF also embarked on a commercial move necessitated by market analyses and traffic forecasts (Klein, 2001). The French government needed neither to initiate the HSR project nor to fund it, since the first French HSL between Paris and Lyon was predicted to be profitable (and it was). However, SNCF still needed formal approval from the state to formally embark on such a large project and to build the HSL. The government eventually opted for the HSR to the detriment of the Aérotrain. Apart from the network argument (the French high-speed train (HST) would be compatible with existing tracks) and the claimed risk of saturation of the Paris–Lyon railway, the argument for supporting HSR was electricity in the context of the oil crisis. It is symptomatic that the decision in favour of HSR was taken at the occasion of an inter-ministry meeting devoted to energy concerns (Troin, 1995). So when President Mitterrand opened the new HSL in 1981, he cited an energy-efficient transportation mode, but in the perspective of geostrategic considerations.[3]

The emergence of environmental advantages potentially offered by HSR actually came later. Worrying about air pollution and, above all, climate change, has progressively led to a new rhetoric embedded in many HSL projects. The reasoning is twofold. First, under certain conditions, notably in terms of travel time, HSR services can compete with oil-based transportation modes and help to reduce their volume of operations. Second, since HSTs require little energy per passenger-km, they emit significantly fewer air pollutants and greenhouse gases (GHGs) than cars and, above all, planes. Indeed, there is a set of inter-modal comparisons interested in emissions induced by various transport modes (e.g., Givoni, 2007; Givoni et al., 2009; García-Álvarez, 2010; Clewlow, 2012). Considering direct emissions, there is no doubt that HSTs are more energy efficient than any other transport mode suitable for medium-distance travel. This has helped many public authorities and pro-HSR lobbies to embellish the 'green' role of HSR to better justify projects submitted for approval. Let us cite only two typical examples. In 2009, President Obama introduced his vision for HSR at the White House. He said:

> We're at the mercy of fluctuating gas prices all too often; we pump too many greenhouse gases into the air. What we need, then, is a smart transportation

system equal to the needs of the 21st century. A system that reduces travel times and increases mobility. A system that reduces congestion and boosts productivity. A system that reduces destructive emissions and creates jobs. What we're talking about is a vision for high-speed rail in America. [. . .] We'll move to cleaner energy and a cleaner environment, we'll reduce our need for foreign oil by millions of barrels a year, and eliminate more than 6 billion pounds of carbon dioxide emissions annually – equal to removing 1 million cars from our roads.[4]

In France, the project of HSLs beyond Bordeaux, towards Toulouse and Spain, aims to "meet growing mobility needs in the South-West, while supporting sustainable mobility".[5] It is also stated that

In a sustainable development perspective, a major issue is to reconcile this increase in mobility with the use of transportation modes that minimise the environmental impacts (including greenhouse effect), and thus to support the use of rail transport rather than planes or road transport.[6]

However, such enthusiastic statements need to be carefully considered. First, only direct emissions (that is, emissions directly attributable to trains, planes and car operations) are usually considered. Actually, indirect emissions – notably related to the construction and maintenance of infrastructures and the vehicles, to fuel production, etc – also need to be included. *Ex ante* life cycle analysis (LCA) suggests that direct emissions account for much more emission of GHGs (or of CO_2 only) than indirect emissions; conversely, infrastructure construction is much more significant than direct emissions as far as carbon monoxide (CO), volatile organic compounds (VOCs) and particulate matters (PM10) are concerned (Chester and Horwath, 2010; Miyoshi and Givoni, 2014). However, it is worth noting that the exact contribution of air travel to climate change and to air quality at the ground level remains a matter for debate, due to gaps in scientific knowledge (Dalay, 2010; Lee et al., 2010). Second, in any case, environmental results are sensitive to load factors. 'Empty' trains are, of course, less environmentally efficient than highly loaded ones. In addition, the total HSR ridership needs to reach a given level that counterbalances the indirect impacts. Considering jointly the whole impacts and load factors, Chester and Horvath's (2010) results confirm than HSR is indeed more environmentally friendly than planes and cars provided it achieves a sufficient load factor. Having said that, one needs to acknowledge that environmental studies are often significantly subject to the hypotheses considered. For instance, Chester and Horvath (2012) updated their 2010 LCA analysis, considering new specifications of HSTs expected to be operated in California, but also new generations of cars and planes. The absolute impact of HSR is thus divided by nearly three, and HSR remains the best option provided its load factor is high. Their conclusions are thus more in favour than they were only two years earlier. Finally, it is also worth noting than access and egress journeys to and from HSR stations and airports can significantly affect the environmental impact of transport modes, depending on whether travellers use cars or public transport (Givoni, 2007; Givoni et al., 2009) (see Section 4).

In short, HSR may be helping to achieve 'greener' mobilities, but only in certain conditions, that is, high ridership and large modal shift from other transportation modes. The remaining sections will investigate the conditions in which HSR can indeed compete with other modes, and raise several constraints that likely limit the scope for HSR as a 'green' solution.

3. HSR competing with airlines: A growing set of evidence

3.1. The need for appropriate assessment

The existing set of evidence about the ability of HSR to compete with air travel is large at first glance. However, serious restrictions need to be reported. First of all, many studies are *ex ante* exercises. Such investigations are needed for planning purpose, but the fact is that in many cases, *ex post* figures show that traffic forecasts were wrong (Nash, 2015). In addition, the remaining portfolio of *ex post* studies is also frustrating. In many cases, a restricted set of routes is considered, if not one only. Surveys conducted in the aftermath of the opening of the initial HSR routes (including Paris–Lyon and Madrid–Barcelona) are continuously cited even two or three decades later.

Figures are often outdated, since surveys were not repeated later after the launch of HSR. In many cases, few factors have been considered when interpreting changes in transport mode use, to a point where all changes are usually considered as a consequence of travel time. The combination effect of a restricted set of routes and of variables has meant that only a few econometric analyses have been conducted to investigate observed changes (Dobruszkes et al., 2014). In short, *ex ante* studies favour econometrics but their results are uncertain, and *ex post* studies favour contemplative postures.

Another issue is the metric used by the authors to investigate HSR-induced intermodal effects and environmental benefits. Some important biases are noticed. First, it is common to consider before/after market shares. This is an issue, because, in the meantime, the total (all modes) market size often increases. The reasons for this increase are new traffic induced by HSR itself (that is, traffic not transferred from other modes but newly generated from scratch) and, subject to a time interval, a growth in cities' population and economy. This means that a large decrease in air travel market share may hide a lesser decrease (or even no decrease) if one considers absolute figures, as evidenced by Table 10.1. Second, most works focus on passengers (the demand), which is of course understandable. However, if the environmental benefits of intermodal effects are pursued, we need to investigate trends in transport means use (the supply). Surprisingly, there is a lack of such evidence. Finally, many authors have investigated HSR against air travel only. As a result, the impacts of HSR on conventional rail, car use and coach services are even less known. In short, the proper investigation of intermodal effects driven by HSR in an environmental perspective needs to

Table 10.1 Comparing trends according to market shares and to absolute figures (millions of passengers).

	1993	2013	2013/1993
London–Paris			
Airlines	0.569	1.822	−50%
	3.665		
	100%	20%	−80%
HSR	0	7.163	
	0%	80%	
Airlines + HSR	3.665	8.985	+145%
London – Brussels			
Airlines	1.160	0.569	−51%
	100%	16%	−84%
HSR	0	2.969	
	0%	84%	
Airlines + HSR	1.160	3.538	+205%

Source: Eurotunnel after BRB, CAA and SNCF.

(1) consider absolute figures and (2) focus on trends in the supply and not only in the demand.

3.2. The available evidence

Bearing these restrictions in mind, Givoni and Dobruszkes (2013) have conducted a review of evidence available from various sources following the launch of HSR services. The conclusions are that:

- About 20 per cent of HSR traffic is induced traffic (although with significant deviations according to routes).
- Subject to routes, the main mode of origin of HSR travellers is either conventional rail or air travel. This suggests that, in many cases, the apparent success of HSR is due to passengers transferred between 'old' and 'new' rail services.
- The drop in absolute number of other mode passengers also varies strongly across routes but, on average, it seems that road transport (cars and coaches) is less affected by HSR than air travel, even though most of the evidence concerns air travel. It also appears that the decrease in numbers of air passengers (or in seats supplied) can be larger than the decrease in frequencies, which is not good news for the environment.
- HSR travel time has a significant impact on HSR vs airline market share, but with high deviations that confirm the role of other factors. These factors include fares, access/egress to/from terminals, group size, schedules, reliability, etc.

Two recent research works go beyond this set of scattered evidence and the lack of econometric analysis. Dobruszkes et al. (2014) considered 161 city pairs across Europe (of which 31 have been deserted by the airlines) to assess the extent to which the actual (2012) level of air service is affected by HSR services. Both the number of airline seats and flights are considered, acknowledging that the number of flights could decrease in a somewhat smaller proportion than the number of seats subject to frequency strategies potentially pursued by the airline through adjusting aircraft size (Givoni and Rietveld, 2009). The main dependant variables considered are HSR travel time (in-vehicle plus boarding time) and HSR frequency. They are controlled by geoeconomic and transport-related variables (city size, countries, airline hub, HSR/airline integration at the airport and HSR station location). The regression model first confirms that HSR travel time significantly affects the provision of air services – namely, the volume of air services increases when HSR travel time increases too. However, the effect is not linear and it appears that the impact of HSR travel time on air services decreases quickly between 120 and 150 minutes, which is less than the three or even four hours often cited. HSR travel time similarly affects airline seats and flights, which suggests that airlines have not reacted to HSR through an increase in frequency, all other things being equal. By comparison with travel time, HSR frequency seems to have a much more limited impact on air services. Airline hubs induce more air services (having allowed for the other factors considered), which is logical since hubs are used by connecting passengers not directly concerned with the air links connected via the hub. HSR/integration has no detectable effect, but this can be due to the fact that such integration takes place at hub airports (spatial overlap). The effect of hubbing would thus be larger than the effect of intermodal integration. Finally, within the sample considered, low-cost airlines have a limited impact, all other things being equal.

This cross-sectional analysis has recently been completed by a panel data analysis covering 180 domestic routes within Europe and interested in changes in terms of frequencies (2002–2010) and numbers of airline seats (2002–2009) (Albalete et al., 2015). The set of independent variables is comparable to Dobruszkes et al. (2014) but for the fact that HSR services are described by a binary (yes/no) variable. This analysis confirms that the presence of HSR affects the provision of airline seats. The effect on the number of flights is not significant, but it is if the fact that no hub airports from Italy are considered. One may regret that this analysis does not consider HSR travel time instead of a dummy for HSR presence. However, the fact that in-vehicle HSR travel time matters is shown by Figure 10.1.

4. The scope for 'greener' mobilities: Reservations and limitations

4.1. Considering global traffics

The results presented above tend to confirm the ability of HSR to compete with other transport modes, or at least with airlines. Hence, global HSR traffic is increasing in various markets. In Europe for instance, HSR passenger-km has been

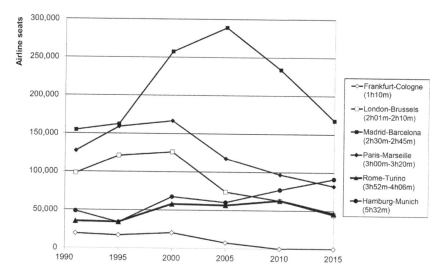

Figure 10.1 Trends in the provision of air services on selected routes.

multiplied by more than seven between 1990 and 2013 (European Commission, 2015). If this has arguably induced local or regional environmental benefits in several cases (less air pollution, fewer GHGs emitted, less aircraft noise), these results need to be put into perspective.

First, trends in HSR traffic have to be compared with air traffic. Doing so for Europe, Figure 10.2 shows diverging trends and significant gaps (only domestic and intraEU-28 passengers are counted). Between 1995 and 2013, air travel experienced an average growth of 3.5 per cent per year, or roughly 6–7 per cent out of crisis times. In comparison, HSR experienced a 12.6 per cent annual increase in traffic. In other words, while HSR services were successful at the expense of less flying between specific cities, this does not prevent the airline industry from continuing to thrive, likely on other markets. And, given the original gap between the two modes, passenger air travel traffic remains five times larger than that of HSR. This suggests that significant, subsequent efforts in terms of building new HSLs could be required. Hence, the European Commission's White Paper on transport (European Commission, 2011) intends to "triple the length of the existing high-speed rail network by 2030". However, given the lack of financial means and austerity policies, the feasibility of this option is open to debate.

Second, the apparent success of HSR masks a fundamental lack in knowledge about the demand. Apart for a restricted sample of routes where surveys were conducted, we simply know nothing about the modal origin of HSR passengers. In other words, there is no information as to the approximately 112 billion of HSR passenger-km split between induced traffic and transferred traffic from planes,

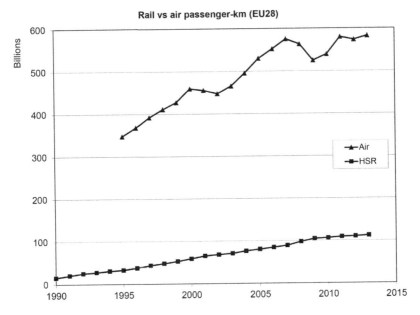

Figure 10.2 Rail vs air passenger-km (EU-28).

cars, coaches and conventional trains. This does not prevent HSR passengers from having potentially generated social, economical and personal benefits. But, in terms of the environment, it is not possible to address *ex post* the basic question of the global benefits.

Third, it could be that the continuous launch of HSR services has had some rebound effects (Givoni, 2007). Provided HSR made it possible to drop short-haul air services that could not survive competition, new airport slots were thus freed. These slots could then be reused for other flights. And in the case of constrained airports, slots freed could likely be reallocated to more profitable long-haul air services operated by larger aircraft. In such a case, the environmental impact of air travel would increase despite (and, in some way, thanks to) HSR, considering that both wide-bodied jets and longer routes involve more total energy and thus more absolute emissions of GHGs and of pollutants (Table 10.2).

Table 10.2 Fuel burnt against distance flown and aircraft size (kg).

Distance	A319	A330–200	A380–800
250 nm (463 km)	2,501	6,484	13,238
1,000 nm (1,852 km)	5,703	14,593	33,082
3,000 nm (5,556 km)	15,401	37,046	88,786
6,000 nm (11,112 km)		78,025	189,022

Source: European Environment Agency, 2013.

4.2. The spatial dispersion of demand

Other chapters in this book and previous sections have shown that HSR can support 'greener' mobilities provided (1) high volumes of passengers can be carried and would come from other transportation modes and that (2) this induces a decrease in the operations of other modes of transport. This raises the issue of the spatial patterns of air and car travel. First of all, the demand needs to fit within the range of distance in which HSR travel times are attractive, especially in a context of free modal choice (this will be discussed below). Short distances favour car use or conventional trains, both being usually cheaper and, above all, more flexible. Conversely, too long a distance makes HSR travel irrelevant, except to some extent for train lovers or for those people who simply do not care about travel time. In this context, Figure 10.3 shows the split of global scheduled air services in January 2015 against great-circle distances.[7] It appears that 44 per cent of flights or 32 per cent of seats correspond to 750 km or fewer. This suggests a great potential of modal shift to HSR.

However, there is second criterion to meet before justifying HSR. The demand needs to be geographically concentrated enough to warrant trains between two cities or along a given corridor. Givoni et al. (2012) performed preliminary analyses based on the shortest distance flown by planes and detours that would be imposed on HSLs by large physical obstacles (including large water surfaces). Results suggest a high sensitivity to market size at the city pair level. Indeed, considering a maximum 750 km travelled by train and a threshold of at least 23,250 seats per month, 16 per cent of flights or 5 per cent of seat-km could be transferred to new HSR services. If the threshold were 163,618 seats per month, these figures drop to 1.7 per cent and 0.6 per cent, respectively. This suggests rather limited

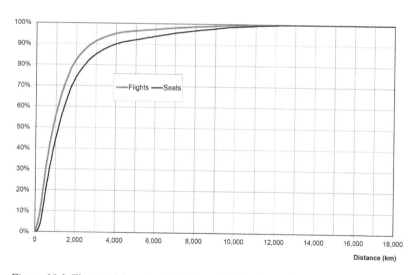

Figure 10.3 The provision of scheduled worldwide air services against distance (January 2015).

potential, especially compared to the growth rate of the airline business. On the other hand, the preliminary analysis conducted by Givoni et al. (2012) does not include the fact that a given HSL can mix the traffic of various city pairs, subject to their relative location of cities compared to the HSL. This can dramatically help to increase HSR traffic density. For instance, the HSL between Paris and Lille (northern France) combines traffic generated by several other city pairs including Paris to cities beyond Lille, Paris–London and Paris–Brussels (and beyond) as well as inter-regional services between Brussels, Lille and the west and south of France. In other words, Givoni et al.'s (2012) work needs to be pursued through GIS-based network analyses. Having said that, an important point in aggregating various city pairs' traffic on a given HSL is whether HSTs are compatible or not with conventional lines. If so, many more origins and destinations can be served through the use of one given HSL without building many HSL branches towards cities nearby (Perl and Goetz, 2015). Such interoperability is thus important to spread the benefits of HSR beyond the sole HSL (Martínez Sánchez-Mateos and Givoni, 2012).

In this context, it is worth noting that the characteristics of urban systems –that is, the size of cities, their absolute and relative positions, their functions and their general interactions– sharply affect both traffic density and the cumulative length of HSLs needed to link main cities with each other. Figure 10.4 illustrates this through three contrasted cases. Within a monocentric urban system as in France or in Poland, a couple of HSLs shaping a star around the largest city make it possible to serve a large part of the country's population. In the case of a linear urban system, as in Italy or along each US coast, a single HSL has great power to serve large markets. By contrast, a polycentric urban system as in Germany would imply a large number of HSLs to link main cities, while traffic would be more scattered (all other things being equal).

Finally, it is also important to note that insufficient traffic may be balanced to some extent by mixed railway operations, namely with conventional passenger trains and/or by freight trains running on the HSL. In Belgium for instance, the HSL between Brussels and Liège (towards Cologne) is even more used by domestic intercity services operated at 200 kph than by HSTs.

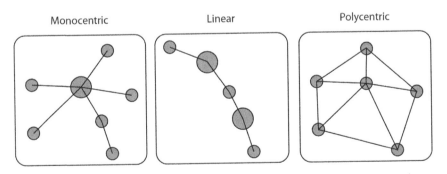

Monocentric   Linear   Polycentric

Figure 10.4 The impact of urban systems on a HSR network required to connect main cities to each other.

4.3. Social impacts and new forms of competition for HSR

It should also be highlighted that HSR ridership can be limited by HSR fares. In virtually all cases, HSR services cost more than standard fares. Furthermore, instead of having a flat fare, many HSR operators increase fares at peak times, or have even adopted yield management techniques. Fare strategies vary across countries. For instance, it seems that fares are always high in Germany, but they don't increase very much when the date of travel is imminent. In contrast, the French SNCF offers significant discounts for tickets booked a long way in advance and without any flexibility, but then fares increase sharply. And, in many cases, there is no discount (or maybe a small one) during peak times. As a result, the cost of travel can be quite high. Delaplace and Dobruszkes (2015) report that a Paris–Marseille return ticket can account for 10–18 per cent of the 2013 per capita median net salary in France. In this context, it is not surprising that upper social and occupational groups are over-represented on HSTs, as evidenced by many surveys. For instance, these groups accounted for no less than 37 per cent of the passengers on the Mediterranean HSR (2003) and 46 per cent on the Northern HSR (2004–2005), but only 8 per cent within France as a whole (RFF/SNCF, 2007). The slogan that SNCF once used "Progress is worth nothing unless it shared"[8] thus appears out of step with social realities.

In contrast, flying has become cheaper. Indeed, a major outcome of air travel liberalisation in many markets has been the advent of low-cost airlines (Dobruszkes, 2013). To date, low-cost airlines have not significantly penetrated markets where HSTs link cities within four hours. Above this rough threshold, they have been keen to enter the market. For instance, EasyJet operates flights between Paris and Toulouse (at least five and a half hours by HSR), between Naples and Milan (at least four and a quarter hours by HSR) and Venice (around five hours by HSR). However, the competition between low-cost airlines and HSR is much higher than it appears. Indeed, intermodal competition does not only take place within a given city pair. Low air fares may also divert potential HSR passengers who are not obliged to travel to a given destination. To give an example, Amsterdam inhabitants may travel by train to Brussels or Paris for a long weekend, but low-cost flights may also attract them to Venice or Barcelona. In other words, low-cost airlines are a threat for HSR as far as geographically flexible passengers are concerned.

As a consequence of rail travel becoming more expensive on various routes, coach services are now expanding again across Europe and have remained in various Asian countries despite HSR services. The product is simple: on the one hand, basic table fares (no or limited yield management), attractive prices, flexible tickets, modern coaches with an electricity supply and free Wi-Fi on board; on the other hand, much longer journeys and lower frequencies. Low fares are usually quoted as a main reason for travelling by coach (e.g., Inoue et al., 2015). Interestingly, a survey conducted by Román et al. (2014) among Madrid–Barcelona passengers reveals that coach users have an average income (€2,220) that is 43 per cent lower than that of air and HSR passengers. In contrast with low-cost airlines, many core HSR routes are now served by coaches too. Even if this market usually remains small if compared to seat capacity offered by HSTs, it nevertheless confirms that HSR travel is not for all social groups. However, it seems that coaches do not affect HSR operators: in several cases, the same companies operate both HSTs and parallel coaches. For instance, SNCF operates OUIBUS coach services across France and to neighbouring countries, and Deutsche Bahn (DB) similarly operates IC Bus coaches. Significantly, both compete with in-house HSR. Considering that HSR infrastructures have been largely paid for by the taxpayers, and that traffic density is critical to justify HSLs, this raises questions. Note that in France, SNCF also operates low-cost HSR services (named Ouigo), that are effectively significantly cheaper, especially for families (Delaplace and Dobruszkes, 2015). However, the use of peripheral stations and a compulsory 30-minute check-in procedure remove some of the key assets of the HSR.

4.4. The free modal choice paradigm

Until this point, the evidence introduced and discussion about traffic density could appear as orthodox. They both make sense within the current political context, where individuals are mostly free to choose their mode of transportation (the freedom being, of course, subject to their income). In addition, the provision of air services is becoming more and more liberalised around the world, thus several governments have lost the right to restrict the expansion of air services even in the case of reasonable rail-based alternatives – provided they intended to do so of course.

One could argue that free modal choice involves flying even in the case of travel by rail being 'reasonable'. The high traffic density observed in several air markets when competing trains need four or five hours to do the same journey is a clear example. Now, let us think out of the box. Take the (likely hypothetical) case that a government would influence the terms of intermodal competition through prices, flying quotas per country, oil prices, appropriate subsidising of HSR systems to create lower rail fares, or whatever. Two changes in favour of HSR would take place. First, the longer journey times of HSR would become attractive too. Second, it could be expected that many travellers would (re) discover the charm of medium-distance tourist destinations accessible by HSR. This discussion is likely hypothetical but it highlights how much the HSR traffic density issue is not only a question of geographical pattern, but also a political one.

4.5. The issue of the location of transport terminals

Finally, the location of transport terminals may also limit HSR ridership. In many cases, HSR systems have been designed to provide efficient services between city centres. Peripheral stations have nevertheless been considered either in the case of a bypass between radial lines (as happens around Paris) or for those cities not large enough to obtain a detour. In the context of European cities with high population densities, central business districts and dense public transport in towns, this probably made sense. Yet, in the meantime, the metropolisation process has induced a redevelopment of cities. This trend has often benefited suburbs to some extent. In many cases, the suburbanisation of housing is now followed by the suburbanisation of jobs, including some advanced service providers and high-tech firms. But for all that, city centres have usually remained vibrant, and dense too. In Asia, very big cities mean that most potential travellers live away from central terminals. And in the US, most of the potential HSR passengers probably live in low-density suburbs with inefficient access to the city centre.

Serving both central and peripheral stations may be possible, but a balance between in-vehicle travel time and door-to-door travel time is unclear. Opting only for a peripheral HSR station would mean that it would be less accessible by public transport and for those people travelling to/from central parts of cities. Conversely, serving only central stations makes HSR more accessible for many travellers, but may also make air travel more attractive for certain inhabitants in the suburbs, as evidenced by Martín et al. (2014). Subject to each mode of transport's travel time and to where people start/end their journeys, planes or HSR are eventually the most attractive solutions.

Transport terminal location is also critical considering the environment. Most intermodal comparisons interested in environmental impacts consider only the travel between transport terminals (linehaul section). However, as demonstrated by Givoni (2007) and Givoni et al. (2009), the access and egress journeys to and from terminals can be worse than flying in certain situations. Similarly, the environmental advantage of HSR travel can be lost if travellers access or egress stations by car rather than by public transport. In this context, HSTs calling at central, incumbent stations (such as Berlin Hauptbahnhof, London St Pancras or Milano Centrale) would favour public transport use. However, given the specific social profile of HSR passengers, it can be reasonably stated that, in many cases, they favour taxis or private cars to access HSR stations. On many occasions, the modernisation of incumbent stations to welcome HSTs went hand in hand with the construction of large car park facilities. At Brussels-Midi station, for instance, despite the central location and connections with a wide range of national and regional trains, the underground, and many tram and bus lines, no less than 1,650 car parking places were nevertheless constructed. It would be interesting to assess the environmental impact of such flows but, of course, this needs time-consuming surveys. In addition, when HSR networks are incompatible with incumbent railways, and/or when peripheral stations are planned to save time and/or the cost of penetrating core cities, there are usually poor connections (if any) between all networks and accessing the station by car is probably even more common.

5. Conclusions

All in all, this chapter confirms that HSR can contribute to significantly decreasing the provision of air services on given markets (that is, large cities neither too close nor too far from each other). Much less evidence is available about the impact on road traffic. However, the success story of HSR against airlines calls for methodological reservations related to the lack of *ex post* comprehensive data and that prevents us from making a definite conclusion as to HSR's global environmental benefits.

Travel time is confirmed as a key factor for intermodal competition. In-vehicle travel time is usually considered by scholars, but of course it is door-to-door travel time (along with experience) that actually matters. In other words, an obsession with peak speed is much less important than the average speed from door to door (Givoni and Banister, 2012). In this respect, the location of transport terminals and smooth connections with other public transport are critical, as is the possibility of HSTs operating on conventional lines connected to the HSLs.

Furthermore, the apparent success of HSR comes up against several limitations. A critical point is the potential of high-density routes. Actually, the HSR would be a more convincing opportunity for 'greener' mobilities if the terms of intermodal competition were affected either by external conditions (including the traffic density) or by voluntary regulations in the name of the environment. New political paradigms could thus be a prerequisite before considering the HSR as a transportation mode that would significantly contribute to 'greener' mobilities. In the meantime, this does not prevent HSR being justified for reasons other than the environment, as discussed elsewhere in this book.

Notes

1   The potential impact of HSR on car travel has surprisingly received less attention. In this chapter, we use the term 'medium-distance' rather than 'long-distance' to make the distinction with medium- and long-haul flights that are basically out of intermodal scope.
2   We could discuss whether the original Shinkansen services in Japan were really HSR since trains were operated at best at 210 kph while 250 kph is now usually considered as a minimal threshold by most observers. However, the original Shinkansen paved the way for subsequent improvements to really high-speed services.
3   Address by President Mitterrand on 22 September 1981, kindly provided by the François Mitterrand Institute.
4   Full speech and transcript available at https://www.whitehouse.gov/blog/2009/04/16/a-vision-high-speed-rail (accessed 3 February 2016).
5   RFF, Enquête préalable à la déclaration d'utilité publique – Grand projet ferroviaire du Sud-Ouest, Pièce D, Notice explicative, Chapitre 1er, juin 2014. Translated by the authors. Available at http://www.enquetepublique-gpso-lignesnouvelles.fr/pieces.html (accessed 3 February 2016).
6   See note 5.
7   That is, the shortest line between two points (also termed orthodromy).
8   "Le progrès ne vaut que s'il est partagé par tous."

References

Albalete, D., Bel, G., Fageda, X. (2015). *"Competition and cooperation between high-speed rail and air transportation services in Europe"*, Journal of Transport Geography, 42, 166–174.

Chester, M., Horvath, A. (2010). *"Life-cycle assessment of high-speed rail: The case of California"*, Environmental Research Letters, 5(1), 1–8.

Chester, M., Horvath, A. (2012). *"High-speed rail with emerging automobiles and aircraft can reduce environmental impacts in California's future"*, Environmental Research Letters, 7(3), 1–11.

Clewlow, R.R.L. (2012). *"Climate impacts of high-speed rail and air transportation: A global comparative analysis"*, Dissertation (PhD – ESD), Massachusetts Institute of Technology, available at http://web.mit.edu/hsr-group [accessed 28 April 2016].

Dalay, B. (2010). *"Air transport and the environment"*, Farnham: Ashgate.

Delaplace, M., Dobruszkes, F. (2015). *"From low-cost airlines to low-cost high-speed rail? The French case"*, Transport Policy, 38, 73–85.

Dobruszkes, F. (2013). *"The geography of European low-cost airline networks: A contemporary analysis"*, Journal of Transport Geography, 28, 75–88.

Dobruszkes, F., Dehon, C., Givoni, M. (2014). *"Does European high-speed rail affect the current level of air services? An EU-wide analysis"*, Transportation Research Part A: Policy and Practice, 69, 461–475.

European Commission, (2011). *"Roadmap to a single European transport area – towards a competitive and resource efficient transport system"*, White Paper, COM(2011) 144 final, Brussels: European Commission.

European Commission (2015). *"EU transport in figures. Statistical pocketbook 2015"*, Luxembourg: Publications Office of the European Union.

European Environment Agency (2013). *"EMEP/EEA air pollutant emission inventory guidebook 2013. Technical guidance to prepare national emission inventories"*, EEA Technical Report No. 12/2013, Copenhagen: EEA.

Fourniau, J-M. (1989). *"La genèse du TGV Sud-Est. Innovation et adaptation à la concurrence"*, Culture Technique, 19, 85–94.

García-Álvarez, A. (2010). *"Energy consumption and emissions of high-speed trains"*, Transportation Research Record: Journal of the Transportation Research Board, 2159(1), 27–35.

Givoni, M. (2007). *"Environmental benefits from mode substitution: Comparison of the environmental impact from aircraft and high-speed train operation"*, International Journal of Sustainable Transport, 1(4), 209–230.

Givoni, M., Rietveld, P. (2009). *"Airline's choice of aircraft size – explanations and implications"*, Transportation Research Part A: Policy and Practice, 43(5), 500–510.

Givoni, M., Banister, D. (2012). *"Speed: The less important element of the high-speed train"*, Journal of Transport Geography, 22, 306–307.

Givoni, M., Dobruszkes, F. (2013). *"A review of ex-post evidence for mode substitution and induced demand following the introduction of high-speed rail"*, Transport Reviews, 33(6), 720–742.

Givoni, M., Brand, C., Watkiss, P. (2009). *"Are railways climate friendly?"*, Built Environment, 35(1), 70–86.

Givoni, M., Dobruszkes, F., Lugo, I. (2012). *"Uncovering the real potential for air–rail substitution – An exploratory analysis"*, in Inderwildi, O., King, D. (Eds), *"Transport and the environment. Addressing the sustainable mobility paradigm"*, London: Springer, pp. 495–512.

Inoue, G., Ono, M., Uehara, K., Isono, F. (2015). *"Stated-preference analysis to estimate the domestic transport demand following the future entry of LCCs and the inauguration of the Linear Chuo Shinkansen in Japan"*, Journal of Air Transport Management, 47, 199–217.

Klein, O. (2001). *"La genèse du TGV, une innovation contempraine de l'épuisement du fordisme"*, Innovations, Cahiers d'économie de l'innovation, 13(1), 111–132.

Lee, D.S., Pitari, G., Grewe, V., Gierens, K., Penner, J.E., Petzold, A., Prather, M.J., Schumann, U., Bais, A., Berntsen, T., Iachetti, D., Lim, L.L., Sausen, R. (2010). *"Transport impacts on atmosphere and climate: Aviation"*, Atmospheric Environment, 44(37), 4678–4734.

Martín, J.C., Román, C., García-Palomares, J.C., Gutiérrez, J. (2014). *"Spatial analysis of the competitiveness of the high-speed train and air transport: The role of access to terminals in the Madrid–Barcelona corridor"*, Transportation Research Part A: Policy and Practice, 69, 392–408.

Martínez Sánchez-Mateos, H.S., Givoni M. (2012). *"The accessibility impact of a new high-speed rail line in the UK – a preliminary analysis of winners and losers"*, Journal of Transport Geography, 25, 105–114.

Miyoshi, C., Givoni, G. (2014). *"The environmental case for the high-speed train in the UK: Examining the London-Manchester route"*, International Journal of Sustainable Transportation, 8(2), 107–126.

Nash, C. (2015). *"When to invest in high speed rail"*, Journal of Rail Transport Planning & Management, 5(1), 12–22.

Perl, A., Goetz, A. (2015). *"Corridors, hybrids and networks: Three global development strategies for high speed rail"*, Journal of Transport Geography, 42, 134–144.

RFF/SNCF (2007). *"Bilan LOTI de la LGV Méditerranée"*, [no place]: [no publisher].

Román, C., Martín, J.C., Espino, R., Cherchi, E., Ortúzar, J.D.D., Rizzi, L.I., González, R.M., Amador, F.J. (2014). *"Valuation of travel time savings for intercity travel: The Madrid–Barcelona corridor"*, Transport Policy, 36, 105–117.

Smith, R. (2003). *"The Japanese Shinkansen: Catalyst for the renaissance of rail"*, The Journal of Transport History, 24(2), 222–237.

Troin, J-F. (1995). *"Rail et aménagement du territoire: Des héritages aux nouveaux défis"*, Aix-en-Provence, France: Edisud.

11 High-speed rail and PPPs

Between optimization and opportunism

Yves Crozet

Introduction

A large number of public–private partnerships (PPPs) have been awarded in the rail sector during recent decades, especially to develop new high-speed lines. However, a lot of these PPPs have failed. The main reason for the failures is well known: strategic behaviours that create an incentive for concessionaires or, more precisely, some members of the consortium acting as the concessionaire in order to make over-optimistic ridership forecasts. Such over-optimistic forecasting is often performed at the instigation of the local public authorities that support the project. The larger the project, the higher the risks that traffic will be overestimated (Flyvbjerg et al., 2006).

In this chapter, we begin by presenting the reasons for PPPs, describing the curse that seems a characteristic of rail PPPs, after which we will present a detailed analysis of the four ongoing projects. How have RFF (the publicly owned rail infrastructure manager) and the French public authorities tried to address the curse that affects rail sector PPPs? Why did the government recommend a concession for the largest project and PPPs (in the strictest sense of the term) for two of the others? We shall see that this decision is the outcome of an attempt to achieve an optimal distribution of the risks. The commercial risks are only borne by the private partner, via a concession, in cases where there is potential for a large increase in traffic. PPPs are used when the anticipated increase in traffic is small. PPPs are thus principally a way of speeding up the construction of the lines by delaying the burden on public budgets. In a manner of speaking, the public decision-maker shows its private sector partners that it wants to build the high-speed railway (HSR) "at any price". In terms of behaviour with regard to risk, this means the state is a risk lover. The result is a situation in which risk analysis dictates that the state should protect itself against its own taste for risk. We shall see in the case of the Tours–Bordeaux concession that even when the state attempts to transfer the maximum amount of risk to the concessionaire, it is the state which, in the last resort, bears the greatest risks, quite simply because it is the source of these risks!

1. PPP: Evidence and ambiguity

Public authorities are more and more attracted to the private sector, not only for building, but also for financing and operating new infrastructures (Bonnafous, 2010). This is the main reason for the success of PPPs as an attractive option when costly new transport infrastructures are planned. A considerable number of reasons are usually given for such private sector involvement, and we can divide these into two categories (OECD/International Transport Forum, 2013).

PPPs appeal to public decision-makers because, under certain conditions, they are a way of providing new transport infrastructures in a potentially more efficient way than traditional public management. Moreover, PPPs also allow new investments without any immediate increase in reported public spending or debt. Even if this second motive is largely illusory (Maskin & Tirole, 2008), it makes PPPs attractive to local and central governments.

The first main explanation for the increasing involvement of private operators in new public facilities is related to the financial concerns of governments. The pressure exerted by excessively indebted public finances acts in favour of systems favouring private financing and debt, even if this involves the redistribution of capital and risk premiums that in the long run are likely to increase the cost of operations for the public finances. The principal task of a PPP is to "mask" public debt. This reflects an opportunistic budgetary strategy to the extent that the commitments of public authorities to partnership contracts are not generally part of debt consolidation (Marty, 2007). This ambiguous attractiveness of PPPs must be balanced by a number of significant gains with regard to some non-financial parts of the project.

The second main justification for PPPs relates to the ability of a private operator to manage the construction and operation of the project more efficiently. This amounts to assuming that the internal rate of return (IRR) of the project is not the same depending on whether it is carried through by a public body or by a private company, which in theory keeps abreast of the continual improvements in optimization techniques. This difference is explained by a number of factors: the private sector pays some categories of staff less well, but is more flexible, offers faster construction times which speed up the return on investment and is sometimes more able to resist political demands which generate additional costs.

Nevertheless, whatever the nature of the operator, there is a target IRR which is closely related to the standard weighted average capital cost (WACC) concept and larger in the case of a private operator because this cost must also include the operator's profit and allow for the higher cost of finance. Thus, if for each public infrastructure project the main criterion for the national government is the need for subsidies, the choice will depend essentially on two opposing factors: the greater efficiency of private operators, and the lower WACC of public operators. For a given project it is therefore necessary to identify the conditions under which a PPP can compensate for the private operator's higher WACC through higher efficiency. Optimal efficiency can be reached by four kinds of improvements provided by the private sector (Bonnafous & Faivre d'Arcier, 2013):

- a reduction of the construction cost,
- a reduction of the project's lead time,
- an increase in the first year rate of return,
- an improvement in the gradient of the annual benefit over time, especially because of a lower maintenance cost.

If these conditions, or at least some of them, are satisfied, the PPP is a valuable option. However, this is not easy to achieve and many PPPs have resulted in huge failures or at least major renegotiations.

2. HSR and PPPs, a quick overview

Julien Dehornoy (2012) undertook a detailed survey of rail PPPs worldwide. He explains that it is necessary to distinguish between two different categories of PPP:

- The "pure" PPP is a traffic-based concession. The concessionaire has to finance and build the infrastructure. During the operating time of the concession, it receives commercial revenue (revenue from rail access charges or fares) and does not receive any payments from the public authority.
- A PPP in a broader sense can also cover "availability-based concession" where the public authority retains the commercial risk. Therefore, the public body receives commercial revenue (rail access charges or leasing fees for asset-only PPPs, or fare revenue for integrated PPPs) but makes payments to the concessionaire based on costs and performance indicators.

The attractiveness of traffic-based concessions depends on the commercial risk sharing mechanisms. For instance, the concessionaire may retain all the risks up to a certain limit, or pay a fixed proportion of its commercial revenue to the public authorities (e.g. Eurotunnel). Experience suggests, however, that transferring the commercial risk to the private stakeholder increases the likelihood that a PPP will fail. Most traffic-based rail concessions have been financial failures.

Rail PPPs and especially HSR PPPs have faced huge difficulties in many countries. The promised benefits of private involvement in the project process are not apparent and very often the public authorities have been forced to rescue projects at a high cost for public finance. The main reason for the total or partial failure of PPPs is a tendency to overestimate traffic and demand (Flyvbjerg et al., 2006). This has not put paid to PPPs but rather led to a kind of learning process that has prompted public authorities to replace "traffic-based concessions" with "availability-based concessions".

If we consider mature concessions, in some representative projects, public authorities had to step in and effectively transform the PPPs into public projects or companies:

High Speed 1 (HS1) (UK) also named CTRL (Channel Tunnel Rail Link, 108 km) is a typical case of PPP failure. The main difficulty relates to the fact that the cost of construction (£80 million per mile), was much higher than in other countries, almost four times more than in France for HSR-East for instance. Two years after construction started (1998), the banks refused to lend more money to the concessionaire and the UK government had to rescue the project by virtually nationalizing the PPP and transforming it into a design and build contract. In 2009, two years after the opening of the line (2007), the UK government decided to sell £16 billion of state assets including HS1 Ltd in the following two years to cut UK public debt. A new concession has been set up in 2010 to operate the line for 30 years. The concessionaire, a consortium of Canadian investors, paid £2.1 billion (to be compared with the estimated cost of HS1, approximately £6.2 billion, undiscounted, at 2007 prices), which included the stations and depot (Colin Buchanan, 2009). Under the concession, HS1 Ltd has the rights to sell access to track and to the four international stations (St Pancras, Stratford, Ebbsfleet and Ashford) on a commercial basis, under the scrutiny of the Office of Rail Regulation (ORR). At the end of 30 years, ownership of the assets will revert to the government.

THSR (Taiwan High-speed Rail) is a line of 339 km along the west coast from the national capital Taipei to the southern city of Kaohsiung. A private company, the Taiwan High-speed Rail Corporation (THSRC) built and now operates the line on the basis of Japan's Shinkansen technology. The total cost of the project was US$18 billion, one of the world's largest rail PPPs. In the initial years of operation the traffic was lower than expected and THSRC accumulated debt due to high depreciation charges and interest paid to the banks. In 2009, the method of depreciation was changed and the government took over the management of the concessionaire which was officially still a private company. This was the final stage in the increase in the proportion of the project that was directly or indirectly financed by the public sector (0 per cent in 1998, 37 per cent in 2005 and 84 per cent in 2009). At the same time, the government asked the banks to reduce the very high interest rates (8 per cent) on private debt.

HSR-Zuid (the Netherlands). The new HSR opened (in 2011) between Amsterdam and Antwerp involved the signing of three contracts:

- for civil engineering (the substructure, earthworks and subgrade), which was passed through seven conventional procurement packages;
- for the superstructure, which was awarded via a concession to the Infraspeed consortium and covered the design, construction, financing and maintenance of the track, stations and signalling for a period of 25 years;
- a concession for the operation of the line, won by the High-speed Alliance consortium (HSA) (90 per cent owned by the Dutch railway company NS and 10 per cent owned by Air France-KLM).

Several issues emerged that were due to poor coordination between contracts. Tenders for the procurement of civil engineering works were 43 per cent higher than budgeted for due to a lack of competition and a certain amount of collusion between bidders (Dutzik et al., 2011). To lower prices, the Dutch government decided to eliminate penalties for the late delivery of civil engineering works, making it liable to pay penalties for project delays in relation to the second contract for the superstructure and the third contract for operating the line. In addition, the state agreed to defray a large part of the additional costs (55 per cent of the originally projected investment). These significant additional costs were mainly due to the lack of coordination between the two firms responsible for substructure and superstructure: the company responsible for the superstructure designed its systems on the basis of design data that was out of date due to changes. Ultimately, the commissioning of the line was delayed for two years. This delay has had an impact on the operating agreement, as under the terms of its concession agreement HSA had to start paying access charges before any services could be operated. HSA was not officially bankrupt, but the Dutch government informed it in the summer of 2011 that the government would take over if necessary. With regard to the risk in relation to traffic, the Dutch government signed a contract in which it took on the risk of last resort. Consequently, the operator seems to have had less incentive to successfully generate profit with optimum quality of service. In fact, demand was low partly because the fares proposed by HSA were exorbitant and non-competitive. This example shows that the structure of the initial contract is paramount in order to organize efficient risk sharing, which is fully consistent with the theory of incomplete contracts.

Perpignan–Figueras HSR (France and Spain). TP Ferro Concesionaria, S.A. is a French–Spanish company, a subsidiary (50-50) of the well-known civil engineering companies Eiffage (France) and ACS (Spain). In 2007, they obtained from the French and Spanish governments a 50-year (extended to 53 years) concession to build and operate the line (44 km), and especially the tunnel (8 km) between France and Spain. The cost of construction was close to 1 million euros but the concessionaire obtained a subsidy of 540 million euros. During the first years of the concession, there was no traffic because the HSR on the Spanish side was not finished. Therefore, TP Ferro obtained new subsidies (128 million euros) to compensate for the losses. The traffic finally started in 2013 but at a level much lower than expected. The result was the bankruptcy of the concessionaire in December 2015.

Eurotunnel (France and UK). Due primarily to traffic overestimates and construction cost overruns, the project's liabilities had to be restructured in 1997 and 2007, with investors and lenders losing more than two-thirds of their investment. The concession also benefited from public support through the extension of the concession duration from 55 to 99 years and the "minimum usage charge", a minimal revenue guarantee, the cost of which was borne ultimately by the owner of Eurostar, that is the French national railway company (SNCF) and the British government jointly.

The list of failures is long and the reasons for this become clear if we return to the four main advantages of PPPs described above (reducing the construction cost, reducing the project lead time, increasing the first year IRR and improving the gradient of the annual benefit over time). We can observe that the advantages stem mainly from a reduction in construction and operating costs. It is, therefore, not surprising that the recent PPPs are more "availability based" than "traffic based". Transferring the commercial risk to a public entity, however, is not enough to ensure the success of a PPP. As shown in Table 11.1, many other reasons can explain the failures. Some examples of complexity are given in Box 1. In the next part of this chapter we will address some political issues characterizing the French case study and the need for innovative solutions to finance the extension of the HSR network.

3. PPPs and HSR network extension in France

In France, HSR has a good share of the market for long-distance travel due to some of its characteristics. In popularity for this type of travel, it lies between the car and the plane.

The average door-to-door speed is much higher than for road and is sometimes equivalent to or higher than the plane.

High-speed trains (HST) are able to use both high-speed and conventional lines which permits journeys between a large number of different stations and dense geographical coverage. HSTs stop in about 200 French cities, some of which are quite a distance from high-speed lines. Moreover, HSTs serve old railway stations, in city centres where employment and population densities are sometimes the highest.

The time travellers spend on HSTs is much more comfortable and profitable than if they travelled by either of the other two modes of transport, especially since security checks now take so much time in airports.

The frequency of services decreases the risk of schedule disruption (23 round trips per day between Paris and Lyon or Paris and Nantes).

Based on the experience of the Paris–Lyon line (opened in 1981), the HSR network has been regularly extended. This has led to a considerable increase in HSR passenger traffic, which now exceeds domestic air transport by a factor of more than ten. In addition, between Paris and London and Paris and Brussels, HSR is dominant. In France, from the middle of the 90s to 2008, HSR traffic increased

Table 11.1 Main causes of PPP failures.

Politics	Complexity	Commercial

• length decision-making processes may cause scope deviations
• failure to execute/interference by public authority
• "political entrepreneur syndrome"
• public and mark acceptance
• involvement in incumbent train operating company
• quality of legal and institutional framework
	• long and complex completion phase
	• technical intensity–proven technologies but complex integration:
	  ○ structures and ground conditions
	  ○ interaction of a variety of systems
	  ○ safety
	  ○ technical interfaces
	  ○ functional interfaces
		• revenue structure
		• demand forecast

Source: Painvin et al., 2010.

by 3.2 per cent per year, whereas the increase for all modes taken together was only 0.5 per cent.

The result has been a considerable enthusiasm in France for high-speed modes of transport (Crozet, 2014) and especially for HSR, both on the part of passengers and public decision-makers. Thus, between 2007 and 2010, a national scheme for transport infrastructures was introduced in France which plans to add 2000 km of new HSR to the existing network by 2020 followed by a further 2000 km more during the following two decades.

It is in this context of HSR mania that the four projects to build new lines have been launched. However, initiating the construction of four new lines at the same time forced the policy makers to innovate. Previously, the construction of HSR lines had been done just one at a time in order to stagger funding which was solely from the public purse. The use of private finance and PPPs was put forward as the solution to being able to build more than one line at once. Hence, despite the evidence of the risks that apply to PPPs in the rail sector, RFF launched two major PPPs and a very large concession between 2010 and 2012, plus a fourth project, the completion of the HSR-East to Strasbourg, which was fully publicly funded.

- **BPL** (Bretagne–Pays de Loire): construction and maintenance of a 182 m new high-speed track between Le Mans and Brittany (a 25-year PPP costing 3.3 billion euros).
- **CNM** (Nîmes–Montpellier bypass): construction and maintenance of a new 80 km high-speed track (25-year PPP costing 1.8 billion euros).
- **SEA** (Sud–Europe Atlantique): concession awarded to a private operator for a 300 km new high-speed track between Tours and Bordeaux (50 years, 7.8 billion euros).
- Completion of the **HSR-East** to Strasbourg: 100 km financed by direct public subsidies (2 billion euros).

The total cost of these four ongoing projects (traffic will start in 2017) is close to 15 billion euros. It was impossible for the state to finance such a large amount and it was therefore necessary to call on regional governments and the private sector for finance. Table 11.2 shows the financing structure of the four projects. The main advantage of PPPs (CNM and BPL) is that public funds are not required during the construction but a lease fee is paid for 25 years. In the case of SEA (concession) and HSR-East, public money has to be provided during the building process, which will end in 2017. For SEA, the amount of private financing is 3.8 billion, a little less than 50 per cent of the total cost. Moreover, in the case of the SEA project, more than two-thirds of the debt is guaranteed by public entities. With regard to public funds, neither concession nor availability-based contracts are free.

But why are there three different financing schemes for just four projects: fully public for the HSR-East, a concession for the SEA and a "pure" PPP for the CNM and BPL? The main explanation is related to the potential traffic and the user's

Table 11.2 Main features and financing structure of the four projects.

	EAST	BPL	CNM	SEA	Total
Total cost (million euros)	2000	3300	1800	7800	14900
Length (km)	106	182	80	303	671
Cost/km (million euros)	18.9	18.1	22.5	25.7	22.2
Paid by RFF (million euros)	520	1400	0	1000	2920
Paid by central gvt (million euros)	680	950	1200	1500	4330
Paid by local gvt (million euros)	640	950	600	1500	3690
Paid by EU + Luxembourg (million euros)	160	0	0	0	160

capacity to pay. Even if none of these four projects are profitable and even if, consequently, public subsidies are necessary to limit rail access charges and consequently passenger fares, the four projects are not in the same position.

The HSR-East project is the extension of an existing line between Paris and the eastern part of France. The main benefit from this line will be a 30-minute time saving between Paris and Strasbourg. But even though Strasbourg is home to the European Parliament, it is only a medium-sized city and the potential increase in traffic is small. In addition, the main time saving was made in 2007 with the opening of the first segment of the HSR-East line[1] which cut the journey time between Paris and Strasbourg from four hours to two and a half.

The situation is more or less the same for the BPL (Paris–Brittany) and the CNM (Nîmes–Montpellier bypass). The first is longer than the second, but both are an extension of existing lines. The time saving for Rennes will be about 30 minutes (one and a half hours instead of two, and there are already 23 round trips per day), and it will be negligible for Montpellier (two or three minutes). Therefore, due to the small potential increase in traffic, it was impossible to have a concession for which the concessionaire assumes the risks. The government and the conceding body (RFF) opted in favour of a PPp. A lease fee of almost 200 million euros per year will be paid to the concessionaire for 25 years. Two French civil engineering firms are in charge of the projects, Eiffage for the BPL project and Bouygues in the case of the CNM project.

The potential traffic increase is higher for the line between Tours and Bordeaux (Paris–Tours is already open). Due to the time saving between Paris and Bordeaux (one and a half hours) and the potential future traffic from Toulouse and the southwest of France, a concession was a genuine possibility. After a tendering process and a long discussion with the three candidates, the concession was awarded in 2011 to a consortium headed by Vinci, France's largest civil engineering firm. From this viewpoint, the increase in the rate of construction on the French HSR network has provided French civil engineering companies with an excellent opportunity to acquire know-how in what is a relatively new field for them. This confirms the French government's traditional support of France's national "champions". But what are the risks, especially the risks of opportunism and its financial consequences?

4. The way to opportunism

The major difficulties encountered by PPPs in the past prompt us to consider the risks that affect them. The main risk comes from the state itself, which too often fails to apply the test described by Karl Popper (1957), requiring alternatives to be built up as powerfully as possible in order that they challenge the preferred project as strongly as possible.

In terms of economic risk analysis, it should be noted that public decision-makers are more risk loving than risk averse. If we express this in terms of expected utility, instead of preferring an expected utility that takes into account the probability of risks occurring, public decision-makers prefer random utility with an uncertain value but with which there is an unknown and generally low probability of making large gains (de Palma et al., 2009). This is the typical attitude of individuals who take part in lotteries (bingo, the national lottery). In this type of game, insofar as a large proportion of the stakes are kept by the game organizer, the rational decision is not to play. The probability of winning is extremely small, even in relation to the size of the maximum prize, and leads to a mathematical expectation of winning a sum that is inferior to the stake. However, millions of individuals regularly take part in these lotteries. Rather than reasoning in terms of expected utility, they focus on the value of the potential gain, even though this is very random. In this way millions of them lose their stake every week.

The same applies in the sphere of transport infrastructures. The public authorities foresee the potential major benefits of new transport infrastructures. The entire economic literature indicates that these effects are largely illusory (Flyvbjerg et al., 2003), but all the public decision-makers believe in them in exactly the same way as national lottery players believe in their luck. This is where the main risk associated with transport infrastructure projects lies. When a project has strong political backing, the individuals who perform the studies are encouraged to come up with traffic flow forecasts that justify the project. In a manner of speaking, because the public decision-maker wishes the project to go ahead "at any price" it places itself in a position of weakness with respect to its private sector partners.

The result is that negotiations between the public authorities and potential concessionaires are asymmetrical. Rail projects are very political and are characterized by three types of pressure: the line must be built, the trains must run and price/quality must be acceptable. Finally, the concessionaire has an extraordinary bargaining power due to the strong desire of the public sector to make the project happen.[2] Public entities are, therefore, ready to accept greater risks, give more guarantees than initially planned or intended and, in the French case especially, provide loan guarantees (the public authority will pay any financial charges the concessionaire is unable to meet).

If we consider the example of the SEA project in terms of the theory of incomplete contracts (Hart, 2003), it is apparent that the main risk is a hidden one that comes from two major sources: the first is differences of interest within the consortium and the second is the strategic behaviour of the rail operator (SNCF).

One major source of incompleteness of contracts is that the different members of the consortium that won the concession may have different long-term interests. Often, the head of the consortium, the construction group, has short-term interests that are limited to the construction period. However, it is less interested in addressing problems that occur during operation, for example traffic-related risk due to macroeconomic trends. However, since the financial crisis of 2008, TGV traffic in France is almost stable and in 2015 long-distance coach services were deregulated. A lot of coach companies, including a subsidiary of SNCF, are now offering coach services between Paris and Bordeaux.

In view of the fact that the current economic slowdown may well continue, traffic levels 2017–2020 are likely to be considerably lower than forecast. In this situation, it may be in the interests of the concessionaire to go bankrupt. In this case, its risk is limited to the loss of the 740 million euros it has invested in the company. This is a significant amount, but not more than 10 per cent of the cost of the works and more or less equal to the profit margin on completion of the works. Finally, the problem is that few concessions are actually led by private companies that want to run a railway business long term. They are led by financiers and construction companies who want the very big returns from such very large projects.

The possibility of risk associated with traffic is made more likely by the fact that the rail operator (SNCF) might be interested in playing brinkmanship. This is explained by the fact that in order to finance the transfer of 1 billion euros to the private operator, RFF has announced very high rail access charges (RAC) on the RFF network (Crozet & Chassagne, 2013) that is connected to the new line. RAC will also be very high on the new privately managed infrastructure. In this situation, the rail operator may decide to limit traffic to business that is profitable to it (during rush hour). Instead of the 30 daily round trips that were planned by the promotors of the project, SNCF announced at the end of 2015 that the service would be only 16 daily round trips. The concessionaire's turnover would then be insufficient. In November 2015, during one month, private banks stopped any payment to the concessionaire in order to alert the French government. SNCF has been obliged to increase the number of daily services.

To avoid the failure of the concession, the state could also ask RFF (SNCF since 2014) to reduce its tolls on the sections connected to the new line. The outcome of this would be that SNCF would be unable, from RAC, to cover the cost of the 1 billion euros it borrowed between 2011 and 2016 and paid to the concessionaire. The result is already a bid increase of the debt of SNCF. The state will probably be obliged to organize a rescue plan for the company. Public subsidies and public debt increases are the common result of opportunism.

Conclusion

In order to speed up the development of HSR, some countries have developed a number of innovative ways of financing. Different solutions have been adopted, taking into account the potential traffic and the capacity of final users to pay. PPPs, instead of direct public financing, have been applied either as concessions, or as availability-based contracts. PPPs are a convenient way to optimize risk sharing between private and public entities and, very often, they are a technical success; the new line is built and opened in good time. But financial issues remain and, more often, public funds are necessary to rescue the project.

Because of the risk of failure and the growing costs of new high-speed lines, a new policy has been adopted by the French government. The financial constraints that weigh on the public finances prompted the Ministry of Transport to appoint a commission in October 2012 to re-examine all the projects. The commission's proposals were made public in June 2013 and have been validated by the French government. In 2017, when all four of the lines that are currently being built will have opened, no new project will be ready to be launched, mainly because of financial shortages.

Notes

1 The air service between Paris and Strasbourg has already been definitely cancelled by Air France.
2 Whenever a concessionaire is granted favours or bailouts that were not explicitly offered to all bidders in the original tender process, then the integrity of that tender process has been terminally compromised and all the other losing tenderers, some of whom were possibly more realistic and less optimistic, are left frustrated.

References

Bonnafous A. (2010). *"Public economics for infrastructures in PPPs"*, paper presented at the 12th World Conference on Transport Research, Lisbon, July 2010.

Bonnafous A. & Faivre d'Arcier B. (2013). *"The conditions of efficiency of a PPP for public finances"*, paper presented at the 13th World Conference on Transport Research, Rio de Janeiro, July 2013.

Buchanan, Colin (2009). *"Economic impact of HS1: Final report"*, London: Colin Buchanan, available at www.lcrhq.co.uk/media/cms_page_media/32/HS1.final.report.pdf [accessed 10 May 2016].

Crozet Y. (2014). *"High speed rail performance in France: From appraisal methodologies to ex-post evaluations"*, in ITF/OECD *"The economics of investment in high speed rail"*, Roundtable Report 155, Paris: OECD, pp. 73–105.

Crozet Y. & Chassagne F. (2013). *"Rail access charges in France: Beyond the opposition between competition and financing"*, Research in Transportation Economics, 39(1), 247–254.

Dehornoy J. (2012). *"PPPs in the rail sector – a review of 27 projects"*, MPRA working paper 38415, Munich: University Library of Munich, MPRA.

de Palma A., Leruth L. & Prunier G. (2009). *"Towards a principal agent based typology of risks in public–private partnerships"*, IMF working paper WP/09/177, Washington, DC: IMF.

Dutzik T., Schneider J. & Baxandall P. (2011). *"High-speed rail: Public, private or both? Assessing the prospects, promise and pitfalls of public–private partnerships"*, Boston, MA: US PIRG Education Fund.

Flyvbjerg B., Bruzelius N. & Rothengatter W. (2003). *"Mega projects and risks, an anatomy of ambitions"*, Cambridge: Cambridge University Press.

Flyvbjerg B., Skamris Holl M. & Buhl S., (2006). *"Inaccuracy in traffic forecasts"*, Transport Reviews, 26(1), 1–24.

Hart O. (2003). *"Incomplete contracts and public ownership: Remarks, and an application to public–private partnerships"*, The Economic Journal, 113(486), C69–C76.

Marty F. (2007). *"Partenariats public–privé, règles de discipline budgétaire, comptabilité patrimoniale et stratégies de hors bilan"*, Document de travail No 2007-29, Paris: OFCE.

Maskin E. & Tirole J. (2008). *"Public–private partnerships and government spending limits"*, International Journal of Industrial Organization, 26(2), 412–420.

OECD/International Transport Forum (2013). *"Une meilleure réglementation des partenariats public-privé d'infrastructures de transport"*, Tables rondes FIT No 151, Paris: OECD.

Painvin N., Kotecha K. & Cherian G (2010). *"High speed rail projects: Large, varied and complex"*, Global Infrastructure and Project Finance, New York: FitchRatings.

Popper K. (1974 [1957]). *"The poverty of historicism"*, London: Routledge and Kegan Paul.

Index

access charges, Spain 28, 54, 144, 184
accessibility: of HSR stations 84, 93–4;
    policies 92–5; of transport 124
ADIF (Administrador de Infrastructuras
    Ferroviarias) 23, 24, 27–8, 34–5, 37–8,
    40–1
administrative centres, and HSR stations
    90–1
Aérotrain project 159–60
agglomeration benefits 57
airline hubs 164
airlines, low-cost 152, 169
air passengers, v. rail 166
air pollution, and modes of transport
    111
air transport/services: and climate
    change 161; competing with HSR
    14–15, 16–17, 159–60, 161, 162–4,
    171–2; cost of 169; emissions 105, 106;
    environmental issues and HSR 102, 166;
    expected trends 113–14, 165; impact of
    HSR 51, 148; marginal costs of 105; and
    rail travel 53, 70
airport services, and HSR 94–6, 97
Akerman et al. 121
Akerman, J. 132
Albalate, D. and Bel, G. 28, 44
Alonso, M. and Bellet, C. 71
Alvia trains 25, 27, 28, 34, 38
Anguera, R. 64
Aschauer, D.A. 7
assessment: lifecycle assessment (LCA)
    122–3, 129–33, 161; of transport
    systems 122
Atkins et al. 59
Austria, open-access services 142
availability-based concessions, public–
    private partnerships (PPPs) 177

AVE (Alta Velocidad Española) 25, 31,
    32, 34, 47
"avoid-shift-improve" model 122

"baskets of goods and services" 77, 78
Basque Y, LCA of 129–33
Bazin-Benoit et al. 71
Bellet, C. and Jurado, J. 89
Bergantino et al. 147, 148
Beria et al. 148
Betancor, O. and Llobet, G. 23
Blum et al. 55
Boletín Oficial de las Cortes Generales
    (BOCG) 24
borders, crossing of 52
BPL (Bretagne–Pays de Loire) PPP 180–2
'build it and see' approach 48
business tourism 70–1
bus services, at HSR stations 94

Campos et al. 46, 53
Campos, J. and de Rus, G. 107
capacity, enhancing 48
capital costs, HSR 53
carbon footprint, Basque Y 131–2
Carbon Footprint of High Speed Rail
    report 131
car travel: to access HSR 171;
    environmental costs 111
Cascetta, E. and Coppola, P. 145, 147, 148
Cascetta et al. 148
central termini 47
Chester, M. and Horvath, A. 161
Chile, Public Investment System (SNI) 18
China: 'build it and see' approach 48;
    environmental issues and HSR 101; and
    HSR/tourism 72, 74; objectives/impact
    of HSR 49

Chinese Taipei, objectives/impact of HSR 48, 49

climate change *see also* greenhouse gas emissions (GHG): and air travel 161; and modes of transport 111; total cost from 112

CNM (Nîmes–Montpellier bypass) PPP 180–2

coach services 93, 169–70, 184

commercial returns, from HSR 63

communications: and HSR/tourism 75–6, 77; stations as a node of 84

competition: and cost leadership 154, 155; and fares 147, 148–50, 169; in HSR 143–4; intermodal 14, 147, 148, 160, 169, 170, 172; intramodal 147, 148; Italy 54; models of on HSLs 153–4; new forms of 169–70; on-track 140–2, 144–7, 151, 153–4, 156n.4; open-access 150–5; and prices 147–8

competitive advantage, strategies for 151–3

connectivity, HSR stations and airports 97

construction costs: inability to recover 23–4, 32, 35, 38; Spain 28

consumer surplus 15

consumption, of land 108

cooperation, in the tourism sector 75–7, 78

cost-benefit analyses: economic evaluation of infrastructure projects through 9–12; HS2 59–63; of HSR in Spain 54–5; by public agencies 17; purpose of 19

cost leadership: and competition 154, 155; of rail newcomers 151–2, 153

cost(s): of air transport/services 169; construction costs 23–4, 28, 32, 35, 38; cost advantage 154; HSR 54; maintenance costs 28, 54; operating costs 54; of rail travel 169; of transport 14

cross-subsidies 151

Crozet, Y. 63

cultural issues, and demand/supply 52

customer care services 152

Czech Republic: competition and fares 147; open-access services 142

D'Alfonso et al. 102

Dalkmann, H. and Brannigan, C. 122

David, P.A. 16

debt, and public–private partnerships (PPPs) 176

decision-makers, public 183

decision-making processes 8

Dehornoy, J. 177

Delaplace, M. and Dobruszkes, F. 169

demand: classic rail services 51; HSR 52–4, 68, 144, 165–6; minimising 124–6; potential user between stations 86–7, 88–9, 96–7; social access demand 121; spatial dispersion of 167–8

de Rus, G. 23, 24, 27, 28, 29, 54, 64, 85

de Rus, G. and Inglada, V. 23

de Rus, G. and Socorro, P. 14, 18

discounting 10

discriminatory practices, to newcomers 150

Dobruszkes et al. 163–4

dynamism, associated with HSR 70–3

Ecoinvent 123

economic effects, of large projects 15–17

economic evaluation: of infrastructure investment 8; of projects 9–12

economic growth: and infrastructure investment 7–8; and transport growth 121

economic impacts, of HSR 52, 55–7

economic planning, of infrastructure 16

efficiency optimisation 128–9

electricity mix, and environmental issues 109, 110

electrification, with renewables 132

emissions: air transport/services 105, 106; direct/indirect 161; EU reduction targets 119–20; greenhouse gas 104, 123–4, 127–8, 129, 130, 135, 160, 161; and HSR 112; rail transport/services 105–7; and transport 105–6, 119, 160

employment, and transport interventions 57–8

energy concerns 160

energy consumption burdens, Basque Y 131

energy consumption, transport sector 103–4

energy costs, HSR 54

energy efficiency: of HSR 134; and load factor 110, 114, 161

Engel et al. 18

environmental impact reduction, calculating 125–6

environmental issues: air travel/HSR 102, 166; car travel/HSR 111; and HSR 49, 52, 101–2, 103–13, 134–5, 160–1; impact of HSR/modes of transport on 112–13; location of transport terminals 171; rail v. other modes of transport 103–8; railway sector 109; and transportation 100–2

European Commission (EC): and HSR 100–1; White Paper on transport 165

European Environment Agency 104, 105

European Life Cycle Database 123

European transport policy 82
European Union (EU): emissions reduction targets 119–20; institutional design in 18; policies 85
Europe, HSR in 83, 164–5
Eurotunnel 179
evaluations, long and short-term 19
exclusion, geographical/economic 52
exclusive exploitation model 46–7
expression, insight of 15

Facchinetti-Mannone, V. 85
fare revenues 50, 51
fares, and competition 147, 148–50, 169
FEDEA (Fundación de Estudios de Economía Aplicada) 23
Ferropedia 24, 27
financial accounts: Madrid–East Coast corridor 37–8; Madrid–North corridor 40
financial IRR, HSR in Spain 43
financial NPV: Madrid–Andalusia corridor 34–5; Madrid–Barcelona corridor 32; Madrid–East Coast corridor 38; Madrid–North corridor 41
financial profitability analysis 31–2
financial profitability, HSR in Spain 23, 26–8
focus strategy 153
France: Aérotrain project 159–60; BPL (Bretagne–Pays de Loire) PPP 180–2; CNM (Nîmes–Montpellier bypass) PPP 180–2; coach services 184; cost of HSR travel 169; environmental costs 111; Eurotunnel 179; HSR/air transport 159–60, 161; HSR construction in 88; HSR-East 180–2; and HSR/tourism 69–78; HSR travel in 180–1; location of stations 89–90, 91, 93, 97; low-cost HSR services 170; model of HSR 143, 144; Perpignan–Figueras HSR 179; public–private partnerships (PPPs) 181–3, 185; railway supply industry 48; SEA (Sud–Europe Atlantique) PPP 180–2; SNCF 76, 160, 170, 179, 184; TGV system 47, 48, 54, 160, 184
free modal choice paradigm 170
freight traffic, and environmental balance 132
Fröidh, O. and Byström, C. 147
fully mixed model 47

García, A. 102
general equilibrium cost-benefit rules 11
Germany: cost of HSR travel 169; environmental costs 111; HSR

construction in 87–8; ICE network 47, 54; location of stations 89, 90, 91, 93, 97; model of HSR 143; on-track competition 156n.4
Givoni et al. 101, 102, 105, 109, 167–8, 171
Givoni, M. 102, 171
Givoni, M. and Dobruszkes, F. 163
global HSR traffic 164–6
governance structures 17–18
governments: and institutional design/ investment 18; and intermodal competition 170
Graham, D.J. 57
Graham, D.J. and Melo, P. 57
greener mobilities, scope for 164–71, 172
greenhouse gas emissions (GHG) 104, 123–4, 127–8, 129, 130, 135, 160, 161
growth, economic/transport 7–8, 119, 121
Guirao, B. and Campa, J-L. 71

Haas, P.J. 113
high-density demand corridors 153
High-speed Alliance consortium (HSA), Netherlands 178–9
high-speed railway (HSR): defined 46; global extent of 48; trends in the provision of 165; types of 46–7
Hoyos, D. 121
HS1, UK 58, 59, 177–8
HS2, UK 57, 58–63
HSR-East, France 180–2
HSR-Zuid, Netherlands 178–9
hubbing 164

Iberian gauge 25
ICE network, Germany 47, 54
IER 102
impact matrix, for a HSR scheme 49–50
impacts: of HSR 63; of HSR projects 48–52
incentives, and institutional design 17–19
income: and choice of transport 169; social marginal utility of 10
indirect utility function, of consumers 11, 12
infrastructure access charges 28, 54, 144, 184
infrastructure, economic planning of 16
infrastructure investment: and economic growth 7–8; Spain 23, 32
infrastructure projects, social appraisal of 12 *see also* projects
insight of expression 15
institutional design, and incentives 17–19

intercity coach services 93 *see also* coach
　services
intercity transport, and HSR users 94
interest groups, political power of 9
intermodal competition 14, 147, 148, 160,
　169, 170, 172
intermodal effects, of HSR 162–3
intermodality *see also* modal shift: and
　connections 76; at HSR stations 82–4,
　93–5; policies 92–5; transport hierarchy
　(TH) approach 127
international track gauge, Spain 24
International Transport Forum Round
　Table 46
International Union of Railways (UIC) 46,
　100
interoperability 168
intramodal competition 147, 148
investment: in HSR infrastructure
　competing with air transport 14–15,
　16–17; infrastructure in Spain 23, 32;
　investment appraisal 102; investment
　curve for HS2 60; irreversibility of 17;
　iso-welfare curves for 54–5; and pricing
　8, 12–15, 19
iso-welfare curves, for HSR investments
　54–5
Italy: competition 54; HSR construction
　in 87, 88; and HSR/tourism 72–3;
　location of stations 89, 90, 91, 93, 97;
　model of HSR 143, 144; NTV 144–7,
　148–50, 154; objectives/impact of HSR
　49; open-access services 142; Trenitalia
　145, 146, 148, 149–50, 155
Ivaldi, M. and Vibes, C. 147

Janic, M. 102, 106, 108
Japan: environmental issues and HSR 101;
　HSR 159; and HSR/tourism 70, 72, 74;
　model of HSR 143, 144; Shinkansen
　services 46
Johansson, P-O. 11, 15
Johnson, D. and Nash, C. 147

Kaldor–Hicks compensation criterion 10,
　12
Kemp, R. 101
Korzhenevych et al. 107
KPMG 57
Kurihara, T. and Wu, L. 72

land, consumption of 108
land markets 52
Levinson et al. 101

lifecycle assessment (LCA) 122–3; of the
　Basque Y 129–33; emissions 161
load factor, and energy efficiency 110,
　114, 161
locations: of HSR stations 89–90, 91, 93,
　97; of transport terminals 170–1
low-cost airlines 152, 169
low-cost HSR services 170

Madrid–Andalusia corridor 25, 34–5, 43
Madrid–Barcelona corridor 24, 25, 28,
　30–3, 43, 111, 128, 129
Madrid–East Coast corridor 25, 35, 37–8,
　43
Madrid–North corridor 38, 40–1
Maibach et al. 105, 106, 107, 111, 112
maintenance costs 28, 54
Major Projects Authority (MPA), UK 18
Mannone, V. 70
marginal costs, of modes of transport
　105–7
market differentiation, and competition
　154
marketing: and HSR/tourism 77; of
　services 151
Marsden, G. 102
Martí-Henneberg, J. 86
Martín et al. 171
Menéndez et al. 84, 89
meter gauge 25
Metz, D. 61
misrepresentation, strategic 9
mixed conventional model 47
mixed high speed model 47
mixed model networks 153
modal shift *see also* intermodality:
　enabling 127–8; and HSR 113, 114,
　134
models of high-speed railways 46–7,
　143–4, 145–7
monetary valuation, of households 10

National Audit Office, UK 59, 61
Netherlands, HSR-Zuid 178–9
Network Rail 102, 112
niche markets, product focus on 153, 154
Nilsson et al. 151
noise pollution 107–8, 111
NTV, Italy 144–7, 148–50, 154

Obama, Barack 160–1
objectives, of HSR projects 48–52
Observatorio del Ferrocarril 24, 27
occupancy rates, and efficiency 129

Okabe, S. 72
on-track competition *see also* competition:
  in the EU 140–2; Germany 156n.4;
  Italy 144–7; models of on HSLs 153–4;
  United Kingdom 151
open-access competition 150–5
open-access services 141–2
operating costs 54
opportunism, and public–private
  partnerships (PPPs) 183–4

Pagliara et al. 52
'paralysis by analysis' approach 48
parking services, at HSR stations 93
passenger rail transport, EC support of 101
passengers, rail v. air 166
patronage thresholds 63
Perpignan–Figueras HSR, France/Spain
  179
Petrazzuolo et al. 111
planning: economic of infrastructure 16;
  transport 82
planning fallacy 9
policies: accessibility and intermodality
  92–5; EU 85; European transport policy
  82; for locating HSR stations 89–92, 97;
  transport 97, 119, 121–2, 133
political power, of interest groups 9
politics: and intermodal competition 170;
  and rail projects 183
pollution 107–8, 111 *see also* emissions
Popper, K. 183
power, political of interest groups 9
Preston, J.M. 113, 147
pricing: and competition 147–8; and
  investment 8, 12–15, 19; short-term
  marginal cost pricing 14; strategic 148;
  variations in 54
product differentiation 152, 153, 155
productivity, and rail connectivity 57
product level, and competition 154
profitability: HSR in Spain 23, 26–8; social
  of HSR in Spain 29–30
projects: economic effects of large 15–17;
  economic evaluation of 9–12; evaluation
  of and social welfare 9, 15; long-term
  effects of 19; objectives of HSR 48–52
public capital, elasticities of productivity
  7–8
Public Investment System (SNI), Chile 18
public–private partnerships (PPPs):
  attractiveness of 176–7; failures in
  175, 177–80, 185; France 181–3, 185;
  and HSR 64, 177–80; provision of

infrastructure 17–18; and risks 175, 177,
  183–4, 185
public transport services, at HSR stations
  94

rail access charges (RAC) 28, 54, 144, 184
rail connectivity, and productivity 57
rail freight market 100
rail operators, key costs/benefits of 49–50
rail passengers, v. air 166
rail revenues 50–1
rail transport/services: and emissions
  105–7; expected trends 114; impact of
  HSR 148
rail travel: and air travel 53, 70; cost of
  169
railway sector, environmental impact 109
railway supply industry 48
RENFE Operadora 23, 24, 25, 27–8, 31,
  34–5, 37–8, 40–1, 44n.3
returns, from HSR 63–4
Reusser et al. 84
revenue yield approaches, pricing 54
Richardson, G.B. 75
risks, and public–private partnerships
  (PPPs) 175, 177, 183–4, 185
road systems, impact of HSR 51
road transport, expected trends 113
rolling stock acquisition 54
Román et al. 169

SEA (Sud–Europe Atlantique) PPP 180–2
segregated systems 47–8
Shinkansen services 46
Shires, J.D. 52
short-term marginal cost pricing 14
Smith, R.A. 110
SNCF 76, 160, 170, 179, 184
social access demand 121
social accounts: Madrid–Andalusia
  corridor 35, 36; Madrid–Barcelona
  corridor 29, 30–1, 32, 33; Madrid–East
  Coast corridor 39; Madrid–North
  corridor 41, 42
social appraisal, of infrastructure projects
  12
social benefits, of development 57
social impacts, of HSR 52, 63–4, 169–70
social IRR, HSR in Spain 43
social marginal utility, of income 10
social NPV: Madrid–Andalusia corridor
  36; Madrid–Barcelona corridor 32, 33;
  Madrid–East Coast corridor 38, 39;
  Madrid–North corridor 42

social profitability, HSR in Spain 29–30
social value, of HSR projects 44
social welfare, and project evaluation 9, 15
Spain: Alvia trains 25, 27, 28, 34, 38; AVE
  (Alta Velocidad Española) 25, 31, 32,
  34, 47; 'build it and see' approach 48;
  cost-benefit analyses of HSR in 54–5;
  demand for HSR 97; environmental
  costs 111; HSR construction in 87, 88;
  HSR in 23, 24–5, 26–30, 44; and HSR/
  tourism 71–2; infrastructure investment
  23, 32; LCA of the Basque Y 129–33;
  location of stations 89–90, 91, 93, 97;
  Madrid–Andalusia corridor 25, 34–5,
  43; Madrid–Barcelona corridor 24, 25,
  28, 30–3, 43, 111, 128, 129; Madrid–
  East Coast corridor 25, 35, 37–8, 43;
  Madrid–North corridor 38, 40–1; model
  of HSR 143, 144; objectives/impact of
  HSR 49; Perpignan–Figueras HSR 179;
  RENFE Operadora 23, 24, 25, 27 8, 31,
  34–5, 37–8, 40–1, 44n.3
stations: accessibility of 84, 93–4; and
  airports 97; intermodality at 82–4,
  93–5; locations of 89–90, 91, 93, 97;
  prioritising the construction of 86–9
strategic misrepresentation 9
subsidies, cross-subsidies 151
supply, HSR 52–4
supply industry 48
sustainability, of transport systems 100,
  120
sustainable development 160–1
Sustainable Development Commission,
  UK 122
sustainable mobility 119, 120–9, 133–4
Sweden, open-access services 142

Taiwan: and HSR/tourism 72; THSR 178
Taiwan High-speed Rail Corporation
  (THSRC) 178
taxation 51, 52
taxi services, at HSR stations 94
technical–regulatory barriers, to
  newcomers 150
termini, location of 47
TGV system, France 47, 48, 54, 160, 184
THSR, Taiwan 178
time savings 55
Todorovitch et al. 71
Tokaido Shinkansen 48
Tomeš et al. 147
tourism, and HSR 69–78
TP Ferro Concesionaria, S.A. 179

track gauge, Spain 24–5
traffic-based concessions, public–private
  partnerships (PPPs) 177
train services costs 54
Trans–European Network 134
transport costs 57–8
transport growth 119, 121
transport hierarchy (TH) approach 122;
  sustainable mobility 122–9, 134
transport interventions, and employment
  57
transport planning 82
transport policies 97, 119, 121–2, 133
transport sector: emissions 105–6, 119,
  160; energy consumption 103–4;
  expected trends 113–14
transport systems, assessment of 122
transport systems, sustainability of 100, 120
transport terminals, location of 170–1
travel time: and HSR/air travel 164; and
  intermodal competition 172
Trenitalia 145, 146, 148, 149–50, 155

underground systems, at HSR stations 94
United Kingdom: emission data 104–5;
  environmental issues and HSR
  101–2; Eurotunnel 179; HS1 58, 59,
  177–8; HS2 57, 58–63; Major Projects
  Authority (MPA) 18; Network Rail
  102, 112; objectives/impact of HSR 49;
  on-track competition 151; open-access
  services 141–2; 'paralysis by analysis'
  approach 48
United States: environmental issues and
  HSR 101, 160–1; 'paralysis by analysis'
  approach 48
urban integration 76
urban public transport services, at HSR
  stations 93–4
urban systems, impact on an HSR network
  168
urban tourism 69–70
Urena et al. 71
utility, monetary valuation of 10

van Essen et al. 102
van Wee et al. 106
Venables et al. 57

Wang, X.C. and Sanders, L. 102
Weidmann et al. 150
welfare approach, of social HSR accounts
  29
white elephants 17

For Product Safety Concerns and Information please contact our EU
representative GPSR@taylorandfrancis.com Taylor & Francis Verlag GmbH,
Kaufingerstraße 24, 80331 München, Germany

Printed and bound by CPI Group (UK) Ltd, Croydon, CR0 4YY
01/05/2025
01858414-0004